Victoria and Vancouver Island

by Dan Klinglesmith

Altitude Publishing

The Canadian Rockies / Vancouver

Altitude Publishing Canada Ltd.

The Canadian Rockies/Vancouver
Head Office:
1500 Railway Avenue
Canmore, Alberta T1W 1P6

www.altitudepublishing.com
1-800-957-6888

Canadian Cataloguing in Publication Data

Klinglesmith, Dan, 1955-
Victoria and Vancouver Island: an Altitude superguide / Dan Klinglesmith

Includes index
ISBN 1-55153-635-8

1.Vancouver Island (B.C.)--Guidebooks.
2. Victoria (B.C.) -- Guidebooks.. I Title.
FC3844.2.K54 2003   917,11'2044
C2003-910265-3   F1089.V3K54 2003

Altitude GreenTree Program

Altitude Publishing will plant twice as many
trees as were used in the manufacturing of
this product.

Front cover: *The Fairmont Empress Hotel and Victoria's
Inner Harbour*
Back cover: *Bamfield*

Project Development

Layout	Daniel Blais
Maps	Hermien Schuttenbeld
Editor	Audrey McLellan

The author would like to thank the following
people who helped review the text and made
valuable suggestions: Anthony Everett, Heather
Jeliazkov, Lana Cheong, Alison Partridge,
Michelle Hynes, Cathy Dyck, Geoff Corbett, Sue
Hopkins, Paul Jonson, Teresa Davis, Dave Hill
and John Walls.

Made in Western Canada

Printed and bound in Canada by Friesen Printers

A Note from the Publisher

The world described in *Altitude SuperGuides* is a
unique and fascinating place. It is a world filled
with surprise and discovery, beauty and enjoyment, questions and answers. It is a world of
people, cities, landscapes, animals and wilderness as seen through the eyes of those who live
in, work with, and care for this world. The
process of describing this world is also a means
of defining ourselves.

It is also a world of relationship, where people derive their meaning from a deep and abid-
ing contact with the land—as well as from each
other. And it is this sense of relationship that
guides all of us at Altitude to ensure that these
places continue to survive and evolve in the
decades ahead.

Altitude SuperGuides are books intended to
be used, as much as read. Like the world they
describe, *Altitude SuperGuides* are evolving,
adapting and growing. Please write to us with
your comments and observations, and we will do
our best to incorporate your ideas into future
editions of these books.

Stephen Hutchings
Publisher

Contents

Maps

The *Victoria and Vancouver Island SuperGuide* is organized according to this colour scheme:

Introduction

Victoria

The Butchart Gardens

South Vancouver Island

The Southern Gulf Islands

South Central Vancouver Island

Central Vancouver Island

The Pacific Rim

North Central Vancouver Island

North Vancouver Island

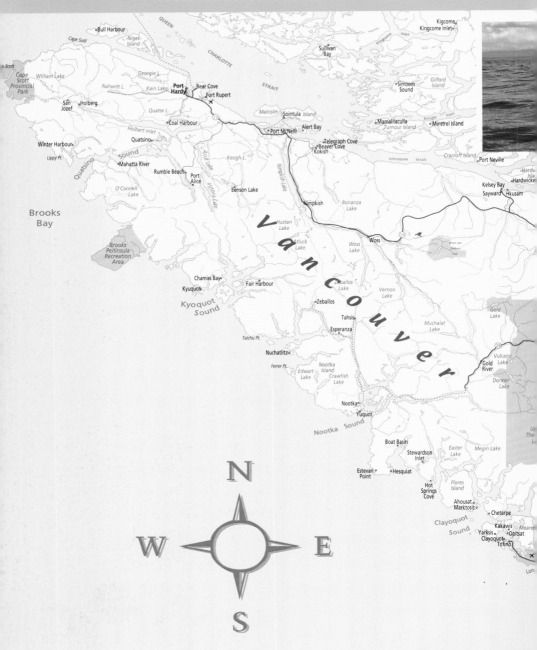

Introduction

The Fisgard Lighthouse dates from 1859 and is British Columbia's oldest.

To simply refer to Vancouver Island as "spectacular" is to utter an understatement. Perhaps nowhere on the planet do the effects of topography, climate, and culture conspire to make a more perfect union of superb natural beauty and genuine hospitality.

Picture deep green forests; cobalt blue seas; long, luxurious stretches of sandy beaches; secluded coves; towering snow-capped peaks; and leafy vales. Envision within all this a smattering of sophisticated metropolitan centres, many lovely towns and hamlets, seaside villages, and relaxing retreats invariably eager to share the wonderful natural gifts of their island with newly found friends. Here it would seem that spectacular is merely ordinary.

Vancouver Island is the largest isle off the North American West Coast, comparable in size to the Netherlands: 460 kilometres long with an average breadth of 100 kilometres, totalling 32,261 square kilometres. A mountainous spine, topped by 2200-metre-high Mt. Golden Hinde, runs its length, while long fiords on the west coast cut deeply into the Island.

The west coast of Vancouver Island is sparsely inhabited, except for a sprinkling of seaside communities nestled about Barkley and Clayoquot sounds. Vancouver Island's major development and roadways are clustered on its south and east coasts where the ocean's weather influence, blocked by the mid-Island mountains, is more constrained. The lush forests and fecund valleys in these areas are the Island's warm spots and market baskets, with dairies, small farms, and orchards. Here, too, in the far south is Victoria, home to the majority of the Island's 700,000 population, as well as to the legislative precinct for all of British Columbia. Southward from Victoria, only 20 kilometres across the Strait of Juan de Fuca, is the United States of America, with Washington State's majestic Olympic Mountains shimmering above the horizon. Up-Island from Victoria, beyond the fertile Cowichan and Chemainus valleys and into the Campbell

River region, "tree country" begins, with kilometre after kilometre of forest.

Long the traditional homeland of First Nations peoples — the Nuu-chah-nulth, the Kwakwaka'wakw, the Coast Salish — Vancouver Island was a realm of miraculous plenty, its forests, lakes, rivers, shorelines, and open sea providing well for the people's sustenance ... and spirituality. Their skills were extraordinary; they were consummate mariners and fishers, industrious, and expressive in basketry and woodcarving. Age-old

BC Ferries

BC Ferries, the province's ferry fleet, in operation since 1960, has grown into one of the world's largest local transportation systems, shepherding millions of passengers in a typical year. More than 40 BC Ferries vessels visit nearly 50 ports of call on 26 different routes linking coastal British Columbia. Ferries offer vehicle transportation, including accommodation for bikes, RVs, trucks, and buses, as well as foot-passenger service. The Spirit class vessels feature many additional amenities: buffet, cafeteria, snack bar, video arcades for the kids, work cubicles for businesspeople, gift shops, and newsstands. The two Spirit class ferries, the *Spirit of British Columbia* and the *Spirit of Vancouver Island*, are the largest ships in the fleet, each measuring more than 160 metres from bow to stern.

While the major BC Ferries routes are Victoria (Swartz Bay) to Vancouver (Tsawwassen), and Nanaimo (Duke Point and Departure Bay) to Vancouver (Tsawwassen and Horseshoe Bay), other popular touring options include:

Mill Bay Crossing – A short scenic route between Brentwood Bay on the Saanich Peninsula and Mill Bay, with access to the Cowichan Valley.

Swartz Bay to Saltspring Island – Delve into Saltspring Island's thriving art scene at many galleries.

BC Ferries call at nearly 50 ports linking coastal British Columbia.

Swartz Bay to the Southern Gulf Islands – Serene and scenic, a self-directed circle tour takes in Pender, Mayne, and Saturna or Galiano islands.

Nanaimo to Gabriola Island – Called the "Queen of the Gulf Islands," Gabriola sports the Malaspina Galleries, fascinating sandstone formations.

Buckley Bay to Denman and Hornby Islands – Art lovers will enjoy the many galleries and craft shops, and sport enthusiasts relish the diving and kayaking.

Campbell River to Quadra Island – Favoured by saltwater fishers, Quadra is also a great place for hikers, kayakers, and divers. A stop by the Kwagiulth Museum and Cultural Centre rewards visitors with a view of the fascinating collection of First Nations masks and potlatch ceremonial objects.

Port McNeill to Sointula – Relax in the quiet of this once-flourishing fishing village on Malcolm Island. Founded by Finnish settlers, the museum is quaint and fun. Bird-watchers won't want to miss the mud-flats at Rough Bay.

Port McNeill to Alert Bay – Marvel at the numerous First Nations totems standing in Namgis Burial Ground at Alert Bay. The U'mista Cultural Centre holds one of Vancouver Island's richest collections of potlatch regalia.

Sunshine Coast Tour – Departing from Comox, catch the ferry to Powell River on the mainland, then travel by car south, taking the Saltery Bay-Earls Cove ferry to the Sunshine Coast. Continue driving south to Gibsons and the ferry terminal at Langdale, where vessels travel to Horseshoe Bay, north of Vancouver. From here, proceed to Vancouver or return to Vancouver Island via the ferry to Departure Bay, near Nanaimo.

BC Ferry Services
1112 Fort Street
Victoria BC V8V 4V2
888- 724-5223 anywhere in BC or 888- 223-3779 in BC outside Victoria or 250-386-3431
www.bcferries.com

customs and honoured traditions filled their daily life with rich ceremony and regalia.

The arrival of the Europeans in the 1700s heralded tremendous change for Vancouver Island and its people. The robust trade in sea otter pelts, and later the pelts of seals and sea lions, lured adventurers from across the globe: Russians, Spaniards, Americans, and in particular captains and merchants of the British Empire. Over the next 150 years, Vancouver Island evolved into a crossroads of commerce as its natural assets fuelled logging, mining, fishing, and farming.

Queen Victoria was still a young woman, and had reigned for less than a decade when, in 1843, the Hudson's Bay Company established a fort where now spreads Victoria's Bastion Square and named it in her honour. The Island became a British Crown Colony in 1849, with its capital at Victoria. Then in 1866, Vancouver Island was joined with the mainland Crown Colony of British Columbia, and that Colony of British Columbia in turn became the Dominion of Canada's sixth province in 1871.

Victoria was merely a frontier settlement in 1858 when it became the staging point for miners hell-bent on reaching the golden prospects of the Fraser River, Cariboo, and Alaskan gold rushes. Brits, Scots, Irish, American, Chinese, Japanese, as well as a host of other immigrants from

Vancouver Island First Nations

Today, census records list 27,175 people — less than 10 percent of Vancouver Island's overall population — as First Nations people. The Nuu-chah-nulth people, who occupy the west coast, are a contemporary alliance of 14 groups whose ancestral land runs from Sheringham Point north to the Brooks Peninsula. On the northeast coast are 15 contemporary Kwakwaka'wakw groups. Vancouver Island's southeastern shores are home to nine communities of the Hul'qumi'num-speaking Coast Salish people and eight belonging to the Straits people.

For thousands of years the ancestors of these people thrived, living on a wide variety of food sources from both land and sea. Largely hunters and gatherers, they banded into strong family groups, leading a semi-nomadic lifestyle and occupying seasonal villages. Not simple camps, their principal towns were actually remarkable cultural centres rich with tradition and ritual. The people's skills were extraordinary — they were consummate mariners and fishers, industrious, and expressive in basketry and woodcarving. Although these people were self-supporting, wars between groups invariably occurred, usually disputes over fishing waters and territories.

Life forever changed for all these First Nations with the arrival of Europeans. Both Spanish and British explorers and traders found welcoming arms at times, while at other encounters there was fierce anger. Over time, European adventurers prevailed, not only exploiting the land's resources, but also displacing a good portion of the First Nations' cultures.

The first onslaught was smallpox. The disease broke out in 1862 in Victoria and quickly spread to the First Nations people. The epidemic continued for three years, with some villages losing more than 90 percent of their population. Commenting on the devastation caused by the outbreak, Haida artist Bill Reid wrote: "It is one of the world's greatest tributes to the strength of the human spirit that most of those who lived and their children after them remained sane, and adapted in part at least to the strange new world in which they found themselves."

There would be much to endure. Beginning in 1884 and continuing until 1952, the "potlatch" was outlawed. This indigenous ceremony had provided their cultures for centuries with far more than a display of wealth, power, and social standing. And for years, missionaries of many Christian persuasions sought to alter age-old beliefs and the traditional ways of the First Nations people.

Nonetheless, First Nations culture over the last two decades has experienced a resurgence and appreciation. Many traditional rites and rituals have been revived. First Nations ceremonies are held frequently and shared with many non-Natives. Arts and crafts produced by First Nations weavers, woodcarvers, and basket makers are increasingly valued not only for their artistic achievement but also for their spiritual quality.

Logging trucks are frequent sights on Vancouver Island.

Australia to Finland flowed to the Island. Fortunes were made and squandered, and even now anyone who strolls down the city's streets and along its Inner Harbour can see the architectural vestiges of those bygone eras. As today's sophisticated capital, Victoria boasts a thriving cultural scene easily accessible at its fine museums and performing arts venues.

South Vancouver Island, encompassing the Saanich Peninsula and the southwestern coast of the Island, offers rural landscapes, quaint seaside towns, and breathtaking nature. Swartz Bay serves as one of the Island's key gateways with its BC Ferries terminal. Farms, meadows, and rolling forested hills delight travellers, as does the Saanich Peninsula's horticultural heaven, The Butchart Gardens, located near Brentwood Bay. Sooke, on the western side of Victoria, is a gateway too, this time to the splendour of Vancouver Island's most southern shores. The West Coast Highway to Port Renfrew is a motor touring pleasure, one of the best scenic drives on the Island.

Scattered throughout the Strait of Georgia are the

Southern Gulf Islands. Saltspring, Mayne, Galiano, Pender, Saturna, Kuper and Gabriola are known for their bucolic bliss and relaxed lifestyle, appealing to artists and nature lovers. Amusements aplenty there are, from artist studio tours and wellness spas to kayaking, hiking, and camping. Parks and recreation areas are a hallmark of the Gulf Islands, with many fine beaches and forested retreats accessible to visitors.

South Central Vancouver Island, from the Malahat north of Victoria into the Cowichan and Chemanius valleys, is country charming with vineyards and farms

Vancouver Island Climate

Vancouver Island's geographic position and topography conspire to create a climate that boasts both North America's wettest spot and Canada's best weather. Lake Henderson near Port Alberni hauls in a whopping 6655 millimetres average annual rainfall, while the isle's sun-blessed southeastern shores can aptly be described as "Mediterranean."

Indeed, Victoria is Canada's least likely locale to have a white Christmas, holding the nation's record for frost-free days — 685 from 1925-26. Springtime comes early to the capital, usually by February, and rainfall here averages only about 700 millimetres annually. Add to this 2082 hours of sunshine and it is little wonder that 90 percent of the Island's population

lives in these cosy southern reaches. Residents like to point out that they get less recorded precipitation than Vancouver or Seattle.

The Vancouver Island Mountains, stretching nearly the length of the Island, create a rain shadow. Storms born in the Pacific Ocean nudge up against the high peaks, losing their blustery gusto and their rain, and leaving the east coast relatively mild.

Moreover, rain and mild temperatures — averaging 15 to 25°C during the summer and 0 to 10°C in winter — have nurtured the development of Vancouver Island's temperate rain forests, sheltering one of the earth's most biodiverse ecosystems.

and irresistible diversions. Drive the Wine Route to discover Vancouver Island's budding viticulture industry at some half-dozen vineyards. Farm gates are bountiful too, proffering agricultural treats from fresh cheeses to apple ciders. Duncan, the region's commercial centre, is the "City of Totems," displaying dozens of this distinctive form of First Nations artistic

expression. Here as well is wonderful Chemainus, world renowned for the larger-than-life murals decorating its buildings. Nearby Ladysmith, with its heritage architecture and setting high above Stuart Channel, has been likened to an early-day San Francisco.

Nanaimo is the Island's second largest city, the energetic historic heart of **Central Vancouver Island** with two key

BC Ferries terminals, Duke Point and Departure Bay. Vacationers favour the region; Oceanside, billed as Canada's Riviera with the resort towns of Parksville and Qualicum Beach, sports the Island's best beaches and warmest waters. Take the pretty Oceanside Highway route from Nanoose Bay up through Lighthouse Country to marvel at glorious coastline views and enjoy

Crossing the Border — Entering And Exiting Vancouver Island

As many of Vancouver Island's visitors hail from other parts of the world — in particular the United States — here's a quick primer of customs regulations and where to find more information.

Entering by Automobile
Both Sidney and Victoria are entry points for motorists and their vehicles coming from Washington State Ferry via Anacortes or the *Coho* from Port Angeles.

Entering by Boat
Victoria, Sidney, Nanaimo, Courtenay / Comox, Campbell River, and Bedwell Harbour on Pender Island have marine customs ports for mariners arriving in pleasure crafts.

Entering by Airplane
Victoria International Airport is the main gateway for international visitors arriving by air and has full immigration and customs facilities. Nanaimo Airport is the second busiest on the Island, and other communities with airports include Courtenay / Comox, Campbell River, and Port Hardy. Many airlines also operate harbour to harbour using floatplanes, which can access more isolated areas.

Declaring Goods
Laws regarding the value and

type of goods international visitors to Vancouver Island are allowed to take home vary by country. Americans visiting Canada for more than 48 hours, for example, can take up to $400 US worth of goods duty free. For stays of less than 48 hours, the duty free allowance reduces to $200 US.

Remember to declare such items as computer equipment, cameras and photographic equipment, audio equipment, and certain types of outdoor / sporting gear for personal use upon entering Canada.

Goods and Services Tax
Most goods and services in Canada are subject to a 7 percent goods and services tax (the GST). Non-residents may claim a rebate of this tax under certain conditions. For more information call 800-668-4748 in Canada.

Firearms
Strict laws apply for bringing firearms into Canada, and many types of weapons aren't allowed at all. Rifles and shotguns used for hunting are permitted, but must be specially licensed.

Contact the Canadian Firearms Centre at 800-731-4000 or www.cfc-ccaf.gc.ca for more information.

Liquor
Drinking alcohol in public places is prohibited in British Columbia, and the legal age for consuming alcoholic beverages is 19. No more than 1.1 litres of spirits or wine or 8.1 litres of beer or ale may be brought into Canada by any adult.

Dogs and Cats
Only dogs and cats older than three months may be brought into Canada from the US, and they must have a valid veterinary certificate stating that the animal has been vaccinated within the last three years for rabies.

Plants
All live plants must be declared and inspected before entry into Canada is allowed. For more information about Canada / US customs contact:

Canadian Customs Regulations
General Inquiries
First Floor, 33 Dunsmuir Street Vancouver BC V6BB 5R3 604-666-0545 or 800-461-9999 Monday-Friday 8:30 am to 4:30 pm 604-538-3610 after hours, and 24-hour information www.ccra-adrx.gc.ca

United States Regulations
604-278-1825 or 800-529-4410 (from Canada)

The Oceanside region on eastern Vancouver Island is home to many fine beaches.

quaint seaside towns.

The Pacific Rim encompasses the central west coast regions of the Alberni Valley, Pacific Rim National Park, Barkley Sound, and Clayoquot Sound. The harbour town of Port Alberni marks the entrance to the area, itself rich with historical attractions such as the Alberni Pacific Railway and McLean Mill National Historic Site. Also from Port Alberni depart the MV *Lady Rose* and MV *Frances Barkley*, two passenger freighters that sail the Alberni Inlet to Barkley Sound.

Pacific Rim National Park is the region's principal draw. Its natural treasures of long sandy beaches, hundreds of offshore islands and islets, and old-growth temperate rain forest are enchanting lures to thousands of recreationalists who annually venture here seeking surf-laden solitude. Along the park's coast migrate gray whales numbering in the thousands, and the shoreline-hugging, 77-kilometre-long West Coast Trail is one of the world's top wilderness

treks. Pretty Tofino on the Esowista Peninsula is the Pacific Rim's darling destination, noted for its great maritime ambiance and access to outdoor recreation of the highest calibre.

North Central Vancouver Island stretches from coast to coast, embracing the Comox Valley up to Campbell River and across to Nootka Sound. Courtenay and Comox are the staging grounds for alpine-to-ocean adventures from skiing to scuba diving. Strathcona Provincial Park spreads its

Boats bob in the gentle currents near the seaside hamlet of Cowichan Bay.

Vancouver Island Accommodations

Vancouver Island offers a wide range of accommodations to suit travellers' needs.

Hotels and Motels
The Super, Natural *British Columbia Accommodations Guide*, free from Tourism Vancouver Island or Tourism BC, lists approved accommodation and prices. Consult the Reference section for contact numbers.

Bed and Breakfast
B&B accommodations are widely available throughout Vancouver Island. Consult the Super, Natural *British Columbia Accommodations Guide* or contact the British Columbia Bed and Breakfast Assocation at 604-734-3486 or www.bcbba.com.

Hostels
Year-round accommodation for individuals or families is available through four Hostelling International (HI) Canada, BC Region, locations.

Hostelling International
Canada, BC Region
402-134 Abbott Street
Vancouver BC V6B 2K4
604-684-7111 or 800-661-0020
www.hihostels.bc.ca

HI-Victoria
516 Yates Street
Victoria, BC
250-537-4149
e-mail: victoria@hihostels.bc.ca

HI-Saltspring Island
640 Cusheon Lake Road
Saltspring Island, BC
250-537-4149
www.beacon.com/ssihostel
e-mail: hostel@saltspring.com

HI-Pender Island
Pender Islands, BC
250-629-6133 or 888-921-3111
e-mail:
info@cooperslanding.com

HI-Tofino
Whalers on the Point

A view out the window at the Wickaninnish Inn

Guesthouse
81 West Street
Tofino, BC
250-725-3463
www.tofinohostel.com
e-mail: info@tofinohostel.com

Commercial Campgrounds
Consult the SUPER, NATURAL BRITISH COLUMBIA *Accommodations Guide* for a directory of commercial campgrounds. **Most facilities** are full service offering flush toilets, showers, electrical hook-ups, laundry centres, supply stores, and children's areas.

BC Parks Campgrounds
Between them, Pacific Rim National Park and the 42 BC provincial parks on Vancouver Island and the Gulf Islands hold 1635 campsites. Amenities vary from wilderness walk-in camping to lodges with showers. In general, most facilities include flush or pit toilets, picnic tables, fire pits with wood supplies, and potable water. At BC Parks there is an overnight fee for most campsites, which are available on a first-come basis, although the busiest areas also have a reservations system. Contact the Discover Camping Campground Reservation

Service at 800-689-9025 or www.discovercamping.ca for more information.

BC Forest Campsites
The BC Forest Service lists 85 backcountry, self-maintained wilderness sites with basic amenities such as pit toilets, picnic tables, and fire rings. For information and passes contact:

BC Forest Service
Box 9513
Stn Prov Govt
Victoria BC V8W 9C2
250-387-1946

BC Forest Service, Vancouver Forest Region
2100 Labieux Road
Nanaimo BC V9T 6E9
250-751-7001

BC Forest Service, South Island Forest District
4227-6th Avenue
Port Alberni BC V9Y 4N1
250-724-9205

BC Forest Service, Campbell River Forest District
370 S. Dogwood Street
Campbell River BC V9W 6Y7
250-286-9300

BC Forest Service, Port McNeill Forest District
Box 7000, 2217 Mine Road
Port McNeill BC V0N 2R0
250-956-5000

254,800 hectares across the region's midsection, providing a wealth of hiking trails and wilderness adventures. From Gold River, the passenger freighter MV *Uchuck III* explores west coast inlets and channels, delivering supplies to the frontier settlements of Nootka Sound.

Campbell River, an undisputed fishing capital, is the region's principal town. For more than a century its favourable east coast location, at the mouth of the Campbell River where it flows into Discovery Passage, has lured sportfishers seeking mighty salmon. Offshore are Denman and Hornby islands, both laid-back destinations for art lovers and outdoor enthusiasts. More adventurous outings await farther out in Discovery Passage; the myriad Discovery Islands, principally Quadra and Cortes islands, present great outdoor recreation amid stunning scenery.

Vancouver Island By Sea

Ten ferry service fleets connect Vancouver Island and the Gulf Island with mainland BC and the United States, as well as points in between.

BC Ferries
1112 Fort Street
Victoria BC V8V 4V2
250-386-3431 (in Victoria or outside BC)
888-BC FERRY (from anywhere in BC, outside Victoria)
888-724-5223 (vehicle reservations from anywhere in BC)
604-444-2890 (calling from outside BC)
www.bcferries.com
BC Ferries' fleet of 40 ships calls at 47 ports along British Columbia's coast. Most routes link Vancouver Island with the Gulf Islands and the BC mainland. For route and schedule information contact the numbers listed above. Reserved boarding may be requested on the Tsawwassen-Swartz Bay, Horseshoe Bay-Departure Bay, and Tsawwassen-Duke Point routes for an extra fee.

Vancouver to Victoria
The flagships *Spirit of British Columbia*, *Spirit of Vancouver Island*, and others make frequent sailings (hourly in June, July, and August) connecting Tsawwassen on the BC mainland with Swartz Bay, Vancouver Island, 38 kilometres north of Victoria. The 44 kilometre crossing takes about 90 minutes. Pacific Coach Lines (800-661-1725) connects Tsawwassen, Horseshoe Bay, and Swartz Bay ferry terminals with Vancouver and Victoria city centres.

Vancouver to Nanaimo
Nanaimo's Departure Bay is linked to Horseshoe Bay, West Vancouver, by sailings every two hours. The 50 kilometre trip takes 95 minutes. Ferries run between Tsawwassen and Duke Point, 11 kilometres south of Nanaimo, frequently each day. The 70 kilometre crossing takes about two hours.

Gulf Islands
Ferries from both Tsawwassen on the BC mainland and Swartz Bay on Vancouver Island make numerous sailings to Saltspring, the Penders, Galiano, Mayne, and Saturna islands. BC Ferries also connects Saanich Inlet communities Brentwood Bay and Mill Bay; Crofton to Saltspring Island; and Chemainus to Kuper and Thetis island. Nanaimo is the departure terminal for crossings to Gabriola Island. The ferry from Buckley Bay, Vancouver Island, links with Denman and Hornby islands. Daily ferry services join Comox and Powell River. Campbell River is the embarkation point for Quadra Island, and from there to Cortes Island. Port McNeill has regular service to Alert Bay on Cormorant Island and to Malcolm Island's village of Sointula.

Inside Passage
Near Port Hardy, Bear Cove ferry terminal is the starting point for a 506 kilometre (15 hours one-way) journey aboard the *Queen of the North* through the Inside Passage to Prince Rupert.

Discovery Coast Passage
The *Queen of Chilliwack* departs Port Hardy for sailings through Discovery Passage en route to Bella Coola.

Alberni Marine Transportation Company
Port Alberni, BC
800-663-7192 or 250-723-8313
www.ladyrosemarine.com
Port Alberni is the home port for the MV *Lady Rose*, a 32-metre-long passenger and cargo ship, and the MV *Frances Barkley*, a 39 metre former Norwegian ferry, both of which link Barkley Sound communities with Port Alberni.

Black Ball Transport Inc.
430 Belleville
Victoria, BC
250-386-2202 (in Victoria)
360-457-4491 (in Port Angeles)
The MV *Coho* makes several daily sailings throughout the year, connecting Port Angeles with Victoria Harbour.

Far up-Island is the pristine natural wealth of **North Vancouver Island.** This is tree country, with vast tracts of timber destined for logging as well as lovingly preserved old-growth forest. The small, hardworking, logging and commercial fishing communities Port McNeill and Port Hardy are the largest towns. Both are good bases from which to launch recreational adventures from saltwater fishing excursions to whale watching. Cape Scott Provincial Park, encompassing the farthest northern tip of the Island, is a wilderness jewel of rugged shoreline, sandy beaches, coves, inlets, lakes, and rivers. Offshore rise Malcolm and Cormorant islands, the latter home to Alert Bay, one of Vancouver Island's most culturally rich First Nations settlements.

Vancouver Island By Sea

The MV Uchuck III *plies the waters of northwestern Vancouver Island*

Clipper Navigation Ltd
250-382-8100 or 800-888-2535 (in Victoria)
206-448-5000 (in Seattle)
www.victoriaclipper.co
Clipper Navigation's fleet of catamarans offers daily service year-round linking Victoria Harbour with Seattle's Pier 69.
Marine Link Tours
Campbell River, BC
250-286-3347
www.marinelinktours.com
From mid-March to mid-October the MV *Aurora Explorer*, a 40 metre freighter, takes passengers along on its working cruise of BC mainland inlets.
Nootka Sound Service Ltd.
Gold River, BC
250-283-2325 or 250-283-2515

www.island.net/~mvuchuck/
The MV *Uchuck III* takes passengers on a working voyage of Nootka Sound, Kyoquot Sound, and Esperanza Inlet out of the community of Gold River.
Victoria Harbour Ferry Co Ltd.
Victoria, BC
250-708-0201
www.harbourferry.com
This service connects Victoria's Inner Harbour with stops in the Gorge Waterway and Esquimalt Harbour.
Victoria Rapid Transit Inc.
Port Angeles, Washington
250-361-9144 (in BC)
360-452-8088 (in Port Angeles)
Connects Port Angeles and Victoria Harbour via the

Victoria Express, with one-hour crossings.
Victoria-San Juan Cruises
Bellingham, Washington
800-443-4552
www.whales.com
Service aboard the *Victoria Star III* connecting Bellingham, Washington, with Victoria.
Washington State Ferries
888-808-7977 (in Washington)
206-464-6400 (outside Washington)
250-381-1551 or 250-656-1531 (within BC)
Washington State Ferries connect Anacortes, Washington, with Sidney (five kilometres south of Swartz Bay terminal) via passage through the San Juan Islands.

Vancouver Island By Land

The shoreline near Bamfield

Vancouver Island is crisscrossed by nearly 10,000 kilometres of public roads, nearly 80 percent of which is paved. This is in addition to more than 1400 kilometres of Forest Service road reaching into the Island's wilderness. The Trans-Canada Highway — at 8047 kilometres the world's longest national highway — begins at Mile Zero in Victoria.

Drivers and passengers in any motor vehicle are required by law to use seat belts. Failure to do so can result in hefty fines. Motorists using any of the backcountry logging roads should be aware that logging trucks and other commercial vehicles have the right of way. Signs posted on logging roads may also note other restrictions and closures. For additional road information contact the BC Ministry of Transportation and Highways InfoLine at 900-565-4997 ($0.75 fee is assessed). To speak to ministry personnel call 604-660-9770 or key into www.gov.bc.ca/th/.

Bus Lines

BC Transit
www.bctransit.com

City bus service operates in the following locales:

Greater Victoria, Sooke, and the Saanich Peninsula
250-382-6161

Duncan, Lake Cowichan, Cobble Hill, Cowichan Bay, Mill Bay, Maple Bay, and Shawnigan Lake
250-746-9899

Nanaimo, Campbell River
250-287-7433

Parksville, Qualicum Beach
250-954-1001

Comox, Courtenay, Cumberland
250-339-5453

Port Alberni
250-723-3341

Gray Line of Victoria
250-388-5248
Travels to Seattle and Vancouver.

Island Coach Lines
250-385-4411
Victoria city-to-city service up-Island to Port Hardy and the west coast communities of Tofino and Ucluelet, and all points in between.

Pacific Coach Lines
800-661-1725
Connects Victoria and Vancouver, departing 75 minutes before BC Ferries sailings.

West Coast Trail Express
250-477-8700
Shuttle bus service connecting Victoria, Nanaimo, and Port Alberni to trailheads of West Coast Trail and Juan de Fuca Marine Trail; also charter service throughout Vancouver Island.

Railways
Approximately 400 kilometres of train track runs along Vancouver Island, notably the 281 kilometre run of the Esquimalt and Nanaimo Railway from Victoria to Courtenay, and the 88 kilometre Canadian Forest Products' Englewood Railway connecting Vernon Camp and Beaver Cove.

The Malahat (E&N Railiner)
250-383-4324 (in Victoria)
800-561-8630 (outside Victoria)
www.viarail.ca
Travelling the 115-year-old Esquimalt and Nanaimo Railway line, this VIA Rail-operated train takes in deep canyons, waterfalls, and historic sites on its Victoria to Courtenay run.

Vancouver Island by Air

Float planes at Tofino

Victoria International Airport is Canada's seventh busiest, annually serving more than a million passengers arriving via major carriers such as Air Canada. Moreover, Vancouver Island and the Gulf Islands are host to a number of smaller regional airlines with scheduled and charter service to many Island and mainland locations. Scenic flight operators are also available.

Air Canada
888-247-2262
www.aircanada.ca
Flights to and from Victoria and Vancouver, Nanaimo, Comox, Campbell River and points beyond

Air Nootka
250-283-2255
www.airnootka.com
Flights departing from Gold River, serving the central and northern coast of Vancouver Island

Airspeed Aviation
250-655-4300
Flights to and from Victoria and Abbotsford

Baxter Aviation
800-661-5599
Flights to and from Nanaimo and Vancouver

Harbour Air
800-665-0212
www.harbourair.com

Flights to and from Victoria and Vancouver, plus Duncan, Nanaimo, and the Gulf Islands
Helijet Airways
800-665-4354 or 250-382-6222
www.helijet.co
Flights to and from Ogden Point / Victoria Harbour and Vancouver plus Seattle

Horizon Air
800-547-9308
www.horizonair.com
Flights to and from Victoria International Airport and Seattle-Tacoma International Airport

Island Hopper
250-753-2020
Flights to and from Nanaimo and Vancouver, plus the Sunshine Coast

Island Valley Airways
877-533-7555
Flights to and from Victoria and Nanaimo, Comox, plus Langley

KD Air
800-665-4244
www.kdair.com
Flights to and from Qualicum Beach and Vancouver, Port Alberni, plus Texada Island

Kenmore Air Seaplanes
800-543-9595
www.kenmoreair.com
Flights to and from Victoria Inner Harbour and Seattle, Nanaimo, Gulf Islands, Campbell River, plus Port McNeill

Klitsa Air
250-723-2375
Charter flights departing from Port Alberni

Long Beach Helicopter Ltd.
250-758-0024
www.longbeachhelicopters.com
Charter flights to and from Nanaimo and Campbell River

North Vancouver Air
604-278-1608 or 800-228-6608
www.northvanair.com

Flights to and from Tofino and Vancouver, plus Seattle
NW Seaplanes Ltd of Canada
888-287-8371 or 250-287-8371
www.air-rainbow.com
Vancouver, Campbell River, Discovery Islands

Pacific Coastal Airlines
800-663-2872
www.pacific-coastal.com
Vancouver, Bella Bella, Bella Coola, Campbell River, Comox, Victoria, Port Hardy

Vancouver Island Air
877-331-2433 or 250-287-2433
www.vancouverislandair.com
Campbell River, Vancouver Island north coast

Vancouver Island Helicopters
250-656-3987
www.vihcom
Sidney, Port Alberni, Campbell River, Gold River, Port McNeill, Port Hardy

West Coast Air
800-347-2222 or 250-388-4521
www.westcoastair.com
Victoria, Vancouver, Victoria Harbour, Coal Harbour

WestJet Airlines
800-538-5696
www.westjet.com
Victoria, Vancouver, and points beyond

Scenic Air Tours
Cooper Air Inc.
PO Box 2082
Sidney, BC V8L 3S3
250-656-3968
800-656-0766
www.copperair.com

Hyack Air (1981) Ltd.
1234 Wharf Street
Victoria BC V8W 3H9
250-384-2411

Juan Air (1979) Ltd.
PO Box 2182
Sidney, BC V8L 3S8
250-656-4312
www.juanair.com

Highlights of History

Dugout canoes plied the coastal waters around Vancouver Island

ONE *HUNDRED MILLION YEARS AGO* – The collision of Wrangelia, a South Pacific continent drifting northward, and Laurentia, the westward-creeping North American continent, gave rise to the Vancouver Island Mountains.

65 MILLION YEARS AGO – Tectonic pressures cleave Wrangellia; one part gives birth to Alaska and the other forms Vancouver Island and the Queen Charlotte Islands (Haida Gwaii).

2 MILLION YEARS AGO – During the Pleistocene Epoch, Vancouver Island undergoes a series of freezes and thaws, causing sea levels to fluctuate and thus forming intermittent land bridges or watery straits.

30,000 TO 20,000 YEARS AGO – Vancouver Island is home to Imperial mammoths, giant bison, and musk oxen — mainland immigrants that crossed to the Island via land bridges across the Strait of Georgia.

14,000 YEARS AGO – Ice, up to a kilometre thick, encases much of Vancouver Island.

10,000 TO 8000 YEARS AGO – The Ice Age thaws, though reminders of that time, such as the Comox Glacier, survive to this day. Animals still familiar today — black bears, killer whales, Steller's sea lions, and others — inhabit Vancouver Island.

4000 YEARS AGO – Evidence exists that humans lived in the Alberni Inlet at this time, though it is probable people had ventured to Vancouver Island shores for millennia.

1579 – Sir Francis Drake, English adventurer and mariner, may perhaps have been the first European to sight Vancouver Island as his expedition skirts the North American Pacific Coast as far north as the Strait of Juan de Fuca. It is possible there were even earlier explorers — Asian mariners hailing from China or Japan.

1592 – Juan de Fuca, a Greek mariner whose actual name was Apostolos Valerianos, is credited as the first European to explore the waters off

James Douglas

Vancouver Island while searching for the Northwest Passage for the Viceroy of Mexico.

1774 – On August 8, Ensign Juan Josef Pérez of the Spanish frigate *Santiago* anchors off Nootka Sound; he becomes the first European to have contact with the indigenous people of Vancouver Island. Pérez did not go ashore, though members of the Nuu-chah-nulth came aboard the ship to trade.

1778 – British seafarer Captain James Cook anchors off Vancouver Island's western shoreline. He, along with then midshipman George Vancouver, is welcomed into the village of Yuquot. Maquinna, the hereditary leader of the Mowachaht, barters sea otter furs for European goods. Later, in China, the sea otter furs are sold at a fabulous profit.

1789 – Don Estevan Martínez claims the North American northwest coast for Spain.

1790 – On June 30, the Native people of Albert Head (now part of Sooke) find Spanish explorer Manuel Quimper wandering their beach; he subsequently claims the land in the name of the King of Spain.

1792 – The village of Yuquot once again welcomes George Vancouver, now a captain and the English representative to negotiate with Spaniard Juan Francisco de la Bodega y Quadra for the sovereignty of the Pacific Northwest coast. They do not reach an agreement, and the region remains open to all nations for trading.

1834 – Humpback, gray, blue, and minke whales are actively hunted for their valuable oil. Such high numbers are killed that it takes less than a century to put the species on the brink of extinction.

1842 – Chief Factor James Douglas of the Hudson's Bay Company completes a detailed examination of Sooke, Becher Bay, Metchosin, Esquimalt, and Victoria harbours. He selects Victoria — known then as Camosack — as the site for a new Hudson's Bay Company depot.

1843 – March 14 finds Douglas off Clover Point, and the following day he decides on the Inner Harbour area for a new fort. By Sunday, March 19, Father Jean-Baptiste Bolduc, a Catholic priest accompanying Douglas, celebrates the first mass in the area. On June 4, the fort's construction begins. It is called initially Fort Camosack, then later Fort Albert, and finally changed to Fort Victoria by June 10.

1846 – The Oregon Treaty establishes the boundary line of the United States and Canada. It runs along the 49th parallel to the Strait of Georgia, then deflects south through the straits to the Pacific Ocean. The demarcation leaves all of Vancouver Island within Canada.

1849 – On January 13, the

Robert Dunsmuir

Imperial Government of the Crown Colony of Vancouver Island is created. Although the Hudson's Bay Company retains a monopoly on the Island's vast natural resources, it must colonize the Island within five years.

Fort Rupert coal mining operations begin, ushering in an industry that will dictate the Island's economy until the 1930s.

1850 – On March 11, Richard Blanshard arrives to take office as Vancouver Island's first governor.

1850-1854 – The amount of Vancouver Island Crown land is substantially increased as James Douglas negotiates land purchase agreements with First Nations leaders. Many aboriginal people are relegated to small reserves.

1852 – A townsite is established around Fort Victoria, and the name is changed to Victoria.

1858 – Some 25,000 gold-hungry adventurers flow through Fort Victoria en route to mainland gold fields. The mainland is declared a new British colony — British Columbia.

1862 – Victoria is incorporated as a city with Thomas Harris as the first mayor. A smallpox epidemic devastates Vancouver Island's First Nations peoples. It has been estimated that the Tsimshian lost half their population, the Kwagiulth two thirds, and the Haida three-quarters. The first industrial sawmill on Vancouver Island — and in BC — opens at the head of the Alberni Inlet. In September, the *Tynemouth*, a "bride ship" hailing from England, pulls into port at Esquimalt, disembarking 61 "well built, pretty-looking women, ages varying from 14 to an uncertain figure; a few are young widows who have seen better days."

1864 – The old Fort Victoria is finally demolished and lots are auctioned off.

1866 – Mainland British Columbia and Vancouver

Emily Carr at her trailer, The Elephant

Captain George Vancouver

Born in England in 1757, George Vancouver enlisted in the Royal Navy in 1771 and sailed with Captain James Cook during Cook's second and third voyages in 1772-75, 1776-80.

In 1790, Vancouver was promoted to commander of the HMS *Discovery*, a 340-ton sloop. Heading a 1791-92 expedition to Australia, New Zealand, and the Hawaiian Islands, Vancouver then sailed to the Pacific Coast of North America, charting the coastline from Cape Mendocino near San Francisco to southern Alaska.

While officially Vancouver was under orders to attend the Nootka Conference to settle sovereignty of the area with the Spanish, he was also instructed to make an extensive exploration of the Pacific Coast. There was still hope of finding the elusive Northwest Passage, or any other means to effectively connect the Pacific and Atlantic oceans. His expedition was well equipped, with a crew of 150 men aboard his flagship and attending vessels, the *Chatham* and the *Daedalus*, plus the latest navigational and scientific instruments.

Meticulous in every detail, Captain Vancouver plotted and mapped his way up the coast, exploring Puget Sound, which he named for one of his lieutenants, Peter Puget. Mt. Baker came by its designation in honour of another of his lieutenants, who first spotted its snowy peak. To make his discoveries official, and also to bolster Great Britain's claim to the lands he surveyed, Vancouver formally assumed possession of the area on June 4, 1792, near the present site of Everett, Washington, proclaiming the region New Georgia after George III, king of England.

Vancouver then proceeded northward to Nootka Sound, where he met with the Spanish commissioner, Captain Juan Francisco de la Bodega y Quadra, to negotiate the conflicting claims on the Pacific Coast. By all accounts the two thoroughly enjoyed each other's fellowship, wining, dining, and deliberating — to no avail. Vancouver and Quadra parted company with no agreement, and it would be almost two decades before discord between the British, Spanish, Russians, and Americans over the Pacific Northwest Coast reached resolution.

Captain Vancouver and company didn't reach home until October 1795, having spent four and a half years sailing some 100,000 kilometres, mapping nearly 3000 kilometres of shoreline, and circumnavigating an island that now is named in his honour. His account of the expedition and his maps were published as *A Voyage of Discovery to the North Pacific Ocean and Round the World* in 1798. Regrettably, Vancouver did not live to see the printed and bound manuscripts; he died that same year.

Canadian Pacific Princess ships in Haro Strait, from the Oak Bay Beach Hotel, about 1930

Island are merged into the combined colony of British Columbia. The capital is at New Westminster.

1868 – Victoria is named the capital of the Colony of British Columbia.

1871 – On July 20, British Columbia enters the Canadian Confederation. Victoria becomes the capital of the Province of British Columbia, in the Dominion of Canada.

Emily Carr is born in December at Carr House at the northeast corner of Government and Simcoe streets.

1877 – Sir James Douglas, Victoria's founder and the father of British Columbia, dies and is interred at Ross Bay Cemetery.

1881 – Vancouver Island population is tallied at 17,292 according to BC's first official census.

1884 – Coal baron Robert Dunsmuir agrees to build what would become the Esquimalt and Nanaimo Railway; the Canadian government pays $750,000 and grants rights, including mineral and timber, on 1 million hectares adjoining the line's route up Vancouver Island's east coast.

1886 – The Provincial Museum of Natural History and Anthropology opens in Victoria; it later becomes the Royal British Columbia Museum. The Esquimalt and Nanaimo Railway from Esquimalt to Nanaimo is completed.

1898 – The provincial Legislative Buildings are completed.

1903 – The Victoria Terminal Railway and Ferry Company initiates service between Sidney and the mouth of the Fraser River, with a rail link between Sidney and Victoria.

1905 – The Canadian Pacific Railway begins construction of the Empress Hotel.

1911 – Strathcona Provincial Park becomes Vancouver Island's first provincial preserve.

1932 – The first Sidney to Anacortes Ferry, the *City of Angels*, completes its inaugural run.

1939 – With the outbreak of World War II, the Patricia Bay Airport is constructed as a training site. It continues today as Victoria International Airport.

1945 – Emily Carr dies in March.

1958 – Ripple Rock, a deadly shipping obstacle off Vancouver Island's east coast, is blown up in the largest humanmade non-atomic explosion.

1994 – Victoria hosts the XV Commonwealth Games.

2000 – The United Nations Educational, Scientific, and Cultural Organization (UNESCO) designates Clayoquot Sound as BC's first World Biosphere Reserve.

2001 – Victoria is awarded the Prince of Wales Prize, named for Prince Charles, for the city's long-standing dedication to preserving its heritage buildings and districts.

2002 – Victoria welcomes Queen Elizabeth II, honouring her Golden Jubilee.

21

Highlights of Nature

Sea lions brave the rocky west coast of Vancouver Island.

Vancouver Island has been blessed with a natural environment of startling beauty. Some 439,000 hectares, about 13 percent of the Island, has been protected. Point the compass in any direction — from far north Cape Scott Provincial Park to the southern tip at

Race Rocks to the western wilds of Pacific Rim National Park to Robson Bight on the east — and discover a bounty of sylvan and maritime treasures.

Old-growth forest, caves, broad blue lakes, salmon-spawning rivers, tide pools, and estuaries are only a few of the ecosystems sheltered within Vancouver Island's 130 provincial parks, two national parks, two world heritage biospheres, six regional district parks, and numerous municipal parks. Some are immense. Strathcona Provincial Park, BC's first, encompasses nearly half Vancouver Island's parkland. Small wonders include such

delights as Botanical Beach on the west coast or Victoria's Beacon Hill. Others contribute to larger dreams, such as Victoria's Galloping Goose Trail, the Island extension of the Trans Canada Trail, which stretches 18,000 kilometres across the nation. Closer to home, the Sea-to-Sea Green-belt, a 200 kilometre swathe of parkland and protected areas, cuts east to west across southern Vancouver Island.

Such an abundance of wilderness and preserve — with habitats ranging from tidal estuaries and rugged coastlines to high alpine glaciers and thick rain forest — allows for a diversity of flora and fauna matched by few

locales across the planet. More than 7000 known species dwell in the Island's watery world alone, including 28 marine mammals such as Pacific gray and killer whales, dolphins, fur seals, and Steller's sea lions. These are in addition to all five species of Pacific salmon, giant red sea urchins, wolf eels, six-gill sharks, crabs, sea anemones, clams, mussels ... and on and on.

On terra firma, 33 land mammals call pristine valleys, river gorges, alpine meadows, and sand shorelines home. Black bears, black-tailed deer, beavers, river otters, raccoons, and Roosevelt elk are frequently spotted, as are

Opposite: Flowers bloom profusely throughout Vancouver Island.

Foxglove

Heirloom Rose

cougars. Vancouver Island has one of the world's densest populations of this majestic cat, an estimated 1000, mostly inhabiting the far north. Less common are such creatures as the Vancouver Island marmot, an indigenous species that evolved on Vancouver Island, or the rare Keen's long-eared myotis bat, which only breeds in two northern Vancouver Island caves.

The avian realm is richly represented too; Vancouver Island is a favoured stop on the Pacific Flyway for migrating birds. Over the course of the year, birders have recorded 387 species on the Island. Of special interest to bird-watchers are the autumn raptor migrations from East Sooke Park and Goldstream Provincial Park; the springtime brant goose migration and festival at the Oceanside resorts of Parksville and Qualicum Beach; the

Courtenay River Estuary festival honouring the yearly residence of trumpeter swans; plus the seasonal shorebird arrivals at Tofino Flats.

Plants
Flowers
Beach Pea
Beach-loving, as its name implies, beach pea tendrils climb along the ground and reach up to 1.5 metres long. Flowers resemble those of sweet peas and range in colour from blue to reddish purple.

Camas
Prized as a food source by First Nations people, the bulbs of these elegant lily-like blue to violet blooming plants were made into starchy cakes. Inexperienced bulb collectors can confuse the edible version with death camas, a poisonous variety.

Calypso Orchid
Preferring mature, moist,

lowland forests, this plant's single slipper-shaped bloom, white with magenta streaks and spots, rises from a 15- to 18-centimetre-long stem with oval leaves. By early summer the plant withers, to re-emerge in autumn.

False Azalea
Actually a type of heather, this species grows to three metre heights. Its flowers are copper coloured and bell shaped, and its leaves are hairy and bunched in whorls.

Foxglove
Commonly seen along roadsides and in clearcut forested areas, these showy 50-centimetre-high spikes are laden with tubular flowers that can be pink, purple, or white. Originally from Europe, foxglove is a source of digitalin, used as a heart stimulant.

Indian Paintbrush
Flowering with clusters of

Blackberries

elliptical bracts that blossom into a number of hues from red to pink to magenta to orange, this widespread plant of the coast and inland meadows was used by First Nations as a lure to catch hummingbirds.

Skunk Cabbage

Heralding the arrival of spring, skunk cabbage blooms with a yellow hood partially enfolding a flowering spike. Sometimes called "swamp lantern," the flowers emit a distinctive odour to attract pollinating insects.

Spreading Dogbane

Large oval glossy leaves cover spreading branchlets that can extend almost a metre across shadier sites. Its pink flowers are quite fragrant and produce 12-centimetre-long seed pods.

Searocket

Sandy beaches are home to this mustard family member, which is most likely an introduced species. Dainty flowers range in colour from white to purple. The name "rocket" stems from the French word *roquette* and Italian *ruchetta*, which describe the Mediterranean species.

Wild Ginger

Found in moist forests, this aromatic plant is unrelated to real ginger, though early pioneers found the tangy flavour to their liking. Brownish purple flowers with three long lobes appear on the short stalks, but are somewhat hard to spot as they are well camouflaged.

Trees and Shrubs

Red Alder

These common trees line the coasts of British Columbia, thriving along stream banks and roadsides. Sun loving, and a rapid pioneering species, alder was widely used by First Nations people for producing red dyes, smoking fish, and carving. The egg-shaped leaves are 7 to 10 centimetres long and have rounded teeth. During late March, male trees bear showy catkins.

Arbutus *(Pacific Madrona)*

Identifiable by its reddish brown bark that peels off in ragged strips, the tree has leathery oblong leaves. In May, arbutus bloom with clusters of white bell-shaped flowers, followed by reddish orange berries in late summer.

Amabilis Fir

Found in coastal forests above 300 metres, this species is also known as Pacific silver fir. The slender trees that reach heights of 50 metres have smooth, ash-gray bark and needles that are flat and notched at the tip. Barrel-shaped cones reaching 10 centimetres in length stand upright along branches.

Douglas Fir

Mature trees are usually two metres in diameter and reach 85 metres into the sky, making this Canada's largest tree. Coastal and interior varieties are the two types found on Vancouver Island, and some individual trees exceed 1000 years in age. Branchlets hold pointed needles, and buds are reddish brown. Cones have three forked bracts and are 5 to 10 centimetres long. The species is named for David Douglas, a Scottish botanist who first described the towering tree.

Garry Oak

The only oak that grows west of the Rocky Mountains in Canada, the species is unique to Vancouver Island's southern coast and the Fraser River Valley on the mainland. Noted for its scaly bark and twisted branches, it is also called the Oregon white oak; south of the border it grows abundantly. It was named by botanist David Douglas for Nicholas Garry of the Hudson's Bay Company.

Sitka Spruce

A large conifer that can reach 70 metres tall and two metres in diameter, these sea-salt tolerant trees are primarily found in the fringe areas along beaches. Branches are long and droopy, with a grayish, scaly bark. Stiff bottle brush-like needles line twigs, and cones are 5 to 10 centimetres long with papery scales.

Western Red Cedar

This is BC's official tree, and long honoured by First Nations people. A primary construction material, the tree also held spiritual importance. It prefers moist soils and is found in low to mid elevations along the coast. Drooping, spreading branches splay out from trunks with stringy bark, and small flower-like cones stand upright on the branches.

Yellow Cedar

Reaching up to 25 metres tall, with a diameter of 90 centimetres, this common tree is also seen in coastal bog environments, though considerably smaller in size. Boat builders favour the tree's straight grain and decay resistance, as well as its warm yellow colouring.

Western Hemlock

This hemlock species has a drooping top and splaying branches covered with small flat needles, blunt and unequal in length. Numerous small cones hang from the branchlets.

Western Yew

This small conifer bears reddish, papery bark and reaches heights of 10 metres. It has flat, pointed needles, two centimetres long, and produces red berries that are toxic to humans, though a compound in the bark is now the focus of cancer research for its taxol content. First Nations people used the wood for a variety of tools and implements, including paddles, clubs, harpoon

Yellow cedar

shafts, and bowls.

Salal

An abundant shrub preferring forest floors, salal may reach dimensions of up to five metres. The evergreen foliage, with its finely-toothed oval leaves, is commercially harvested for flower arrangements. The blue berries are edible and were gathered by Native people.

Dwarf Dogwood

Bunchberry is this plant's other name, referring to its clusters of red berry-like fruit. The shrub tolerates both moist and mixed forest areas, as well as bogs. It bears white flowers in spring.

Labrador Tea

Well adapted to acidic, boggy areas, the plant can grow to one metre tall and bears rust-coloured leaves with a woolly underside. First Nations people made tea from the fresh or dried leaves.

Kinnikinnick

"Bear berry" to some folks, this low evergreen grows into thick mats along sandy dunes. While the bright red berries are edible, they're not tasty — except to bears. First Nations people dried the leaves for smoking.

Arbutus

Pacific Crabapple

This shrub thrives along lakeshores and streambeds, producing white or pink flowers, followed by tart green apples. First Nations people gathered the apples, storing them in water to help preserve them. The shrub's wood lends itself to making tool handles, wedges, digging sticks, and bows.

Red Elderberry

Soft, pithy stems mark this shrub, which blooms with clusters of yellowish cream-coloured flowers. Humans should not eat the berries produced in July and August, but birds do just fine by them. A large shrub, it can reach 45 centimetres high, with leaves in groups of five to seven sprouting from opposing branches.

Salmonberry

Brown stems produce scattered spines, with leaflets usually in threes. Dark pink flowers bloom from April to June, and come June to July there are yellow to orange-red berries.

Killer whales frequent the waters off Vancouver Island

Animals

Marine Mammals
Humpback Whale
Weighing in at 40 tonnes, growing to more than 12 metres in length, and displaying dorsal fins of five metres, this leviathan is an endangered species — and nearly two-thirds of the world's population of 10,000 call the northeast Pacific home. Humpbacks are baleen whales and feed on small fish and krill. "Bubble netting," in which they emit a screen of air bubbles to act like a natural net, is one of their most frequently used hunting techniques.

Pacific Gray Whale
Another baleen whale, grays are mottled gray in colour and often have barnacles and yellow lice attached to their bodies. Travelling some 15,000 kilometres annually, gray whales have the longest migration of any mammal. Vancouver Island welcomes a population numbering in the thousands in March and April. They come close to shore, offering excellent spotting opportunities.

Killer Whale
Vancouver Island waters support three resident pods of killer whales, in all about 300 individual whales. Transients come and go, moving up and down the coastline. Residents feed only on fish, but transients also hunt seals and other whales. A male adult killer whale exhibits a prominent dorsal fin. The individual pattern of scars on each whale's dorsal fin is used by researchers to easily identify specific whales. Killer whales, with their distinctive black-and-white colouring, are actually members of the dolphin family.

Pacific White-Sided Dolphin
Active and playful, these speedy dolphins display a black back and chin with a white stripe running forehead to tail; they are light gray to white from forehead to lower sides and belly. Gregarious and acrobatic, they are noted too for their curved dorsal fin with a white patch and black tip.

Pacific Harbour Porpoise
Measuring about 1.5 metres long and weighing about 40 kilograms, these porpoises are commonly seen off Vancouver

Sealing

Baby harbour seal

For generations, First Nations people harvested seals for their pelts, meat, and blubber, never taking them in great numbers. However, the seals' and sea lions' fate took a turn for the worse in the 1860s. Sea otters had made Europeans wealthy, but their diminishing population turned entrepreneurs to seals and sea lions as alternate commercial pelt sources.

Victoria became a sealing centre, with fleets of schooners exploiting the sealing grounds, and later the rookeries, to meet an increasing demand for the soft fur. Over time, the decline in seal and sea lion populations intensified competition, even leading to escalating tensions between Canada and the United States over access to sealing grounds in Alaskan waters. Not until 1911 was a treaty signed by the two nations that banned the fur sealing harvest, rescuing the seal and sea lion species from the brink of disaster.

Island's coasts. They frequently travel in small groups and can be spotted by their short bursts of blowing. They maintain their distance from boats and swimmers.

Dall's Porpoise

Travelling in pods of 20 or so, these porpoises are the boat "bow riders" and all-around aquatic acrobats frequently seen off Vancouver Island. They feed on fish, squid, and crustaceans when not entertaining humans.

Sea Otter

Hunted to near extinction for their luxurious pelts, these comical creatures have now re-established small colonies north of Clayoquot Sound. The sea otter's reviving population, transplanted from Alaska, means it has once again become an important indigenous species of Vancouver Island.

California Sea Lions

Spied along the southern and western coasts of Vancouver Island, these sleek mammals migrate from as far away as Mexico to refresh themselves after the summer breeding season. California sea lions are dark brown, weigh up to 500 kilograms, bear a prominent forehead protrusion, and bark.

Elephant Seal

After facing extermination by sealers in the 1880s, elephant seals are now occasionally seen in the waters of southern Vancouver Island and Barkley Sound during the winter months. The coasts of California and Mexico are their warmer-climate homes, where they breed. Expert divers, they can descend to depths of 200 metres and stay under without surfacing for air for 40 minutes.

Black bears inhabit many areas of Vancouver Island.

Steller's Sea Lion

Vancouver Island holds many haul-out points where these sea lions (also known as the northern sea lion) congregate and growl. Massive in size, males can exceed a tonne in weight. They are blond in colouration and don't have a bulging forehead like their California cousins. Feeding on a wide variety of sea life from squid to crab to tiny shrimp, they are in turn vigorously hunted by killer whales.

Harbour Seal

These widely dispersed denizens of the coastal waters of Vancouver Island are also called "hair seals." They are voracious hunters of salmon and were considered a threat to human commercial fishing interests. Hence, in earlier times a bounty was placed on these seals. They can remain underwater for up to an hour, though typically they only dive for a few minutes before resurfacing for air.

Pine martens are agile tree climbers.

Vancouver Island holds a large population of cougars.

Northern Fur Seal

This seal's southward migration in December to January brings them to Vancouver Island's west coast shores, and then in April to May they move offshore. They feed on mainly squid and herring.

Land Mammals

Black Bear

"Black" bears can also be brown or cinnamon in colouration. They average a height of 1.2 to 1.9 metres when standing on their hind feet, and can weigh up to 250 kilograms. Their wide-ranging diet is their principal survival technique; they will eat insects, green vegetation, wild berries and fruit, salmon, even carrion. Late November is when black bears den, emerging again in April. In the wild, black bears may reach the age of 20 years, and some individuals have lived 30 years.

Cougar

Male cougars can top 90 kilograms, stretching to 2.7 metres long, including their 90 centimetre tails. Females are somewhat smaller, averaging 35 kilograms and 1.5 metres long. Cougars are slender with small heads and are predominately tawny brown with white underbelly and facial markings. In the wild, these big cats live an average of 10 years.

Black-Tailed Deer

The most commonly seen deer on Vancouver Island, this is actually a dark-hued subspecies of mule deer. Fawns are light brown with spots on their sides and back; the calving season is between March and November.

Roosevelt Elk

Roosevelt elk, sometimes known as Olympic elk, are larger and darker in colouration than Rocky Mountain elk. A mature bull may weigh as much 450 kilograms. Their antlers are shorter and heavier, with a narrower overall spread. Huckleberry, wild blackberry, salal, and other shrubs are favourite foods during most of the year. Weeds and grasses are their preferred staples in the spring and early summer.

Raccoon

Common throughout Vancouver Island, raccoons hunt and scavenge for food. Their opposable thumbs make them dexterous; their tracks look like tiny human handprints.

Pine Marten

Semi-retractable claws make these small weasels agile tree climbers, and they use this ability to hunt insects and small rodents, and escape from predators. Reddish brown, with paler ears, adults can reach 62 centimetres in length, including a 15-centimetre-long tail.

Red Squirrel

Feisty red squirrels respond to threats with aggressive chattering. Autumn finds them cutting cones from trees for winter storage in caches or "middens."

Mink

These water-loving weasels are found along lakeshores and streams, and in wetlands. Partially webbed feet and short legs enable them to swim efficiently and gracefully. Their lustrous brown, lush, and rather oily pelt insulates them from the cold.

River Otter

These weasels are nomadic, following their favourite foods whether in freshwater or seawater habitats. An unpleasant, acrid scent is a sign of river otter presence. They can be aggressive if threatened, but usually they are simply a delight to watch, their playful natural antics are constantly amusing.

Birds

Bald Eagle

These regal birds can be observed daily at some locales around Vancouver Island. Impressive hunters, they'll also scavenge. Juveniles are mottled brown; only after three years of age do the distinctive white hoods appear. Both males and females bear the marking, in addition to white tail feathers. Bald eagles' calls are high-pitched, stuttering cries. Vancouver Island is home to more bald eagles than the continental United States.

Osprey

As this bird of prey primarily hunts fish, it is frequently spotted along beaches and mudflats, hovering, then plunging into the shallow water, talons first, to snatch a meal. Interestingly, ospreys have an outer "opposed" talon that enables them to grip wriggling, slippery fish more securely.

Pilated Woodpecker

With a solid black head and back adorned with a red crest, this is the largest woodpecker in North America. Its slow drumming resounds throughout the forest as it pounds its strong bill into tree trunks, drilling square holes in its search for insects. Woodpeckers perch upright when foraging, unlike warblers and hatches that perch head down.

Western Screech Owl

This eared owl with feathery tufts on its head ranges in colour from gray to orangish brown. Coastal British Columbia and southern Ontario are the only places in Canada where these owls are found.

Common Raven

The large cousin to the crow,

Sea otters have been successfully re-established to Vancouver Island.

the jet-black raven is omnivorous and will eat almost anything it spots. Ravens are year-round Vancouver Island residents and one of the most frequently seen birds.

Varied Thrush

Coniferous woods throughout the Island are home to these year-round residents. Their bell-like whistle ring is a familiar rainforest sound.

Steller's Jay

Aggressive and noisy, this is the only crested jay west of the Rocky Mountains. Smoky blue in colouring, the species can easily imitate other bird's calls, warding off predators. They nest in conifers and feed on seeds, nuts, fruits, and insects.

Glaucous-Winged Gull

A nesting resident of the islands, it can been seen daily all year long. Mature adults are white plumed with gray wings. Younger gulls are brown with black bills. Note the absence of black wing tips; herring and California gulls bear these markings while glaucous-winged gulls don't.

Dunlin

Dunlins are winter beach residents, brownish grey, with white underbellies and long beaks, which they use to probe

the sands in search of worms and larvae.

Killdeer

Beach inhabitants, these birds are consummate actors. When nests are threatened, killdeer divert predators by flying a short distance away, then faking an injury by dragging one wing along in the sand.

Semipalmated Plover

A common migrant to Vancouver Island, these birds arrive in July and stay until late August. Sandy beaches are their habitat. They use their light-footed approach to sneak up on sand-burrowing prey.

Western Sandpiper

Flocks of these birds are commonly seen on beaches and mudflats, feeding on small invertebrates exposed by the shifting tides.

Brandt's Cormorant

This is a year-round resident of Vancouver Island's west coast, which is the northern range limit of this Pacific Rim bird. Cormorant young are born naked in nests of eel grass and seaweed, and are totally dependent upon parents for warmth and food.

Black Oystercatcher

Rocky headlands, exposed reefs, and islets are the habitat

Bald eagle

Canada goose

Osprey

of this bird, which uses its formidable bill to plunge into shells and skewer crabs.

Western Grebe
Seen primarily between October and May, these grebes use protective breeding grounds in interior forests, but are frequently spotted along the coastline.

Pigeon Guillemot
Usually spotted offshore and along rocky outcroppings, these "alcids" are related to auks and murres. Broad, white-coloured wing patches identify these predominately black birds.

Sooty Shearwater
Sometimes spied in flocks numbering in the thousands, this Pacific Rim oceanic bird nests in New Zealand and Australia, but migrates to the North American Pacific Coast come April, returning home via Japan in October.

Black-footed Albatross
The so-called "goony bird" is a Vancouver Island offshore summer resident, most often spotted by boaters in open water.

Pelagic Cormorant
Often seen off the west coast, these birds nest on steep cliffs, cozy in their well-protected homes made of mud, guano, and various aquatic vegetation.

Chestnut-backed Chickadee
Stands of Sitka spruce are a good place to see this forest dweller, which dwells year-round on Vancouver Island.

American Widgeon
This small dappled duck with a white forehead and black eye-stripes is sometimes seen in flocks of more than 1000, feeding on eelgrass mudflats. Its migration pattern brings it to Vancouver Island from September to October.

Canada Goose
Tidal flats are a good place to observe flocks of this signature bird of Canada. The long days of summer, warm but not hot climate, and abundant food sources bring them northward, travelling in flocks of 100 or so. When migrating, these birds adopt the distinctive V-formation; a goose in this shaped flock can travel more than 70 percent farther than one flying solo. Flock speeds average about 80 kilometres per hour at altitudes of up to 2400 metres. Honking is their flying language, used to communicate direction changes and dangers.

Mallard
Shallow water inlets and mudflats are the places to find these common Vancouver Island visitors, identified by their brilliant green hoods and yellow beaks. October to April is their season, as they arrive in late fall to feast on dying salmon and salmon spawn along rivers and streams.

Bufflehead
The Pacific Rim's most abundant diving duck, these white-bottomed, black-topped birds favour shallow, protected waters, congregating in flocks of 100 or more from October to May.

Fish
Saltwater
Pacific Salmon
Each Pacific salmon species is called many names. Chum, for example, are also known as dog, keta, fall, or calico salmon. They reach lengths of 102 centimetres, weighing on average 15 kilograms, and ranging from southern California to Korea. Coho salmon are also known as silver, jack, hooknose, blue-back, or silversides salmon. This type ranges from the northern Baja to the Aleutian

Islands to northern Japan. As adults they can weigh 14 kilograms and grow to 98 centimetres. Coho are used for canning, smoking, and freezing, and are also eaten fresh. Sockeye salmon are the most commercially important species in the Pacific Northwest. On average, sockeye or red salmon can grow to 84 centimetres and weigh 6.8 kilograms. Pink salmon, also known as humpback or "humpies" due to their distinctive curved back which appears during spawning season, grow to 76 centimetres and can tip the scales at 6.8 kilograms. Chinook salmon are true kings, growing to weights that can exceed 57 kilograms. Chinooks over 13 kilograms are also known as "tyee," a name bestowed upon the mighty fish by the Tyee Club of B.C., founded in 1924 to honour fishers' skills at landing the feisty fish using light tackle from a rowboat. Chinook are identifiable by their blue-green back and spotted tail. Chinook snouts become hooked and their teeth enlarged when they return to fresh water to spawn.

Pacific Halibut

Sought by commercial fishers and sportfishers today, Pacific halibut have a rich history with First Nations peoples. The elongated flatfish with both eyes on its upperside is often depicted on totem poles and other objects. Grayish in colouring, halibut uppersides are darker than bottomsides, helping them avoid detection by both predator and prey. Halibut spawn in deep water primarily from December through February. Females lay two to three mil-

Millions of Pacific salmon migrate annually to Vancouver Island rivers.

lion eggs and the fertilized eggs hatch after 15 days to become free-floating larvae. Younger halibut are very migratory, but after age 10 they tend to stay in smaller regions. Female halibut can live up to 40 years, and males may reach age 30. Most halibut weight about seven to 10 kilograms, though catches of over 50 kilograms are not rare, and some halibut grow to a hefty 200 kilograms.

Pacific Cod

Alaska cod or gray cod to some, this species tops the scale at 22 kilograms and grows to 117 centimetres long. Ranging from southern California to the Bering Strait and across to Japan, the fish is an important food source for marine animals and humans alike. Females release over 6 million eggs, which are fertilized by the males and then abandoned to the currents to hatch.

Red Tide

Heed the warnings for red tide closings before collecting or eating shellfish. Paralytic Shellfish Poisoning (PSP) is the reason — and in humans this can be fatal.

Red tides occur naturally when dinoflagellates, single-celled microscopic organisms that live in the sea, spontaneously bloom under certain conditions during the summertime. The population of dinoflagellates increases dramatically, turning seawater visibly red. Dinoflagellates also produce toxins that are accumulated in large amounts by water-filtering bivalves such as clams, oysters, and mussels. These toxins do not harm the bivalves, which can take months to fully expel the taint from their systems.

However, people ingesting clams, oysters, or mussels containing these toxins can experience the symptoms of PSP within minutes. Initially the lips and tongue tingle, followed by the spread of the numbing sensation to toes, fingers, and perhaps arms and legs. In severe cases of PSP, paralysis can occur and lead to death.

An Orca surfaces in the open ocean.

Pacific Herring

Widely dispersed throughout the northern Pacific Rim, these silvery fish are often seen jumping from the water. When viewed from above, schools of herring flash as they dart in near perfect unison beneath the water. Herring are commercially harvested, in particular the female egg mass, which is served as roe in Japanese cuisine.

Fresh Water
Trout

Vancouver Island holds several types of trout. Elongated and reaching up to 1.1 metre and up to 19 kilogram, rainbow trout have large heads. When inland they are olive above, their sides bear a wide red stripe and black spotting, and they are yellowish to white in the belly area. In marine form (steelhead), they are silvery blue above, with black spotting, silvery sides, and a pink wash on the front half of the sides. Rainbow trout have a triangular dorsal fin and a crescent-shaped tail fin with black spotting. Brown trout reach one metre in length and weigh about 18 kilograms. They are elongated, brown above with olive-coloured sides bearing dark brown and red spots, and silver bellies. The brown's dorsal fins are rounded and the tail fin squarish. Brook trout grow to about 53 centimetres and weigh 6.6 kilograms. They are olive green on their backs, with dark lines; their sides are olive coloured with large yellowish spots. Bellies are white, but reddish in adult males. Their dorsal fins are spotted and triangular, and the tail fin is squared.

Smallmouth Bass

Introduced from the United States, this favourite catch of fishers is elongated and grows to an average of 33 to 44 centimetres. Smallmouth bass have brown backs and a whitish belly. Sides are greenish yellow with brownish bands. Dorsal fins are spiny and the tail fin notched.

Other Marine Creatures
Crabs

While Dungeness crab is commercially harvested off Vancouver Island, the beaches support several species of crab. Starting in late May, crab shells are often spotted amidst surf debris at high tide.

Sand Dollar

A relative of the starfish and sea urchin, the dried white skeletons of sand dollars are commonly discovered on sandy beaches. These flattened creatures actually prefer deeper waters offshore. They use their short velvety tentacles to feed.

Razor Clam

Tiny volcano-like hills scattered across the beach indicate the presence of these tiny bivalve molluscs. Their thin brown shells, which look like a straight-edge razor, give them their name.

Butter Clam

The Island's most commercially harvested mollusc inhabits deeper waters primarily. Shells are noted for their concentric rings. They are yellowish when young, but white as the clam ages.

Purple Sea Urchin

Dwelling along the rocky coastline, urchins like the low tide line. Urchins are not fixed in place, but move around, their long spines in constant motion. They feed on seaweed and kelp. Urchins are a favourite food of sea otters, and humans commercially harvest the red urchin for sushi.

Recreation

Surfers flock to the beaches of western Vancouver Island.

Choose a sport or activity — whether it be on land or sea — and chances are Vancouver Island can deliver the experience in excellent form and superb setting. Home to some 130 provincial parks, including the immense Strathcona Provincial Park, plus the incomparable Pacific Rim National Park, Vancouver Island is truly an unmatched destination for outdoor enthusiasts.

Land
Mountain Biking and Cycling
According to Canadian government statistics and studies, Victoria is the "Cycling Capital of Canada." There are at least 2.5 times more commuter cyclists in Greater Victoria than in any other city in Canada. Bike lanes on Victoria downtown streets, and bike racks on buses, encourage cycling to and from suburban communities. Popular cycling areas include many locations on the Gulf Islands, the Comox Valley, and the Galloping Goose trail system meandering through southern Vancouver Island.

Bike Rental & Tour Resources
Cycle Victoria Rentals
950 Whart Street
Victoria BC V8W 1T3
250-385-2453
www.cyclevictoriarentals.com

Harbour Rentals
(Island Boat Rentals)
811 Wharf Street
Victoria BC V8W 1T2
250-995-1661
www.greatpacificadventures.com

Coastline Eco-Tours
40 King George Terrace
Victoria BC V8S 8J9
250-595-8668
www.coastlinetours.com

Hiking
Vancouver Island is covered with wonderful hiking trails. Truly challenging wilderness experiences such as the famous West Coast Trail or the Juan de Fuca Marine Trail test the limits of experts, yet, there are many, many easy and scenic trails perfect for enthusiasts and families.

Hiking Resources
Coastal Connections Nature Adventures Inc.
1027 Roslyn Road
Victoria BC V8S 4R4
250-480-9560 or 800-840-4453
www.island.com/~coastcon/

Go Green Adventures
PO Box 1139
Cumberland BC V0R 1S0
250-336-8706 or 888-32-GREEN

Nature Calls Eco-Tours Ltd.
12 Falstaff Place
Victoria BC V9A 7A5
250-361-4453
877-361-4453
www.members.home.net/ecotours/

Camping

As more than 90 percent of Vancouver Island is owned by the government, it has become home, over the years, to one of the most extensive publicly owned park systems in Canada. These provincial parks and wilderness areas support a wide range of camping options. Expect to find no electrical, sewer, or water hookups — that wouldn't be camping. But outdoor enthusiasts will find well-maintained tent areas, picnic tables, fire pits, access to firewood, flush or pit toilets, and, of course, potable water. Some campsites also have showers and sani-stations. Wilderness areas won't be as fancy, with primi-

tive campsites at which to pitch a tent and places to replenish water supplies.

Many parks do charge a fee during the summertime camping season, usually paid via self-registration envelopes and drop boxes located at campground entrances. Canadian currency is appreciated. Campsites are generally available on a first-come basis, however some do require advance reservations. You can make a reservation through British Columbia Discover Camping at www.discovercamping.ca.

Golf

Tip a hat to Vancouver Island's British heritage for the isle's passion for golf. Throughout the Island — north to south and east to west — duffers can discover remarkable links from full-scale championship level to smaller, more forgiving courses. Owing to the Is-

land's mild climate, golfers can pursue their sport year-round, and they play on some of Canada's most comely and challenging courses. For listings of golf courses by area see individual chapter "Tee Times."

Golf Tours & Reservations
B.C. Golf Safaris
666 Jones Terrace
Vancouver BC V8Z 2L7
250-889-4653
www.bcgolfsafaris.com
GolfBC
1800-1030 W. Georgia Street
Vancouver BC V6E 2Y3
604-681-8700
www.golfbc.com
Golf Central
3204 Browning Street
Victoria BC V8P 4C4
250-380-4653
www.golfcentraltours.com

Snow Sports / Skiing
While Vancouver Island is better known as a place for

Victoria and Vancouver Island Scenic Drives

While it could be argued that almost any road on Vancouver Island offers a scenic drive, here are three that are deservedly well regarded.

Scenic Marine Drive
Starting at the Ogden Point Breakwater, the route follows Dallas Road east beside great beaches, parkland, and walking paths with stunning views across the Strait of Juan de Fuca towards Washington State. Dallas Road becomes Beach Drive heading into Oak Bay and Uplands. Farther on it changes its name a few more times and finally runs through the lovely rural Saanich Peninsula community of Cordova Bay.

West Coast Highway
Highway 14, also called the West Coast Road, delivers a superb scenic experience as it winds along the southwest shoreline of Vancouver Island from Sooke to Port Renfrew. Lush rain forest and rocky cliffs, lighthouses, and spectacular beaches are its rewards, in addition to many, many options for hikes, from short casual strolls to full-day treks and sojourns for expert campers. Wildlife lovers will not be disappointed. Bird-watchers can take in Whiffen Spit, a natural breakwater between the Strait of Juan de Fuca and Sooke Harbour. Scenic views abound.

Oceanside Route
The Oceanside Route, the original coastal Highway 19A, strings together several of the more popular resort areas from the Nanoose Peninsula in the south to Deep Bay in the north. Look for the official Oceanside Route "starfish" signs pointing the way. You can set a leisurely pace, off the beaten track, and take detours to explore the headwaters of the Englishman River, French Creek, and the Big and Little Qualicum rivers, flowing down from Mt. Arrowsmith and other peaks. From ocean to alpine is only 18 kilometres.

marine or forest recreational outings, alpine snow sports on the Island aren't neglected. Excellent downhill and cross-country skiing, snowboarding, snowshoeing, tobogganing, and inner-tubing are also available. Mt. Washington, Vancouver Island's premier ski resort, is about four hours north of Victoria by car.

Equestrian / Horseback Riding

Vancouver Island saddles up at several locations where riding enthusiasts can take in farmland and woodland trails imbued with rustic charm and stunning views. Most outfitters offer one- to two-hour rides, and some even support day-long or overnight expeditions to more remote locales. Western or English equipment is usually available.

Equestrian / Horseback Riding Resources

Aldercreek Stables
4986 West Saanich Road
Victoria BC V8X 4M6
250-744-3906

Alpine Stables
3700 Holland Avenue
Cobble Hill BC V0R 1L0
250-743-6641
wwwalpinestable.com

Aspen Park Stables (Oak Meadow Stables)
4085 Prospect Lake Road
Victoria BC V9E 1J2
250-479-6843
www.members.home.net/ bcgray/aspenparkstables.html

Lakeside Stables
Pipeline Road
Victoria BC V9E 1J2
250-479-8191

Woodgate Stables & Peninsula Trail Rides
8129 Derrinberg Road

Victoria and Vancouver Island Gardens

Come February every year, residents of Victoria band together in a special springtime ritual — the Annual Flower Count. Folks from all walks of life engage in the time-honoured task of stooping over flowerbeds and climbing into flowering fruit trees to tabulate the number of blossoms blooming. Lately, the total has topped four billion!

Happily, then begins the gardener's calendar. Early springs heralds the blooming of bulbs and the first flowers peeking out from fruit trees. Millions upon millions of daffodils follow in March and April. In May, gardens are a riot of tulips. Rhododendrons unfurl their lovely petals in April, and in May, lilacs, cherry trees, and dogwood burst into flower. Roses take the stage in June, and by midsummer, gardens are crowded and bright with annuals and perennials. Late summer and autumn are enlivened with dazzling displays of begonia, gladiola, dahlia, and chrysanthemum.

Blame it on the climate;

The Sunken Garden at The Butchart Gardens

the Island's sub-Mediterranean weather makes Vancouver Island a gardener's paradise. From Victoria in the south to the Pacific Rim and all the way up to the northern reaches, Vancouver Island is blooming with interesting gardens.

The most prestigious example is The Butchart Gardens, deservedly world famous for its 23 enchanting hectares of manicured-to-perfection formal plantings and beds, encircled by lawns and decorated with fountains and gates and arbours. Beacon Hill Park in downtown Victoria

Victoria BC V8M 1T5
250-652-0287
www.woodgatestables.com

Caving

Vancouver Island's coastline and interior karst formations encompass several excellent underground cavern systems. The two most popular spelunking locations are:

Horne Lake Caves
Provincial Park
Horne Lake Road, west off Highway 19 — about 60 kilometres north of Nanaimo or 55 kilometres south of

Courtenay, then 12 kilometres to the entrance along a gravel road

Educational guided and self-guided tours reveal the park's fascinating caves filled with karst formations and crystalline features. Guided tours include the Triple Cave Adventure, which visits three caves in three hours; "High Adventure," a challenging five-hour trek that includes basic rock climbing; and "Underground Extreme," which features a rappel down the seven-storey-deep Rain-

barrel. The Horne Lake Main and Lower Caves are accessible for self-exploration outings year-round. None of the caves are lighted, so flashlights are the only source of illumination. Trails are rocky and uneven, and the caves are cool, making them possibly difficult for the elderly or very young. Call 250-248-7829 for guided excursion reservations, or visit www.hornelake.com.

Upana Caves
Head Bay Forest Road, 17 kilometres west of Gold River
Take flashlights and don

Victoria and Vancouver Island Gardens

is renowned for its Garry oak, camas, and daffodils. Government House in the Rockland neighbourhood features stunning gardens with stunning views, while the collection of rhododendrons at the University of Victoria is unsurpassed. The Abkhazi Gardens reward visitors with a woodland retreat of 100-year-old rhododendrons, a sunny south lawn, stands of majestic Garry oak, and rocky terraces bursting with flowers. At the Horticultural Centre of the Pacific more than 20 demonstration gardens allow visitors to delight in seeing something in bloom at any time of year.

Hatley Park, 2005 Sooke Road in Colwood, is a national historic site that features stately trees, italian gardens, japanese gardens and an English natural garden. Set in this lush setting is Hatley Castle, now part of Royal Roads University.

Up-Island there are more horticultural treats. Outside Qualicum Beach lies Milner Gardens & Woodlands. This 28 hectare site was once the home

of Ray and Veronica Milner, wealthy and passionate gardeners. (Veronica, incidentally, was related to Queen Elizabeth II.) The Milners' estate and artist's gardens are now overseen by Malaspina University, which is restoring the wondrous rhododendrons and other exotic plantings the Milners favoured.

On the Pacific Rim side of Vancouver Island, drop into Tofino Botanical Gardens, about 1.5 kilometres from the town's centre. Bird blinds and a viewing tower help visitors explore the natural wonders of the Island's west coast presented by this five hectare garden and forest site abutting a 2000 hectare wildlife sanctuary and shoreline habitat. Also on the wild west coast is Cougar Annie's Garden. Ada Annie Rae-Arthur, a legendary recluse who lived at the head of Hesquiat Harbour, is best known for her deadly aim, dispatching some 70 cougars in her day. Rae-Arthur's life inspired Margaret Horsfield's acclaimed book, *Cougar Annie's*

Garden. The heritage garden dating back to 1915 has been preserved and can be visited via charter boat or floatplane tour.

To the far north is one of the Island's more unusual gardens. Ronning's Garden, 14.5 kilometres west of Holberg, encompasses a thick forest that shelters the horticultural legacy of Bernt Ronning, a bachelor who set up home here in 1915 and stayed until his death in the mid-1960s. BC's largest and oldest Chilean "monkey puzzle" trees, rare Himalayan rhododendrons, plus scads of daffodils, bluebells, and sweet woodruff still flourish, thanks to the care and upkeep of retired lighthouse keepers Ron and Julia Moe.

Garden Tours
Victorian Garden Tours Ltd.
2-145 Niagara Street
Victoria BC V8V 1G1
250-380-2797
www.victoriangardentours.com
Victoria's Secret Gardens
3150 Midland Road
Victoria BC V8R 6E9
250-595-5333
877-595-5333

Garry oaks grace Victoria's lovely Abkhazi Gardens.

totals in Victoria at over 240 species. Visiting birders are likely to record up to 150 species in a three-week stay. Victoria, or rather the Victoria International Airport, is home to one of North America's most important skylark populations, and Victoria and Vancouver Island host a number of avian-oriented festivals: Eagle Extravaganza at Goldstream Provincial Park, East Sooke Hawk Watch, the Brant Festival at Parksville, the Trumpeter Swan Festival in the Comox Valley, and the Shorebird Festival at Tofino.

Marine
Fishing
Vancouver Island has long been lauded for its unparalleled freshwater and saltwater fishing. Depending upon the season the catch can be salmon, halibut, cod, sole, crab, or shrimp, but autumn is the most spectacular as millions of Pacific salmon leap up the streams of the Pacific Northwest to spawn, then die. Of the five species of North American Pacific salmon, the chum salmon is

rubber-soled boots for self-guided spelunking through the rooms and passages of the Upana Caves. There are 15 known entrances to the extensive cave system. In all, passages run for some 450 metres and take approximately one hour to cover.

Wildlife Watching
Vancouver Island offers excellent wildlife viewing opportunities throughout the season, both on water and on land. Several types of whale can be sighted all along the coasts of Vancouver Island and the Gulf Islands, and otters, seals, sea lions, and dolphins can also be spotted. Adventurers can even go snorkeling with migrating salmon in Campbell River. Sightings of land mammals such as black bears, cougars, and deer are also common. Of particular interest are the majestic Roosevelt elk, found only on Vancouver Island. Further, many

grizzly bear tours of the BC central coast (on the mainland) depart from the north central and far north regions of Vancouver Island.

Nature enthusiasts have long favoured Vancouver Island for bird-watching. Over 380 different species of birds have been recorded in the southern Vancouver Island region, with average annual

Island Autumn Colours

From late September to mid November, Vancouver Island bursts into autumn colour: mottled yellows of alder; the yellows and oranges of broadleaf maples; the vivid reds of dogwood; and the yellows and tans of poplar, oak, and larch. Several locations throughout Vancouver Island offer superb views of the fall show.

- Beacon Hill Park, downtown Victoria
- Government House, Rock-

land neighbourhood of Victoria
- Fort Rodd Hill National Historic Site, near Esquimalt Lagoon
- Goldstream Provincial Park, north of Victoria off Highway 1
- East Sooke Park, 15 minutes off Highway 14 near Sooke
- Newcastle Island Provincial Marine Park, via ferry from Nanaimo
- Collier Dam Park, Nanaimo

Kayaker

Canoeists enjoy Vancouver Island's many lakes.

the most common, though coho and chinook salmon and steelhead and cutthroat trout are also abundant. The migrating species teem in the rivers and bays of Vancouver Island, delivering some of the greatest sportfishing in the world. One species in particular — steelhead — is the "Holy Grail" of flyfishers due to its rarity and feistiness.

Vancouver Island Myths & Legends

Sasquatch

Sasquatch, a massive ape-like creature standing 2.4 metres tall and weighing more than 200 kilograms, is said to roam the forests from northern California to the Yukon and east to the Rocky Mountains. Vancouver Island is apparently its home too. Incredible 40-centimetre-long footprints were discovered in Strathcona Park in 1988, and ape-like whooping was heard near Comox Lake in 1992.

Empirical evidence of Sasquatch existence is scant, however some researchers believe that it might be a descendant of *Gigantopithecus*, a primate documented in fossil records dating back 500,000 years.

Cadborosaurus

Often described as "sister to the Loch Ness Monster," sightings abound of this creature with its reported long, greenish-brown looped body topped by a horse-like head rising from a long, slender neck. For more than a century folks have claimed to spot the beast in calm waters at dusk or in the early morning. "Caddy" for short, the creature was last seen in 1933 when the clerk to the Legislature, Major W.H. Langley, spied it dipping through the waters off Victoria.

Mermaid of Active Pass

In 1967, passengers aboard a ferry sailing through Active Pass claimed to have seen a mermaid — a comely female with long blond hair flowing down to the body of a porpoise — who was reclining on the rocks, munching on a salmon. Aerial photos taken by a pilot and later published by the *Times Colonist* newspaper appear to support the assertion of witnesses.

Note that Vancouver Island offers the only year-round fly fishing in Canada.

Both residents and visitors can tackle this pastime easily as there are a number of guided tour operators and bareboat fishing charter outfits on the Island. Guided freshwater fishing excursions to lakes and rivers are available as well.

Fishing Resources

A River Runs by Flyfishing
1419 Lang Street
Victoria BC V8T 2S6
250-598-3441
www.ariverrunsby.com

Adam's Fishing Charter
19 Lotus Street
Victoria BC V9A 1P3
250-370-2326
www.adamsfishingcharters.com

Calypso Fishing Charters
383 Simms Road
Campbell River BC V9W 1P2
250-923-2001
www.bctravel.com/calypsocharters/

Captain Hook's Fishing Charters
Westbay Marina
Victoria BC V8W 3H9
250-598-5697
www.bc-biz.com/hooksboatcharters

Vancouver Island fishing lodges offer guests superb accommodations.

Sailing along the coast

Chinook Charters
450 Campbell Street
Tofino BC V0R 2Z0
250-725-3431
www.chinookcharters.com
Cuda Marine Sportfishing Adventures
463 Belleville Street
Victoria BC V8V 1X3
250-995-2832
www.whalewatchingadventure.com
Duffy's Salmon Charters
5789 Sooke Road
Sooke BC V0S 1N0
250-642-5789
Island Outfitters
2438 Selwyn Road
Victoria BC V8Z 3L2
250-475-4969
www.fishingvictoria.com
Kingfisher Charters Ltd.
2823 Murray Drive
Victoria BC V9A 2S6
250-888-0233
www.kingfisher1.com
Oak Bay Charters Ltd.
2141 Newton Street
Victoria BC V8R 2R9
250-598-1061
www.members.home.net/sunbeam/OAKBAYCHARTER.html
Reel Action Fishing Charters
961 Haslam Place
Victoria BC V9B 4T1
250-478-1977
www.vanisle.net/users/ehatcher

Reel Excitement Salmon Charters
PO Box 222
Sooke BC V0S 1N0
250-642-3410
www.sookenet.com/reelexcitement
River Quest Charters
5650 West River Bottom Road
Duncan BC V9L 6H9
250-748-4776
www.web-merchants.com/riverquest
Searun Cutthroat Fishin' Charters
307-390 Waterfront Crescent
Victoria BC V8T 5K3
250-381-3295

Kayaking / Canoeing / River Rafting

With some 3500 kilometres of ocean coastline, 700 lakes, 160 rivers, and 890 streams, there is no shortage of environs in which to experience Vancouver Island from a low-slung vantage. Not only is the pace laid-back, but exploring the Island from a kayak offers access to many place inaccessible by foot or car. And there is perhaps no better way to encounter marine life in its natural setting, from sea lion colonies to pods of killer whales.

Kayaking Resources
Adventures Unlimited Kayaking Corp.
2060 Megan Court
Victoria BC V9B 6A8
250-727-1714
E-mail: letsgokayak@home.com
Balstar Adventure Tours
3203 1st Avenue
Port Alberni BC V9Y 1Y8
877-449-1230
www.balstar.com
Coastal Connections Nature Adventures Inc.
1027 Roslyn Road
Victoria BC V8S 4R4
250-480-9560
800-840-4453
www.islandnet.com/~coastcon/
Coastal Spirits Sea Kayaking & Lodge
1069 Topcliff Road
Quadra Island BC V0P 1N0
250-285-2895
888-427-5557
www.adventure-canada.com
Gorge Kayaking Centre Ltd.
105-2940 Jutland Road
Victoria BC V8T 5K6
250-380-4668
877-380-4668
www.gorgekayaking.com
Into the Current Kayaking
PO Box 212
Qualicum Beach BC V9K 1S8
250-752-8693
www.intothecurrent.com

Vancouver Island Drive Times

Approximate Drive Times from Victoria

Campbell River	4 hours	264 kilometres / 158 miles	
Courtenay	3.5 hours	219 kilometres / 131 miles	
Duncan	1 hour	60 kilometres / 36 miles	
Gold River	5.5 hours	55 kilometres / 213 miles	
Nanaimo	1.5 hours	111 kilometres / 66 miles	
Port Alberni	3 hours	195 kilometres / 117 miles	
Port Hardy	7.5 hours	502 kilometres / 301 miles	
Qualicum Beach	2 hours, 15 min.	158 kilometres / 95 miles	
Sidney	30 minutes	26 kilometres / 16 miles	
Sooke	40 minutes	37 kilometres / 22 miles	
Tofino	5 hours	316 kilometres / 190 miles	
Ucluelet	4.5 hours	291 kilometres / 175 miles	

Island Escapades
118 Natalie Lane
Saltspring Island BC V8K 2C6
250-537-2571
888-529-2567
www.islandescapades.com

Ocean River Sports
1437 Store Street
Victoria BC V8W 3J6
250-381-4233
800-909-4233
www.oceanriver.com

Vancouver Island Canoe &
Kayak Centre
575 Pembroke Street
Victoria BC V8T 1H3
250-361-9365
877-921-9365
www.voyageurcanoe.bc.ca

Victoria Kayak Tours
950 Wharf Street
Victoria BC V8W 1T3
250-216-5646
www.kayakvictoria.com

Rafting Resources
Endless Summer Adventures
PO Box 8068
Victoria BC V8W 3R7
250-704-9305
E-mail: endsums@yahoo.com

Kumsheen Raft Adventures Ltd.
PO Box 30, Highway 1
Lytton BC V0K 1Z0
250-455-2296
800-663-6667
www.kumsheen.com

Boating / Sailing

Some say that the only way to truly experience Vancouver Island's remarkable beauty is to see it from water. The crenellated coastline tufted with tall spruce and fir, and the inevitable sightings of eagles afloat on thermals or whales breaching, are only a few of the reasons to take to the water. Chartered boat operators and tour companies abound on the Island, offering a wide range of options from dinner cruises to sightseeing excursions to nature sailings. This is in addition to many bareboat operators specializing in self-sail rentals. Marinas are plentiful, particularly on the east coast, taking advantage of the Strait of Georgia's calmer waters.

Boat Charter / Tour Resources
Captain Jim's Adventures
214-827 North Park Street
Victoria BC V8W 3Y3
250-920-3533
www.members.home.net/captain.jims

Pacific Eco Tours
75 Cook Street
Victoria BC V8W 3W7
250-480-0773
www.pacificeco.com

Sooke Charter Boat
Association
8760 West Coast Road
Sooke BC V0S 1N0
250-642-3904
www.sookefishing.com

Blackfish Wilderness
Expeditions
2886 Ilene Terrace
Victoria BC V8R 4P1
250-216-2389
www.coastnet.com/~blackfish

Nootka Sound Service Ltd.
PO Box 57
Gold River BC V0P 1G0
250-283-2515
www.island.net/-mvuchuck/

Victoria Harbour Ferry
Co. Ltd.
4530 Markham Street
Victoria BC V8Z 5N3
250-708-0201
www.harbourferry.com

Sailing Resources
B.C. Yacht Charters Corp.
Inner Harbour
Victoria, BC
250-389-0770
800-708-SAIL
www.sailbc.com

Explore! Charters
6669 Horne Road
Sooke BC V0S 1N0
250-642-6669
www.explorecharters.com

Great Northwestern
Adventure Co.
PO Box 57
Cowichan Bay BC V0R 1N0
250-748-7374
800-665-7374
www.great-northwestern.com

Pacifica Sailing Charters
2200 Oak Bay Avenue
Victoria BC V8R 1G0
250-744-7305
www.pacificacharters.com

Vancouver Island Sea to
Sky Adventures
PO Box 2574
Sidney BC V8L 4C1
250-881-3559 or 877-389-SAIL
www.afinemadness.com

Numerous marinas dot the coastline of Vancouver Island.

Scuba Diving

Two time-honoured accolades proclaim Vancouver Island's status as a scuba diving nirvana. *National Geographic Magazine* declared Vancouver Island one of the best cold-water diving destinations in the world. And the Jacques Cousteau Society rates the Island's waters as second only to the Red Sea for diversity of marine life and water clarity. Add to this a number of interesting shipwrecks and reefs (natural and human-made) and it's easy to understand why hundreds of deepwater enthusiasts annually take the plunge.Although scuba divers can don their gear year-round, winter is the favoured season as the cooler water increase the clarity. Outfitters and charter operators can provide not only equipment rental, but also lessons and guided excursions.

Scuba Diving Resources
Ogden Point Dive Centre
199 Dallas Road
Victoria BC V8V 1A1
250-380-9119
www.divevictoria.com

Marine Wildlife Watching

Nature lovers marvel at Vancouver Island's marine wildlife watching opportunities. And while it's certainly possible to see sea lions, seals, dolphins and porpoises, it is whale watching for which Vancouver Island is world-renowned. A number of wildlife viewing expeditions are available from high-speed Zodiacs to easy cruises.

Whale Watching Resources
SOUTH VANCOUVER ISLAND / VICTORIA

Cuda Marine Whale Watching Adventures
463 Belleville Street
Victoria BC V8V 1X3
250-995-2832
www.whalewatchingadventure.com

Eagle Wing Whaling Fleet
2419 Teresa Place
Victoria BC 9B 4M7
250-391-9337
800-353-3344
www.bc1.com/users/eagle

Fantasea Charters Ltd.
1243 Miramar Drive
Victoria BC V8X 5E5
250-658-6052
888-721-100
www.Fantaseacharters.com

Fiesta Cruises Whalewatching
1234 Wharf Street
Victoria BC V8W 3H9
250-389-2628
877-389-2628
www.victoriawhalewatching.com

Five Star Charters
706 Douglas Street
Victoria BC V8W 3M6
250-386-3253
800-634-9617
www.5starwhales.com

Great Pacific Adventures
811 Wharf Street
Victoria BC V8W 1T2
250-386-2277
877-SEE-ORCA
www.greatpacificadventures.com

Naturally Salty Excursions
Box 5595
Victoria BC V8R 6S4
250-382-9599
www.naturallysalty.com

Ocean Explorations / Whale Watching
532 Broughton Street
Victoria BC V8W 1C6
250-383-6722
888-442-6722

Orca Spirit Adventures Ltd.
PO Box 5441, Station B
Victoria BC V8R 6S4
250-383-8411
888-672-ORCA
www.orcaspirit.com

Pride of Victoria Cruises & Tours
1175 Beach Drive
Victoria BC V8S 2N2
250-592-3474
800-668-7758
www.oakbaybeachhotel.com

Prince of Whales Whale Watching
812 Wharf Street
Victoria BC V8W 1T3
250-383-4884
888-383-4884
wwwprinceofwhales.com

Seacoast Expeditions Ltd.
45 Songhees Road
Victoria BC V9A 6T3
250-383-2254
800-383-1525
www.seacoastexpeditions.com

Seafun Safaris
950 Wharf Street
Victoria BC V8W 1T3
250-360-1200
877-360-1233
www.seafun.com

SeaKing Adventures Inc.
950 Wharf Street
Victoria BC V8W 1Y3
250-381-4173
www.seakingadventures.com

Springtide Whale Watching &
Charters
4336 Crownwood Lane
Victoria BC V8X 5E4
250-386-6016
800-470-3474
www.springtidecharters.com

Spyhopper Whale Watching
Tours Ltd.
950 Wharf Street
Victoria BC V8W 1T3
250-388-6222
877-388-6111
www.spyhopper.bc.ca

Victoria Marine Adventures
Centre Ltd.
950 Wharf Street
Victoria BC V8W 1T3
250-995-2211
800-575-6700
www.marine-adventures.com

Wildcat Adventure Tours
1234 Wharf Street, Water Lot
Victoria BC V8W 3H9
250-384-9998
800-953-3345
www.wildcat-adventure.com

PACIFIC RIM
Cypre Prince Tours
PO Box 149
Tofino BC V0R 2Z0
250-725-2202
800-787-2202
www.island.net/~cypre/

Whale watching by high-speed Zodiac

Jamie's Whaling Station
606 Campbell Street
PO Box 129
Tofino BC V0R 2Z0
250-725-3919
800-667-9913
www.jamies.com

Remote Passages Zodiac
Whale Watch
71 Wharf Street
Tofino BC V0R 2Z0
250-725-3330
800-666-9833
www.remotepassages.com

Seaside Adventures / Whale
Watching
300 Main Street
Tofino BC V0R 2Z0
250-725-2292
800-332-4252
www.seaside-adventures.com

Sea-Trek Tours &
Expeditions Ltd.
441B Campbell Street
PO Box 627
Tofino BC V0R 2Z0
250-725-4412
800-811-9155
www.seatrektours.bc.ca

NORTH VANCOUVER ISLAND
Robson Bight Charters
PO Box 99
Sayward BC V0P 1R0
250-282-3833
www.robsonbightcharters.bc.ca

Stubbs Island Whale Watching
PO Box 2-2
Telegraph Cove BC V0N 3J0
250-928-3185
www.stubbs-island.com

Mackay Whale Watching
PO Box 66
Port McNeill BC V0N 2R0
250-956-9865
877-663-6722
www.whale-time.com

Catala Charters
PO Box 526
Port Hardy BC V0N 2P0
250-949-7560
800-515-5511
www.catalacharters.net

Sea Legend Charters Ltd.
PO Box 5227
Port Hardy BC V0N 2P0
250-949-6541
800-246-0093

Seasmoke Whale Watching
PO Box 483
Alert Bay BC V0N 1A0
250-974-5225
800-668-6722
www.seaorca.com

Victoria

The BC Parliament Buildings are resplendently illuminated at night.

Gracing Vancouver Island's southern tip, Victoria and its surrounding communities well deserve their reputation for fine living in a splendid natural setting. The city is bounded by ocean on three sides and is blessed with a mild maritime climate. The landscape is rolling lowland

out of which rise granite rocks reaching heights of up to 300 metres. To the south are Washington State's magnificent Olympic Mountains, only 20 kilometres away across the Strait of Juan de Fuca. Downtown Victoria wraps around the Inner Harbour, a firth of protected waters that forms the nucleus not only of the Island, but also of all British Columbia, as Victoria is the capital of the province and seat of the provincial government. Presided over by the majestic Parliament Buildings and the Fairmont Empress Hotel, the Inner Harbour is the centrepiece of the city, exuding a dignified yet cheerful disposition.

Founded in 1843 by the Hudson's Bay Company as a British fur-trading post, Fort Victoria was established in the midst of First Nations' tradi-

tional homelands. Bastion Square marks the spot where Fort Victoria once stood. Not until 1862 was Victoria officially incorporated, with the motto

Victoria Recommendations

- Explore Victoria's Inner Harbour and historic downtown; at Chinatown, stroll down Canada's narrowest street, Fan Tan Alley.
- Take in the exhibits at the Royal BC Museum, filled with impressive artifacts and displays depicting the natural and human history of British Columbia.
- Wonder at the priceless memorabilia in the Maritime Museum of British Columbia,

especially the *Tilikum*, a dugout canoe that endured a 65,000-kilometre voyage around the world.
- Explore Victoria's historic homes including Helmcken House, Emily Carr House, Point Ellice House, and Craigdarroch Castle.
- Plan time to see the Art Gallery of Greater Victoria, showcasing treasures drawn from some 15,000 celebrated works and *objets d'art*.

Opposite: A totem pole greets visitors to Victoria's Inner Harbour.

Semper Liber or "Always Free." The gold rush years of the latter half of the 1800s filled Victoria with would-be miners, wild-eyed and eager to reach the ore fields of the Fraser Valley, the Cariboo, and the Klondike. Market Square in those days bustled with shops and saloons, hotels and street hawkers. Victoria's colourful Chinatown dates from those heady days as well, making it Canada's oldest.

Nature is never far away from the city; nearby are 48 regional, provincial, and national parks totalling more than 7600 hectares. Spring begins as early as February, ushered in with Victorians' annual count of the blossoms in their gardens — a citywide total bursting with some 4 billion blooms. Summertime is warm and dry, never too hot, with refreshing evenings. Autumn comes in late September, with riots of colour as trees and bushes melt into golds and crimsons. Winter is moderate, oftentimes rainy, yet there are still many sunny days perfect for strolling.

Indeed, the mild climate guarantees flowers bloom perpetually, and it's little wonder that Victoria has a reputation as the "City of Gardens." One has only to witness the incomparable profusion gracing The Butchart Gardens, the hundreds of flower baskets swinging prettily from 19th-century lampposts downtown, the romantic Abkhazi Gardens, the meandering pathways of Beacon Hill Park, or the six hectares of manicured landscape at Government House, home to BC's lieu-tenant-governor, to attest to the truth of the moniker.

Shoppers will delight in a world of merchandise — not only imports from across the globe, but also a wealth of locally produced goods. Stroll Government Street to peruse English bone china, Scottish tartans, and Irish linen in ad-dition to famed hand-knit Cowichan sweaters and other First Nations creations. Some 65 percent of Canada's artists live on Vancouver Island and the Gulf Islands, and art aficionados will relish the many fine galleries and boutiques displaying indigenous works and fashions.

Victoria Parks & Recreation

Thunderbird Park is renowned for its totem poles.

Thunderbird Park
Corner of Belleville and Douglas streets
This tiny park set behind the Royal British Columbia Museum is renowned for its fine collection of totem poles. During the summer months, First Nations craftspeople demonstrate their skills carving new poles.

Beacon Hill Park
Downtown between Douglas and Cook streets
Beautifully landscaped with gardens, fountains, trails, duck ponds, and walkways, this is Victoria's principal park. Playing fields, a children's petting zoo, and plenty of perfect picnic places round out the features. Springtime brings thousands of daffodils and wild blue camas flowers. The views of the Strait of Juan de Fuca and Washington State's Olympic Mountains are stunning.

Thunderbird Park

Victoria Proper

Inner Harbour, Old Town, Chinatown, James Bay, Fisherman's Wharf, Fairfield, Rockland, Beacon Hill

Tourism Victoria
812 Wharf Street
Victoria BC V8W 1T3
250-953-2033
800-663-3883
www.tourismvictoria.com
Visitor Centre: 812 Wharf Street
Population: 350,000

"Genteel" is a word used often to describe Victoria proper, and it is clearly an apt appellation for a city named in honour of Victoria, Queen of Great Britain from 1837 to 1901.

The centrepiece of the city is the Inner Harbour, bustling day and night with marine activity and sightseers along the wharf, taking in museums and nipping into shops, boutiques, and galleries. Grand legislative building and hotels rise up like palace facades around the harbour. Most of Victoria's principal attractions can easily be reached from here on foot, and there are also numerous touring (self-guided and guided) options ranging from horse-drawn carriages, double-decker buses, boats, and even floatplanes. Victoria's Old Town encompasses several city blocks and is a wonder of historic architecture. Chinatown, just north of Market Square, is the oldest such community in Canada and brims with exotic specialties.

James Bay, south of downtown, is Victoria's oldest neighbourhood. Quiet and residential, it's bordered by the waters of the Strait of Juan de Fuca on three sides, and on the fourth side rises Beacon Hill Park. Fisherman's Wharf Park in James Bay is the place to see the catch-of-the-day straight off commercial fishers' boats, and there are concession stands serving up the blue briny's treats. Fairfield, off Beacon Hill's east side, used to be farmland, but is now an urban neighbourhood, and the shops, pubs, and cafes in the area known as Cook Street Village are delightful. Rockland sits east of downtown and is an upscale residential area filled with stately homes, including the magnificent Craigdarroch Castle and Government House.

With so much to see and do, the best starting place is the Tourism Victoria Visitor Info Centre located beneath the clocktower at the Inner Harbour. Staffed by knowledgeable personnel, the facility has up-to-the-minute touring tips, maps, and even tickets for upcoming events.

Victoria Harbour Ferries

Refitted logging boom tugs ferry guests along Victoria's Inner Harbour.

These funny little boats (actually refitted logging boom tugs) are an excellent way to take in Victoria by water. Departing from the Inner Harbour every 15 minutes (or thereabouts), the tiny tugs scoot along for a 45-minute excursion around the harbour and up the Gorge Waterway. Sights along the way include shipyards, marinas, fishing boats, floating homes, and the occasional wildlife. Ferry stops are located at the Inner Harbour Causeway in front of the Fairmont Empress Hotel, at the Delta Victoria Ocean Pointe and Spa, and at the Coast Harbourside Hotel. Passengers may disembark at any of the stops and then hop on again later

BC Parliament Buildings

Belleville Street at Victoria Harbour
250-387-3046
www.parl-bldg.gov.ca
Open daily, June-September; tours every 20 minutes
Admission free
Look to the copper-sheathed domed top of this commanding architectural fancy to spy a gilded statue of Captain George Vancouver, the first

Old Victoria Walking Tour

Maritime Museum at Bastion Square

❶ Bastion Square

Once, and now once again, one of Victoria's principal gathering places, this square is where the Hudson's Bay Company built Fort Victoria. The old fort was demolished in 1864, but plaques on building walls and on the pavement below your feet mark its outline. Take notice of two historic buildings at the square's northwest and south corners: the Burns Building, built as a classy hotel in 1887 at the staggering cost of $20,000; and the 1892 Board of Trade Building, a classic Romanesque-styled facade designed by architect A.M. Muir. The Maritime Museum resides in the building that once housed the Supreme Court of British Columbia, on the site that was originally the old jailhouse and public execution yard. The 1889 building of Moorish-Mediterranean styling was designed by H.O. Tiedemann, with later additions by F.M. Rattenbury.

❷ Wharf Street

During the gold rush days, Wharf Street was the street of dreams for many a miner. Storefronts brimmed with supplies and whatnots to satisfy many a fortune seeker. The Rithet Building at 1117 to 1134 Wharf, built in several phases beginning in 1861 is the site of Fort Victoria's original well. At 1107 Wharf is the old Carr Warehouse, the successful wholesale market run by Richard Carr, father of Emily Carr. Embedded in the wall across the street are the mooring rings used by the Hudson's Bay Company to secure its ships. Dating from 1874, the Dominion Customs House at 1002 Wharf bears a decidedly French appearance with its mansard roof. It was the Canadian government's first federal building in British Columbia.

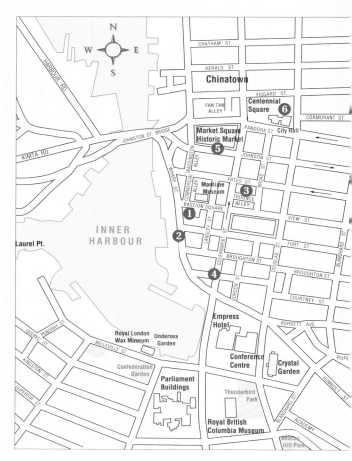

Old Victoria Walking Tour

❸ Trounce Alley
Named after Thomas Trounce, the architect who designed Victoria's first police station, this is where a more famous architect, John Teague, kept his offices.

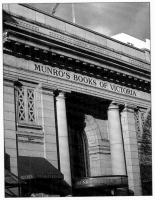

The facade of Munro's book store on Government Street

❹ Government Street
Several period buildings and vintage businesses line this historic thoroughfare. Munro's Books at 1108 Government is deposited in the one-time Royal Bank building of 1909, while at 1200 Government is another bank, the 1896 Bank of Montreal designed by F.M. Rattenbury with French-chateaux styling, a precursor to the Empress Hotel which he also designed. On the west side of Government at View Street, notice the paving stones that mark what was the northeast corner of Fort Victoria. Farther north at 1312 Government is the 1892 New England Hotel, designed by architect John Teague as a luxury hotel.

❺ Market Square
Market Square's incarnation as an open civic space dates from the 1970s. Fort Victoria Properties retained an architect to connect and restore eight heritage buildings centred around an inner courtyard. In pioneer days, the area was known for its bordellos. Back then, Victoria sported 100 men for every woman. Prostitution was tolerated, though police raided the houses on a regular basis to collect fines.

City Hall at Centennial Square

❻ Centennial Square
The resplendent Victoria City Hall anchors the square's southeast end. It is a John Teague-designed building that many consider among his best architectural work. It was built in three phases: in 1878 the Pandora Street side; the rear section, used as the fire hall, in 1882; and in 1892 the Douglas Street facade. At 625 Fisgard is the 1914 Victoria Police Station, formidable with its Italianate Renaissance fortress design facade . At the corner of Douglas and Fisgard streets is the 1914 Hudson's Bay Company building, built in a neoclassical style and former home of the department store.

Chinatown

The Gate of Harmonious Interest announces the entry to Victoria's Chinatown.

Tan, and Chuck Luck gaming parlours flourished. Fan Tan Alley buzzed with Fan Tan gaming fever. Rumoured (though unverified) is the tale of three tunnels — used supposedly for smuggling contraband and Chinese immigrants — that once connected Chinatown to the Empress Hotel, Wharf Street, and the Inner Harbour. At 636 Fisgard stands the 1909 Chinese Public School, constructed in response to a city edict that prohibited Chinese children from attending public school.

Canada's first Chinatown

spreads over a two-block area just north of downtown Victoria, though the first Chinese immigrants who arrived here in 1858 initially settled farther south along lower Cormorant Street. Drawn by the lure of gold, the newly arrived men and women found employment as labourers. By the 1870s, Chinese merchants did brisk business — grocery stores, butcher shops, bakeries, and other Chinese-oriented businesses proffered products from the faraway homeland.

In the 1880s, more than 16,000 Chinese nationals arrived to toil on the construction of the Canadian Pacific Railway. By 1910, Victoria's Chinatown had swelled to some six city blocks, and at its peak an estimated 3000 Chinese dwelled here. More than 150 firms catered to the specific Chinese cultural needs. Two theatres offered entertainment, and there were three Chinese schools, a hospital, two churches, five temples and shrines, a score or more of opium factories, plus various gambling dens and brothels.

Today's Chinatown is Canada's third largest after those in Vancouver and Toronto, offering a rich introduction to the vibrant Chinese culture. Shoppers will delight in the tiny, interesting shops displaying curios. Fan Tan Alley, the nation's narrowest street at only a couple of metres across, once prospered with opium dens, but now does quite well with its quaint shops and boutiques. Top off a stroll with a visit to any several Chinese eateries.

In the days of Chinatown's population peak, the spot where the Gate of Harmonious Interest (1981-83) now stands would have been the ethnic area's centre. Chinatown then was five times as large as it now is. The boiling potato-like scent of processed opium pervaded the district, and Mah Jong, Fan

Fan Tan Alley

Emily Carr House

Pacific Undersea Gardens on Victoria's Inner Harbour

European to circumnavigate the isle that bears his name. Completed in 1898, honouring the Diamond Jubilee of Queen Victoria, the impressive facade cost $924,000. Stroll the grounds, vivid in summer with flower gardens, to admire the formal entry fountain and statuary. Inside, tours take in the public galleries. Beautifully illuminated at night, a total of 3333 white lights ornament the building's exterior.

Emily Carr House

207 Government Street; four blocks south of the BC Parliament Buildings
250-383-5843
www.heritage.gov.bc.ca
Open Wednesday to Monday, mid-June to mid-September; Costume Christmas, December 18-24
Admission charged
Furnished rooms and homey exhibits make the former home of Emily Carr not only a visual delight, but also an interesting peek into the life and times of this world-renowned artist and writer. Now a BC Heritage Site, this 1864 Italianate house, built of California redwood, was saved from the wrecking ball in the 1960s. Today, visitors enter through the one-time back porch and kitchen, then amble through the parlour, sitting room, and upstairs bedrooms and bath. Couches and divans, dining set and chairs, lamps and tables, plus a wealth of everyday items similar to what Emily Carr would have used during her life, make the artist's presence palpable and give a human touch to her enduring legacy. See also the Emily Carr box.

Royal London Wax Museum

470 Belleville Street
250-388-4461
www.waxworld.com
Open daily
Admission charged
In the tradition of the famous Madame Tussaud's of London, the Royal London Wax Museum presents more than 300 life-sized wax figures ensconced behind glass or atop exhibit pedestals. Take peeks at icons of historic and popular culture such as Queen Victoria, Princess Diana, Mother Teresa, Anne of Green Gables, Albert Einstein, Martin Luther King, and Christopher Reeve as Superman.

Pacific Undersea Gardens

490 Belleville Street
250-382-5717
www.pacificunderseagardens.com
Open daily
Admission charged
At the Pacific Undersea Gardens, next to the Inner Harbour causeway, visitors descend beneath the water to peek at Vancouver Island's indigenous marine animal and plant life.

Royal BC Museum

675 Belleville Street
250-356-7226 or 888-447-7977
www.royalbcmuseum.bc.ca
Open daily
Admission charged
This world-renowned institution is Canada's most visited museum, and it's easy to see why. Housed here is an impressive and extensive permanent collection of artifacts on the natural and human history of British Columbia. In addition, the Royal BC Museum is frequently the host for major travelling exhibitions from national and international collections. From May to September at the adjacent Thunderbird Park, the museum hosts "Echoes of

Francis Mawson Rattenbury, Victoria's Architect Extraordinaire

Victoria's vintage architectural cityscape can be traced to one man, Francis Mawson Rattenbury (1867-1935). At the precocious age of 25, the British-born youth captured the honour of designing British Columbia's second Parliament Buildings, the regal edifices anchoring the Inner Harbour's southern view. Completed in 1898 for the princely sum of $924,000, the complex instantly garnered acclaim. Over the next three decades, Rattenbury would add to his triumphs: the Bank of Montreal at 1200 Government Street (1896), the centre block of the Empress Hotel (1908), a collaboration in the design of the Canadian Pacific Marine Terminal (1925) and the Crystal Gardens (1925), many fine residences (including his own at 1701 Beach Drive), plus several other western Canadian buildings.

Rattenbury's personal life was as flamboyant as the facades he created. While he was celebrated in his earlier years, his later life was marred by financial hardship and alcoholism, in addition to scandal and ultimately his own murder.

It all started with Alma Victoria Clarke Dolling Pakenham. Author and historian Terry Reksten describes her as "Thirty years his junior, beautiful, giddy, a gifted pianist and a twice-married woman who smoked cigarettes in public." Rattenbury or "Ratz" was roguish enough to take up with her, despite the fact he had a wife, Florence. He even entertained his mistress at home while Florrie lay ill in bed upstairs. Alma, it is said, played funeral marches on the piano downstairs.

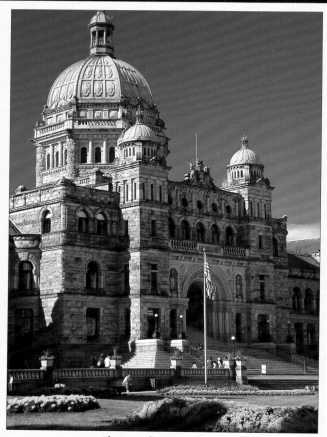

The BC Parliament Buildings

Little wonder then that when Rattenbury finally divorced Florrie and married Alma in 1925, the newlyweds became social pariahs. They subsequently moved to Bournemouth, England, in 1930, where their fortunes continued to decline.

In 1934, the couple engaged a 17-year-old chauffeur by the name of George Stoner. Within weeks, Alma had seduced the young man and installed him as her lover-in-residence. On the night of March 28, 1935, Stoner, in dread fear of the affair becoming public, crept into the living room and, discovering Rattenbury dozing in his favourite chair, bludgeoned him to death.

Both Alma and Stoner were charged with the murder, and the trial that ensued caused a sensation. In the end, Alma was acquitted, while Stoner was sentenced to hang. Besotted with grief, Alma committed suicide, stabbing herself repeatedly while walking into the water to her death. Stoner's sentence was later commuted to life in prison, though he only served seven years before being released.

Ancestry" in partnership with the Victoria Native Friendship Centre. Kwakwaka'wakw and Coast Salish carvers share their talents at the Carving Studio. Guest interpreters round out the program, and in August the First Nations Peoples Festival takes place around Thunderbird Park. See the Royal BC Museum box, page 58.

Helmcken House

At Thunderbird Park next to Royal BC Museum
250-361-0021
www.heritage.gov.bc.ca
Open daily, May to October;
Victorian Christmas, December 18-31 (except December 25-26)
Admission charged
Listen to the story of Dr. John Sebastian Helmcken during an audio tour of this BC Heritage

Site — the oldest house in British Columbia on its original site. Built in 1852, the house is now a museum, with plenty of the good doctor's medical memorabilia on display, along with mementos of his wife Cecilia, daughter of Governor James Douglas.

Shopping Victoria

Pick your pleasure: English linen or fine bone china, teas from Asia, Scottish tartans, Irish lace, Shetland Island sweaters, and arts and crafts from across Canada, especially Pacific Coast First Nations. Compact downtown Victoria delivers a wide range of shopping and browsing, notably along the old streets of Government, Johnson, Fort, Wharf, and Broad.

Lovely Government Street is Victoria's Old Town shopping central. Here boutiques and shops proffer merchandise from around the world behind the quaint facades of heritage buildings. Within the eight-block area from Humboldt to Fisgard sits Victoria's oldest bookstore, Munro's Books, with more than 50,000 titles; Roger's Chocolates, in business since 1885; and the city's most adored tea shop, Murchie's Tea & Coffee. There are plenty of souvenir shops elsewhere on Government Street, as well as many galleries. Just off Government Street at Johnson is Market Square, a two-storey arcade where more than 40 shops await behind their historic entrances. Nearby Bastion Square features superb browsing opportunities in addition to a lively, outdoor craft market of local vendors.

Fort Street, running east from Government, is the home of the Bay Centre, the downtown's indoor galleria-style marketplace. Broad Street, which runs north and south from the Bay Centre, is also worth a look. The south side is stuffed with interesting shops selling everything from home furnishings to clothing, while to the north is a scattering of small boutiques. Trounce Alley, between Government and Broad streets, dates back to the 1860s and feels a bit like New Orleans or perhaps Paris with its wrought-iron railings, ornate lampposts strung with flower baskets, and cute outdoor cafes. "Antique Row" starts on upper Fort Street, stretching from Blanshard to Cook streets, and will thrill the heart of anyone looking for that one-of-a-kind collector's item or memento.

Chinatown, to the north of downtown, offers gift shops and galleries. Fan Tan Alley is Victoria's narrowest street, but compensates with a nice variety of boutiques. West of downtown is Oak Bay Village, a tidy row of shops lining Oak Bay Avenue, that offers many English-made items. Farther afield, Mattick's Farm at Cordova Bay houses a wonder-

ful collection of small shops: an old-time general store, a gourmet food shop, an art gallery, a wine store, plus lots of crafts with a country flair. Don't leave out Sidney-by-the-Sea. The seaside village at the top of the Saanich Peninsula is a book lover's paradise. It has been called the "Second Hand Bookstore Capital of Canada," and its "Booktown" area features seven diverse used (and new) book outlets.

Some final shopping scenes worth noting. If it's summertime, then it's public market time. Moss Street Market is held every Saturday, and the Government Street Market is on Sunday. Victoria's largest shopping mall is the Mayfair Shopping Centre on Douglas Street between Finlayson and Tolmie, while two other malls vie for the distinction of being second largest: the Hillside Shopping Center on Hillside at Shelbourne, and the Tillicum Mall at Burnside. All three are only minutes from the city centre, and major retailers are well represented. As to auction houses, Lunds Auctioneers and Appraisers Ltd. at 926 Fort Street (250-386-3308) is the best-known, convening every Tuesday.

Crystal Garden Conservation Centre

713 Douglas Street
250-381-1213
www.bcpcc.com/crystal/
Open daily; Admission charged

This vintage glass-roofed social centre once housed the largest saltwater swimming pool in the British Empire. That was in 1925, but the landmark remained a popular gathering place until its closing in 1971. Nearly a decade passed before it was renovated and reopened as a miniature, luxuriant rain forest complete with ballroom. While it often is the site for social functions such as weddings and receptions, day visitors don't need an invitation to come and marvel at the exotic flora and fauna. Some 65 species of birds are housed here, plus free-flying butterflies. There are mammals too, such as the pygmy marmoset, only 12 centimetres long when fully grown, and four species of bat.

Crystal Garden Conservation Centre also shelters animal species that are endangered, using its resources in the Species Survival Plan of the American Zoo and Aquarium Association. Catch glimpses of hyacinth macaw, Bali mynah, the golden lion tamarin, pygmy slow loris, radiated tortoise, and ring-tailed, ruffed, and mongoose lemurs.

St. Ann's Academy Historic Interpretive Centre and Chapel

835 Humboldt Street; interpretive centre in main foyer
250-953-8828
www.bcpc.com/stanns
Open daily; Admission free

Reopened in 1998 after an

Crystal Garden Conservation Centre features rain forest habitat.

extensive $16.2 million restoration, St. Ann's Academy now holds arts and government offices. Its origins date back to 1858, when four Sisters of St. Ann reached the rugged outpost of the Hudson's Bay Company. The Catholic nuns assumed the task of educating the Company children and also dedicated the city's first Roman Catholic chapel. By 1871 the French Provincial styled main edifice had been erected (the first four-storey masonry building in Victoria), and in 1886 and 1910 respectively, the elegant east and west wings were added. St Ann's welcomed students until 1973, when declining enrollment forced its closure. Today the gardens are a pretty place to stroll, and inside the building are the restored 1858 Roman Catholic chapel (now deconsecrated) and the magnificent 1910 auditorium.

Fairmont Empress Hotel

721 Government Street
250-384-8111
www.fairmont.com
Open daily

With its distinctive French chateau-style architecture, the now ivy-covered facade of the Fairmont Empress Hotel has presided over Victoria's Inner Harbour since 1908. While the hotel offers 496 Edwardian-Victorian styled rooms, most visitors know the Empress for its afternoon tea; the hotel serves in excess of 100,000 teas annually. Popular, too, are drinks at the Bengal Lounge or dinner in the Empress Room, a haven of haute West Coast cuisine. See the Fairmont Empress Hotel box.

The Fairmount Empress Hotel

The venerable Fairmont Empress Hotel

Gracing Victoria's Inner Harbour, the Fairmont Empress has been the social centrepiece of the city for nearly 100 years. Over its history, the palatial urban retreat has hosted kings, queens, movie stars, and industrial moguls.

It was January 20, 1908, when the first guest registered at the newly completed hotel, the work of noted Victoria architect Francis Rattenbury. It was to be the quintessential respite, a quiet hub of the Canadian Pacific empire. Guests arriving from across the Pacific Ocean aboard Canadian Pacific steamships would have an opulent Canadian Pacific hotel in which to luxuriate before boarding Canadian Pacific railcars on the mainland and embarking on a journey into the Canadian Rockies and beyond.

Clearly, tycoon William Van Horne spared little expense in creating his chain of grand hotels, and the Fairmont Empress only improves with age. An extensive renovation over the last half-decade has restored its High Victorian grandeur. Millions of dollars were spent to redecorate all 460 guestrooms and add 36 posh new suites with their own private check-in and concierge team. In addition, the Empress Room has been spiffed up to enhance the fine dining experience, staged in a classic Edwardian gentlemen's club atmosphere tricked out in Tudor arches, intricate columns with elaborate plasterwork, stained glass medallions, and an impressive fireplace. The Bengal Lounge, originally the Writing Room, takes its cue from colonial India, with elegant leather furniture, marble fireplace, and a Bengal tiger skin, more than 30 years old, on the wall. Then there is the Crystal Ballroom for elegant soirees and grand private dinners. Add to the list of amenities a 12 metre lap pool, a fully equipped fitness area, and a much appreciated resort spa, and it's easy to understand why the Fairmont Empress is considered a truly regal destination.

Most people, however, know the Empress for its afternoon tea, a notion born during the reign of Queen Victoria, initiated by the Duchess of Bedford, who suffered a chronic "sinking feeling around five o'clock." The good Duchess started taking tea with thin sandwiches and dainty cakes, and afternoon tea became *de rigueur*.

It is, indeed, a pleasant pastime, and ever so popular. The Fairmont Empress serves over 100,000 afternoon teas annually in its Tea Lobby. There, beneath twinkling chandeliers, at tables set with crisp linen, gleaming china, and sparkling silver, guests blissfully ease into refined relaxation. Melodies drift out from a string quartet and piano, mingling with the cheery conversation. Sweet indulgences arrive: petite sandwiches of smoked salmon, deviled egg, cucumber, and watercress, and plump scones with strawberry preserves and thick cream. Silver teapots steam with the Empress's own blend of China black, Ceylon, and Darjeeling teas. Soon, fresh seasonal berries appear, as well as irresistible light pastries almost too pretty to eat. Yes, the elegance of a long-ago era lives on.

Avast Matey! Whales, Dolphins, and Porpoises

Collectively known as cetaceans, whales, dolphins, and porpoises are marine mammals: they must breathe fresh air, unlike fish that absorb oxygen from water; they are warm-blooded and must maintain a body temperature of about 35 to 37°C; and they give birth to live young, which they feed with milk from mammary glands. There are two types of cetaceans: those that have teeth and those that don't. And interestingly, cetaceans evolved from deer-sized land mammals some 60 million years ago. Today, their closest living land-dwelling relatives are the even-toed ungulates including deer, sheep, and bison.

Of the 80 recognized species of cetaceans, seven types are most commonly seen in the waters encircling Vancouver Island: humpback, minke, gray, and killer whales; Pacific white-sided dolphins; harbour and Dall's porpoises. Some are resident throughout the year and some come and go with the seasons. Each spring thousands of gray whales migrate past Vancouver Island en route to Arctic feeding grounds. Three killer whale groups stay within Vancouver Island waters year-round, but there are other pods that simply drop by for a visit. There are also occasional sightings of sperm, fin, and even the immense blue whales.

Humanity's relationship with cetaceans has taken many forms, running the gamut from deep reverence to atrocious brutality. For centuries, Native populations relied on whales for food and as a source of materials for any number of household requirements.

Whale watching is one of Vancouver Island's best marine adventures.

Cetaceans were held in awe and respected, prominently depicted in their mythology and art. Conversely, European and American whalers of the 19th century engaged in wholesale slaughter of the animals for their commercial value — they were used for everything from lamp oil to piano keys.

Today, whale watching excursions are one of Vancouver Island's hottest tickets to magnificent adventure, and whale watching is a thriving multimillion dollar industry from Telegraph Cove in the north to Tofino on the west coast, and especially around the city of Victoria. It is indeed thrilling to climb aboard a Zodiac and bounce into the waves and whitecaps, feel the sea spray, gaze at lighthouses and sailboats, and then come upon a pod of titanic and mesmerizing creatures of the deep blue briny.

Vancouver Island's specialty is undoubtedly killer whales. Their distinctive markings and animated antics deliver an unparalleled nature experience. They exhibit an incredible repertoire of behaviours that visitors may witness:

- Breaching – Whales leap, partially or entirely, out of the water. This is often repeated 20 times or more.
- Spyhopping – Whales stand vertically in the water, their heads rising up out of the water as if they are scanning the surroundings.
- Flippering – Rolling on their sides, whales repeatedly slap the surface water with their flippers.
- Blowing – Surfacing after a dive, whales exhale powerfully, expelling water vapour.
- Lobtailing – Hanging upside down, whales slap their tail flukes repeatedly against the water's surface.

Whether on a professional whale watching excursion, in a private boat, or in a kayak, the following rules of etiquette apply:

- Never approach whales closer than 100 metres.
- Approach whales from the side, not from the front or rear.
- Approach slowly, leave slowly.
- Minimize noise, especially motors, and do not sound horns or whistles.
- Limit time spent with whales to 30 minutes or less.
- Never crowd whales along shorelines or other boats.
- Never chase whales.

See Highlights of Nature, page 31, Marine Mammals, for specific species descriptions. See Vancouver Island Recreation, page 48, Whale Watching Resources, for a list of companies offering excursions.

E&N Railiner

Operated by Via Rail, the E&N Railiner offers scenic rail service along Vancouver Island's east coast from Victoria to Courtenay, with stops in communities along the way.

The Esquimalt and Nanaimo Railway came about as the result of converging interests. Prime Minister Sir John A. Macdonald wished to complete a long-promised condition of BC's confederation with Canada by giving Vancouver Island its portion of the national rail system, and Robert Dunsmuir needed to provide transportation for his coal-mining operations. In exchange for $750,000 and nearly 1 million hectares of land, inclusive of all mineral and timber rights, Dunsmuir embarked on construction of the Esquimalt and Nanaimo Railway.

At the height of the project, some 1000 men, many of them Chinese, toiled laying track and building trestles and stations. Sir John A. MacDonald drove in the last spike on the line connecting Victoria and Nanaimo in 1886.

In 1905, James Dunsmuir, a son of Robert Dunsmuir, sold the E&N and its land grant to the Canadian Pacific Railway for $2.3 million. VIA rail was formed in 1977 to take over CN and CP passenger service and continues to operate the railway.

E&N Railiner (VIA)
450 Pandora Avenue
888-VIA RAIL
250-953-9000 ext. 5800

Lively Bastion Square occupies the former site of Fort Victoria.

Miniature World
649 Humboldt Street
250-385-9731
Open daily; Admission charged
Enthusiasts of model trains, dollhouses, and toy soldiers will delight in the extensive displays of Lilliputian realms of fancy and fact such as the World of Dickens or the Enchanted Valley of Castles. There are over 80 attractions including Space 2201 AD, a pint-sized universe complete with a spaceship to the stars, and, for something more down to earth, a scale model of the route of the Canadian Pacific Railway across Canada. Sets and figurines are all hand-carved by Canadian artists, inspired by historic events and nursery rhymes.

Government Street
Principal shopping and pedestrian area parallels Wharf and Broad streets between Humboldt and Fisgard streets
Government Street is awash in history and also features some of Victoria's best shopping. Indeed, from the 1860s to the 1890s, Government Street was the city's key commercial corridor, with shops and storefronts, banks and booksellers, tobacconists and taverns. A stroll down this pleasant thoroughfare today presents a similar experience.

Bastion Square
Off Langley Street, between Yates and Fort streets
At one time the site of Fort Victoria, surrounded then by warehouses, shops, saloons, hotels, and bordellos, Bastion Square has shed its gritty past and replaced it with galleries, museums, offices, and restaurants. Notice the heritage buildings such as the 1882 Board of Trade Building or the Burns Building, both lovely examples of High Victorian style. The Maritime Museum of British Columbia occupies the building that was the city's first courthouse, on the site that originally held the old Fort Victoria jailhouse. Between 1860 and 1885, nine men were hung in the jail yard and later interred in the square itself. The bodies were moved

Royal British Columbia Museum

Dedicated to collecting, displaying, and researching the human and natural history of British Columbia, the Royal British Columbia Museum shelters an extraordinary collection of artifacts on one of the world's most fascinating areas.

The museum holds some 10 million objects — from fantastic totem poles to the psychedelically painted Rolls Royce once owned by Beatle John Lennon — but only a selection of the extensive collection makes up the displays seen in its principal galleries. There are plans to enlarge the exhibit space to share more of the holdings with visitors and to illustrate the results of the museum's research programs.

The Royal British Columbia Museum

Natural History Gallery

Fascinating, realistic, life-sized dioramas and displays bring to life the drama and spectacle of British Columbia's birth, from tumultuous tectonic forces to frigid ice age to more temperate times and the arrival and dispersal of the region's varied flora and fauna. Stroll through the "Living Land, Living Sea" exhibit to marvel at the impressive bulk of a full-scale woolly mammoth, gaze into the soulful eyes of harbour seals basking in a tidal pool, or spy on a lumbering grizzly inspecting a shallow creek bed. At the "Open Ocean" exhibit visitors descend, figuratively speaking, into British Columbia's briny deep, home to vampire squid, snub-nosed pomfret, flapjack devilfish, and iridescent jellyfish bristling with poisonous tentacles.

First Peoples Gallery

Long before the encroachment of Europeans, the First Nations cultures of British Columbia's coasts and interior thrived on the endless bounty of land and sea. Elegant ceremonial houses and a wealth of everyday and ritual artifacts displayed in the gallery rooms provide an amazing glimpse into the richness of their beliefs and lifestyle. Interpretive exhibits, such as the scale model of the 1880 Haida village of Konna (Skedans), or the enlarged black-and-white historical images by 19th-century photographer Edward Curtis, along with numerous totem poles, masks, textiles, and basketry make this an unsurpassed experience.

Modern History Gallery

During the last 200 years, British Columbia raced into the industrial age, and the lifelike installations here re-create the heady times of discovery and settlement. Step aboard the aft deck of the HMS *Discovery* and duck into the relatively spacious quarters of Captain George Vancouver.

Amble through Old Town past the Grand Hotel, peek into the North Pacific Saloon, ogle the City Garage's 1913 Ford Model T, then head over to Chinatown, modelled after Victoria's own. At the 20th Century Hall, scads of artifacts await perusal, and visitors can browse through interactive stations for anecdotes and stories of British Columbia.

Also housed within the Royal British Columbia Museum complex is a National Geographic IMAX Theatre with a six-storey-tall screen. Special exhibits drawn from national and international collections are also frequently on show at the museum.

Royal BC Museum
675 Belleville Street
250-356-7226 or 888-447-7977
www.royalbcmuseum.bc.ca
Open daily
Admission charged

A fisherman sculpture greets guests to the Maritime Museum of British Columbia.

to the Ross Bay Cemetery in the1930s.

Nowadays the tight quarters are brimming with vendors hawking everything from T-shirts to handmade jewelry, while in the background street musicians — sometimes Peruvian pipe bands, other times a lone saxophonist — keep passers-by entertained for spare change.

Maritime Museum of British Columbia
28 Bastion Square
250-385-4222
www.mmbc.bc.ca
Open daily
Admission charged
The Maritime Museum of British Columbia, ensconced in BC's original courthouse, pays homage to life and the sea with engaging exhibits and priceless memorabilia — some 5000 artifacts in total. Cruise up and down three floors of displays featuring themes focussed on BC's coastal heritage — Exploration, Adventure, Commerce,

Passenger Travel, Floating Palaces, and the Dominion's Fleets. Of special interest is the *Tilikum*, a dugout canoe rigged for sail that endured a 65,000-kilometre voyage around the world. Save time to visit the Shipbuilding Room as well, a fascinating look at some of the museum's storehouse of 30,000 ship plans and models. On the third floor is a restored Vice-Admiralty Courtroom where once presided Sir Matthew Baillie Begbie, Chief Justice of British Columbia, and perhaps better known as the "hanging judge."

Victoria Bug Zoo
631 Courtney Street
250-384-2847
www.bugzoo.bc.ca
Open daily; Admission charged
Children (especially), as well as curious adults, will be fascinated by the displays of live insects — from spiders to scorpions to praying mantis — in addition to Canada's largest ant farm.

Market Square
Downtown Victoria at Johnson, Store, and Pandora streets
250-386-2441
www.marketsquare.victoria.bc.ca
This is the heart of Old Town Victoria, once the city's bustling commercial centre, anchored by the Grand Pacific, the Strand, and the Senator hotels, staging points for many a fortune seeker heading towards the Klondike in the late 1800s. The lower Johnson Street side served the white immigrants with prospecting supplies and bottom-dollar housing and meals. Opium merchants also thrived at Market

Square, as did prostitutes, plying their trade from several bawdy houses. The lower Pandora side, at one time separated by a ravine from Johnson Street, was home to Victoria's burgeoning Chinese community until Chinatown settled onto Fisgard Street in the 1880s. Market Square is still a vibrant part of downtown Victoria's commercial scene with more than 40 restaurants and cafes, boutiques and galleries.

Chinatown and Fan Tan Alley
Fisgard and Government streets
The Gate of Harmonious Interest marks the entrance to Victoria's Chinatown, the oldest in Canada and, in 1858, the country's largest, with some 3000 residents. Where once opium dealers rubbed shoulders with men toiling in laundries, now restaurants and shops do brisk business. Fan Tan Alley, a narrow passage

Race Rocks

Anchoring the southern tip of Vancouver Island, and long known to mariners, Race Rocks is now the Race Rocks Ecological Preserve. It was Canada's first marine protected area, sheltering an abundance of marine life — gray, humpback, minke, and killer whales, sea lions, seals, porpoises, and many species of birdlife. In 1860, Race Rocks Light Station was built here to warn sailors of the treacherous reef. It was completed only days after the Fisgard Island Light Station, and therefore it is the second oldest lighthouse on the coast of British Columbia.

59

Victoria's Flower Baskets

Some 1,000 flower baskets decorate Victoria's lampposts each summer.

From spring to the end of summer, some 1000 flower baskets festoon Victoria's lampposts. It's a tradition that originated in 1937 during the city's celebration of its 75th anniversary.

Each basket weighs in at about 25 kilograms, and it takes six gardeners to assemble the arrangements during April. Hardy species such as petunia and schizan-thus, viscaria, ivy-leafed geranium, lobelia, and various marigolds are the preferred blooms, but baskets hung in shadier areas might contain impatiens and rhodochiton.

Craigdarroch Castle

Point Ellice House displays some 10,000 Victorian-era items.

linking Fisgard Street and Pandora Avenue, is Canada's narrowest street. See the Old Victoria Walking Tour box.

Centennial Square
Entrance off the intersection of Pandora and Government streets
During the 1960s, Centennial Square hosted a public market for Saanich Peninsula farmers who hawked their fresh goods around the square's fountain. Two of the three monoliths represent birth and youth, while the largest depicts St. George slaying a dragon, symbolizing the triumph of good over evil. City Hall also graces the square, a marvelous example of architect John Teague's extensive work in Victoria. The clock faces measure more than two metres across, a third the size of those on London's Big Ben.

Victoria City Hall
Douglas and Pandora streets, by Centennial Square
Constructed in 1897, Victoria's City Hall is beautifully Victorian. From mid-June to September there are free noon-

hour concerts in the Square to entertain visitors and locals alike. See the Old Victoria Walking Tour box.

Congregation Temple Emanuel
Blanshard and Pandora streets
A National Historic Site as well as a place of worship, Temple Emanuel opened in 1863 and is Canada's oldest synagogue in continuous use.

Antique Row
Fort Street between Blanshard and Cook streets
Look for several half-timbered, mock Tudor-style buildings to find the centre of Victoria's antique business. Collectibles aplenty await discerning buyers seeking anything from Victorian silver to Chinese Ming Dynasty silk scrolls.

Christ Church Cathedral
Quadra and Courtenay streets
250-383-2714
Self-guided tour brochures; guided tours available by prior arrangement
Free admission
From July to August, the free Saturday afternoon concerts here are a delight. Stop by any

season, however, to experience one of Canada's few remaining churches with real working bells. Or enjoy services accompanied by a massive 3000-pipe organ. The spectacular pulpit of this 1929 cathedral was crafted from a 500-year-old oak tree.

Craigdarroch Castle
1050 Joan Crescent
250-592-5323
www.craigdarrochcastle.com
Open daily
Admission charged
Scottish-born tycoon Robert Dunsmuir built Craigdarroch (meaning "rocky oak place" in Gaelic) between 1887 and 1889, though he never saw it finished as he died in April 1889. His widow, Joan, completed the massive project and lived there until her death in 1908. It then became a military hospital, a college, offices for the school board, and a music conservatory before rightfully becoming a treasured national historic site.

Visitors today are treated to a delightful glimpse into the lives of Vancouver Island's entrepreneurial aristocracy. Dunsmuir's industrial kingdom, centred round Nanaimo coal mines, fuelled the construction of this ornate 39-room mansion commanding the high point of the prestigious Rockland area near Government House. The grounds were once far more extensive, encompassing nearly 11 hectares of parkland strewn with quiet ponds and meadows. Inside, restoration has recaptured its glory days as a private residence. Guided and self-guided tours take visitors into rooms lavishly finished with worked granite, marble, and sandstone, in addition to intricate wood panelling of walnut, mahogany, cedar, and spruce.

Art Gallery of Greater Victoria

1040 Moss Street; off Fort Street
250-384-4101
www.aggv.bc.ca
Open daily
Admission charged

Galleries occupy the 1889 Spencer mansion, as well as six modern exhibition halls, and showcase treasures drawn from some 15,000 celebrated works and *objets d'art*. Contemporary artists such as Emily Carr and Max Maynard are featured, in addition to many excellent Asian artifacts: a 19th-century Chinese embroidered silk robe, a Japanese Edo-period hanging scroll, or an 18th-

century Burmese lacquer depicting a monk praying, to name only three splendid examples. Rain or shine, the outdoor Shinto shrine — the only one of its kind outside Japan — provides a soothing respite for quiet contemplation.

Point Ellice House

2616 Pleasant Street; just before Bay Bridge
250-380-6506
ww.heritage.gov.bc.ca
Open daily, mid-May to mid-September
Admission charged

A BC Heritage Site clinging to the past in the midst of an industrial warehouse area, the former home of magistrate

Abkhazi Garden, A Heritage Garden That Love Built

Abkhazi Gardens

Star-crossed lovers Marjorie (Peggy) Pemberton-Carter and Prince Nicholas Abkhazi of the country of Georgia fell in love in Paris in the 1920s. Their romance blossomed, but fate separated them with the onset of World War II. He was destined to suffer in a German POW camp, while she was imprisoned in a Japanese internment camp near Shanghai.

During her ordeal in China, Peggy managed to retain a sum of travellers cheques, which she kept hidden in a talcum powder bottle. At the end of the war, Peggy made her way to Victoria, using her funds to purchase a rocky home site in Victoria. Soon she was reunited with her great love, and she and Nicholas were married in Victoria in 1946.

Together at last, the couple lavished attention on designing and building their simple home set amidst a stunning garden. Years of careful nurturing ensued, and "the garden became our child," according to Peggy. By all accounts they were proud parents, and their garden opened to the public in 1949.

Although both Peggy and Nicholas have died, that generous tradition remains today under the auspices of The Land Conservancy of British Columbia. In 2000, the TLC saved the home and gardens

from housing development, and it is now well into the property's restoration. Visitors today are treated to what Peggy likened to a Chinese scroll, which, when unrolled, reveals a beautifully sequenced landscape in view, mood, and character. Indeed, even though it is no more than a half hectare in size, the garden rewards visitors with a woodland retreat holding 100-year-old rhododendrons, a sunny south lawn, stands of majestic Garry oak, and rocky terraces bursting with flowers. Peggy once remarked, when asked about her process of gardening, "When you are very much in love you don't go wrong."

Abkhazi Garden
1964 Fairfield Road
250-598-8096
www.conservancy.bc.ca
Open Wednesday, Thursday, Friday, and Sunday afternoons, March to September
Admission charged

Emily Carr

Born in the James Bay area of Victoria on December 13, 1871, Emily Carr is celebrated as one of Canada's foremost artists and writers. Her drawings, paintings, and pottery are proudly held in collections throughout the world, while her books are exquisite memoirs of Victoria's Victorian era.

Emily Carr grew up in a family of six, the youngest of five daughters. Her father, Richard Carr, ran a wholesale grocery store located on Wharf Street, but, sadly, both her father and mother died before her 16th birthday. Still, by her own account she led an idyllic life with her sisters, exploring Birdcage Walk, nearby Beacon Hill, New Field, Mrs. McConnell's cow farm, and Pond Place, where "primroses and daffodils grew on its bank and leaned over the bank so far to peep at themselves that some of them got drowned."

Carr began her artistic career in the 1890s and continued to paint until 1913; however, the lack of encouragement and financial support resulted in her painting very little in the subsequent 15 years. Carr received her education in San Francisco, London, and France, where she studied post-impressionist techniques that she applied to her own vision of the Pacific West Coast. She is particularly respected for her interpretations of coastal landscapes and First Nations villages.

At the age of 41, still unmarried and destined to remain that way, Carr built a boarding house at 646 Simcoe Street (now a private residence), and for the next 23 years she relished her time in her "House of All Sorts." Here she hooked rugs, fired pottery, bred and sold sheepdogs, and doted on her gardens. Later, in 1936, she moved to a place on Beckley Street before taking over Alice Carr's schoolhouse on St. Andrews, once the site of the family vegetable garden.

Carr's painting style evolved significantly after 1927; indeed, the bulk of the work she became noted for was completed in the last 17 years of her life. Several events are credited with her expanding talent. The much acclaimed exhibition of 1927, "Canadian West Coast: Native and Modern," held in Ottawa, in which Carr showed several pieces, brought her praise and renewed her dedication to painting. Then in 1928, American painter, Mark Tobey, whom Carr had already known, came to Victoria to teach and lived in Carr's "House of All Sorts" for several weeks. Tobey's modernist ideas mixed with spirituality melded well with Carr's own philosophies and she increasingly searched for stronger structure and design in her work, while also more freely expressing the landscape's natural rhythms. "What I am struggling most for is movement and expanse — liveness," she wrote in 1934. In the following decade, she refined her understanding and expression of the spirit of the landscape.

The painter was also respected for her writing. Carr's first book, *Klee Wyck* (1941), a collection of short stories about her visits to First Nations villages, received the Governor General's Award. *The Book of Small* was published in 1942, and its reminiscences of her Victoria childhood still entertain readers, as does her later work, *The House of All Sorts* (1944), about life in the boarding house.

Emily Carr died March 2, 1945, at St. Mary's Priory, now the James Bay Inn, and is interred at Ross Bay Cemetery (Block H plot 85E), near the northwest corner by the junction of Fairfield and Arnold roads. Her legacy lives on in many national and international collections. Of particular note is the substantial permanent collection of Carr's work at the Art Gallery of Greater Victoria. The artist's birthplace and childhood home is now a museum and open for tours. Further, lectures and special events highlighting Carr's work are frequently held in Victoria, especially during the annual October Emily Carr Festival of the Arts.

Peter O'Reilly is a matchless treat. The fact that the house displays some 10,000 Victorian-era items is reason enough to visit. The heritage gardens, re-established based on notes left by Kathleen, the daughter of Peter and Caroline O'Reilly, are alive with heirloom roses and native oaks. Plan to take high tea, served at the gallery / cafe, for a memorable afternoon. Save time for a game of croquet on the lawn, too.

Ross Bay Cemetery

Fairfield Road and Memorial Crescent; east of Clover Point Contact Old Cemeteries Society of Victoria for tours 250-598-8870 www.oldcem.bc.ca Open daily during daylight hours Donations accepted

This is more of a "living" cemetery, as the 11 hectare site is popular with joggers and amblers. Eternally at peace here are some 28,000 souls, including such notables as artist / author Emily Carr, tycoon Robert Dunsmuir, and BC's early governor Sir James Douglas. Indeed, so rich in historical internment is the Ross Bay Cemetery that organized tours are conducted by the Old Cemeteries Society of Victoria. Its volunteers are also frequently on site to point the way to interesting graves, such as that of Mary Laetitia Pearse, Ross Bay's first inhabitant, laid to rest here in 1872, or the Hon. John Hamilton Gray, Canada's only Father of Confederation buried in western Canada.

Clippity-Clop Victoria

To experience Victoria at the leisurely pace of a horse-drawn carriage is to recall one of the city's most genteel eras.
Black Beauty Carriage Tours
180 Goward Road, RR7
250-361-1220

Tally Ho Horse Drawn Tours
Menzies and Belleville
250-383-5067
www.tallyhotours.com
Victoria Carriage Tours
251 Superior Street
250-383-2207
www.victoriacarriage.com

Victoria Arts

Pacific Opera Victoria presents imaginative productions from October to May at the resplendent 1913 Royal Theatre. The venerable stage is also one of the homes of the Victoria Symphony, which offers a full schedule of traditional concerts, as well as special events such as the summertime Cathedral Fest and Symphony Splash. Look, too, for performances at the University of Victoria or at the Victoria Conservatory of Music as well as any number of other local venues. Check local newspapers or at the Tourism Victoria Visitor Info-Centre for up-to-date listings of current engagements.

Of historic note are the Belfry Theatre, renowned for contemporary productions, and Langham Court Theatre. The Belfry's home is a one-time church that was recently refurbished to its heritage state, while the original buildings of the Langham Court Theatre (ca.1880) were the carriage house and barn from the Robert Ward family estate.

Every July, more than 75 well-known and emerging artists converge upon the entire length of Moss Street — from the Art Gallery of Greater Victoria down to the Pacific Ocean — to celebrate the visual arts. Artists work at "stations" along Moss Street, while some 20,000 interested visitors enjoy the free festivities.

The inspirations of contemporary artists can also be found on a self-guided walking tour of six Victoria galleries: Alcheringa Gallery, Fran Willis Gallery, Starfish Gallery, Stephen Lowe Gallery, West End Gallery, and Winchester Galleries. Pick up a Victoria Gallery Walk map and brochure at any of the participating galleries.

Sir James Douglas

An illegitimate son born in the Caribbean West Indies in 1803 to a Scottish father and a mother of mixed race, James Douglas rose from his humble beginnings to become a man of power and prestige. He not only founded Victoria, but also became His Excellency, the governor of both the Crown Colony of Vancouver Island and the Crown Colony of British Columbia. When he died in 1877 he was Sir James Douglas, Vancouver Island's wealthiest man, both revered and feared.

Douglas came to Vancouver Island in his capacity of chief factor (head trader) for the Hudson's Bay Company. He chose the site for Fort Victoria, supervised its construction, and headed its operations. In 1849, he and his wife, Amelia, settled at Victoria, raising the six of their 13 children who survived infancy. From this hardscrabble frontier the tireless and autocratic Douglas fashioned a prosperous British commercial bastion.

Described as "a handsome specimen of nature's noblemen — tall, stout, broad-shouldered, muscular, with a grave bronzed face," Douglas enjoyed the finer points of civilization, was literate yet tough-minded, and brooked little opposition from liberal democratic proponents. Eventually, with the maturity of the colony and its evolution from hinterland to a stable and profitable bureaucratically run British institution, Douglas retired from power, becoming increasingly reclusive and obsessed with his wealth.

Touring Victoria

There is no shortage of unique ways in which to experience this city by the sea.

Victoria Bobby Walking Adventures
812 Wharf Street, Visitor InfoCentre
250-995-0233
www.walkvictoria.com
Join a former English bobby for a lighthearted stroll through Victoria's history.

Ale Trail
Victoria's breweries are garnering an international reputation. Learn brewmasters' secrets on this fun-filled excursion to several micro-breweries and brewpubs to sample ales and lagers as well as meals prepared with beer. Occurring the first Saturday of every month, the self-guided Ale Trail takes in four microbreweries: Swans, Hugo's, Spinnakers, and the Canoe Club.

The Vancouver Island Brewing Company at 2230 Government Street also offers brewery tours on Fridays and Saturdays.

Victoria's Heritage Pub Tour
250-386-2264
Take in two excursions, "Sooke and Suds" or the "Sidney Slosh," for a truly "hoppy" experience of local brewpubs.

Classic Car Tours
250-885-2221 or 250-383-2342
www.classiccartours.net
Ride in style aboard a classic convertible to visit Victoria's notable sites, while the driver / narrator relates tales of the city.

James Bay Heritage Walking Tour
Victoria Heritage Foundation
250-383-4546
www.vhf.city.victoria.bc.ca
Pick up a map / brochure at the Visitor InfoCentre and take in a self-guided jaunt to see 51 of the dozens of historical buildings in Victoria's oldest residential neighbourhood.

Victoria Architectural Walking Tour
Community Arts Council Sussex Building
1001 Douglas Street
800-667-0753
Operating from July to September, this free guided tour strolls around Victoria, highlighting the city's history as seen through its architecture.

Ghostly Walks
634 Battery Street
250-384-6698
www.discoverthepast.com
Sign up, if you dare, for a storyteller's evening jaunt down the haunted memory lanes of Old Town and Chinatown.

"To realize Victoria you must take all that the eye admires in Bournemouth, Torquay, the Isle of Wight, the happy valley at Hong Kong, the Doon, Sorrento and Camp's Bay — add reminiscences of the Thousand Islands and arrange the whole around the Bay of Naples with some Himalayas for the background."
Rudyard Kipling

Victoria Festivals & Events

FEBRUARY

Victoria Independent Film and Video Festival
Various venues
The festival screens over 100 features and shorts in all genres over ten days.

Flower Count
Mission Control at Victoria Eaton Centre
Victoria residents examine front gardens, backyards, and city parks to count flowers.

MARCH

Dancearts
University Centre Auditorium
Eight days of exciting dance performances, provincial competitions, master classes, and workshops.

APRIL

Greater Victoria Performing Arts Festival
Various venues
Categories in the festival include: dance, piano, vocal, brass, woodwinds, speech, strings, accordion, ukulele, harp, classical guitar, choral, and bands.

Victoria International Blossom Walks
Throughout Victoria
Choose from seven different blossom walks, ranging from 5 to 42 kilometres, that lead participants along waterfront walkways and through picturesque neighbourhoods.

TerrifVic Jazz Party
Various venues
The TerrifVic Jazz Party strikes up five music-filled days with a lineup that includes over 20 international bands.

Uno Festival
Various venues
Uno is Canada's one and only festival of solo theatrical performance.

Bastion Square Festival of the Arts
Bastion Square
Local artists and artisans display and demonstrate their wares.

MAY

Fort Rodd Hill Historical Military Encampment
Fort Rodd Hill National Historic Site
Military re-enactments and displays of vehicles, uniforms, and equipment reflect British Columbia's naval and military history from the 1850s to the 1950s.

Luxton Pro Rodeo
Luxton Fairgrounds
Featuring world and Canadian champion cowboys, plus dances, a midway, craft sale, blacksmithing demonstrations, and antique farm equipment.

Victoria Harbour Festival
Inner Harbour
This celebration bridges two holiday long weekends, Canada's Victoria Day and US Memorial Day. Activities range from the Victoria Day parade to concerts and other events around the harbour, including the internationally renowned Swiftsure International yacht race.

Victoria Highland Games
Royal Athletic Park
Traditional Scottish games, music, dancing, and entertainment.

Bastion Square Cycling Grand Prix
Downtown Victoria and Saanich
A criterium-style race featuring a closed-loop circuit on which professional riders, as well as those in Categories 1 and 2 (the next notches down from the pros), compete.

A bagpiper skirls at Victoria's Inner Harbour.

JUNE

Jazzfest International
Various venues
Features over 50 performances of jazz, blues, and world music with over 200 musicians.

Victoria Conservatory of Music's Garden Tour
Various venues
Eight to ten of the finest private gardens in Victoria open their gates to the public.

Folkfest
Ship's Point, Inner Harbour
A celebration of professional and amateur multicultural entertainment, food, and festivities.

Summer in the Square
Centennial Square
Enjoy local music and dance talent in daily performances throughout the summer months.

Victoria Festivals & Events

The Dragon Boat Festival attracts dozens of contestants for its dragon boat races.

JULY

Luminara Victoria
Beacon Hill Park
A community lantern celebration, held annually, includes paper lanterns, candlelight, outdoor art and performances.

The Great Canadian Family Picnic
Beacon Hill Park
Featured attractions are over 25 local artists and entertainers including clowns, buskers, and stage performances. Feast on the huge Canada Day cake.

Victoria Symphony Summer Music Festival — Summer Cathedral Fest
Christ Church Cathedral
Two weeks of fantastic classical music in the stained glass splendour of the magnificent Christ Church Cathedral. The 11 concerts feature all kinds of classical music, including works for orchestra, chamber ensemble, quartets, quintets, and solo performers.

Moss Street Paint-in
Moss Street
This annual festival of the visual arts is orchestrated by the Art Gallery of Greater Victoria. More than 75 well-known and emerging artists work at "stations" along Moss Street, using a wide variety of media and styles.

"A Bite of Victoria" Food Festival
Government House
A showcase of Victoria restaurants and eateries, with a tasty variety of food and beverages for sampling. Buskers, musicians, and local artists provide additional treats for eyes and ears.

AUGUST

Latin Caribbean Music Festival
Market Square
Includes over 100 performers from Latin America, the Caribbean, and North America.

Symphony Splash
Inner Harbour
Seated on a barge moored in the middle of the Inner Harbour, members of the Victoria Symphony delight a crowd of 40,000 with their perfect blend of orchestral classics and popular favourites, including a rendition of Tchaikowsky's "1812 Overture" complete with cannons and fireworks.

First Peoples Festival
Royal BC Museum and surrounding sites
Canada's largest annual urban celebration of aboriginal tradition, art, and culture showcases the talents of approximately 350 aboriginal artists, storytellers, dancers, musicians, and fashion designers.

Dragon Boat Festival
Inner Harbour
The dragon boat festival has ancient Chinese cultural and spiritual roots, but has been celebrated in North America only in recent years. The centrepiece of the festival is the famed dragon boat races, in which crews of 24 paddlers in full dragon boat regalia race head-to-head in a 650-metre sprint, with timing drums thumping away.

Classic Boat Festival
Inner Harbour
Over 100 boats, all built before 1955, line the docks for a maritime open house. Special events include the sailpast and the Sunday schooner race.

OCTOBER

Ghost Festival
Throughout Victoria
Members of the Old Cemeteries Society escort participants on spook-filled tours of Victoria's best haunts.

NOVEMBER–JANUARY

Victoria Christmas
Various Venues
Decorations, carolers, and lots of twinkling lights deck out the holiday season.

The Butchart Gardens

The magnificent Sunken Garden at The Butchart Gardens was once a limestone quarry.

Descend through a magnificent arbour of more than 500 flowering Japanese cherry trees along Benvenuto Avenue to enter The Butchart Gardens, easily one of the world's most flower-bedecked and beloved horticultural wonders.

The gardens bloom on the one-time estate and residence of Robert Pim and Jennie Foster Butchart. The Butchart family's roots reach back to the Forfar district of Scotland. It was one George MacLauchlan Butchart who immigrated to Canada, settling in the Owen Sound area of Ontario around 1850. Here he started a successful hardware business, and here was born Robert Pim in 1856, the eldest son of a family of ten. Robert entered the family business when he came of age, and after his father's death he and his brother

continued the business.

Jennie Foster Kennedy was born in Toronto, Ontario, in 1866. When she was orphaned at an early age, an aunt in Owen Sound brought her to live there, and it was at Owen Sound that Jennie blossomed into a fine young women, known for the talent and enthusiasm she brought to her every undertaking. In 1884, Jennie Foster and Robert Pim were married in Buffalo, New York, and the twosome honeymooned inEngland, a trip that would mark new beginnings in their life together in many ways.

Indeed, it was on this journey to Great Britain that Robert learned the process for making Portland cement, an endeavour that would lead to fortune and new frontiers. Back at Owen Sound, less than four

years later, Robert and his brother David formed the Owen Sound Portland Cement Company, its first mill situated at Shallow Lake. Later the business venture expanded to include another plant at Lakefield, Ontario, and then a third in Montreal, Quebec. The Butcharts' Portland cement, along with their innovation of packaging the cumbersome product in easy-to-handle sacks rather than the customary and invariably awkward barrels, laid a strong foundation for their plants' growth.

Farther horizons beckoned as Robert foresaw the need for cement production in western Canada, a budding industrial frontier at the turn of the century. Disembarking at Victoria in 1902, Robert soon discovered a good limestone deposit at Tod Inlet, 20 kilometres north

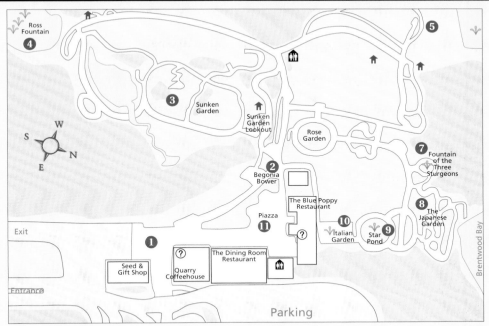

of the city. The location not only provided this critical ingredient of cement, but also had an ample water supply for production. The site's seaside access offered excellent transportation and distribution possibilities, too. The Tod Inlet Cement Plant was established in 1904, and within the short span of a year the first sacks of cement were shipped out to form the foundations for the burgeoning growth of coastal cities and towns.

Jennie and their two daughters, Jennie, age 21, and Mary, age 19, moved to Vancouver Island with the founding of the plant. With characteristic verve, the Butcharts built the first phase of their new home, Benvenuto ("welcome " in Italian), near the factory site to allow for careful oversight by Robert Pim. Still, it was far enough away to offer privacy and retreat

Pink chrysanthemum

from the duties of plant management. The formative sprouting of the garden beds began, and over time Benvenuto expanded to become their permanent residence.

The Butcharts' horticultural endeavour started with a gift, a new friend's housewarming offering of a few sweet peas and a single rose plant. Thus began The Butchart Gardens.

Gracious Jennie welcomed guests to the family gardens from the outset. Indeed, the household served tea to everyone who stopped by — that is until the vast number of visitors made this hospitality impractical. Nonetheless, the welcome respite was reintroduced as teahouses and summerhouses were nestled amongst the gardens. In 1915 alone, tea was served to some 18,000 people. Vancouver Island residents and visitors alike couldn't resist the alluring combination of socializing and spectacular flower arrangements. *Maclean's* magazine described The Butchart Gardens in 1931 as "more than twenty acres in which every flower and shrub of the temperate zone grow at their best."

In 1939, Pim and Jennie presented the gardens to their grandson, R. Ian Ross, on the occasion of his 21st birthday,

The Butchart Gardens

though he didn't assume directorship until 1948. The Butcharts moved to Victoria in 1940, and during World War II the gardens were maintained, albeit minimally. Mr. Butchart died in 1943, and Mrs. Butchart in 1950.

The task of reclaiming, restoring, and expanding the gardens fell to Ian Ross and Ann Lee Ross, his Chicago-born wife. Imagination and vigour directed their vision as they established a variety of entertainment diversions to enhance the experience of the gardens, not only during the prime summer months but throughout the year.

Seasonal displays enliven the stunning landscape. Springtime heralds the arrival of azalea and rhododendron blooms, and an abundance of tulips — some 135,000 bulbs from Holland — burst into showy harbingers of warmer weather. Come summertime, sensational fireworks grace the skies in a true spectacle of pyrotechnic art. This is in addition to the year-round nighttime illuminations begun in 1954 to commemorate the garden's 50th anniversary. Holiday festivities begin on December 1, with thousands of lights twinkling and glowing. Later, carpets of poinsettias herald the arrival of ChristmasTime, and carolers and brass ensembles offer background accompaniment to the wonder of the gardens' winter radiance.

❶ Patio Garden and Entrance
The Visitor Centre located here houses an information station, first aid station, lost and found, luggage storage, postal services, and washrooms. In addition, several items are

The Italian Garden features a cross-shaped lily pond.

available on a loan basis for patrons including strollers, wheelchairs, umbrellas, and even cameras. The garden's visitor guide is available in 19 languages: Arabic, Chinese, Danish, Dutch, English, French, German, Greek, Hebrew, Hindi, Italian, Japanese, Korean, Polish, Portuguese, Russian, Spanish, Swedish, and Ukrainian.

As most plants in the gardens are left purposely unmarked, in keeping with the spirit of a family versus a botanical garden, the Plant Identification Centre offers visitors access to the knowledgeable staff who can answer horticultural questions. Further, at the Benvenuto Seed & Gift Store, guests may purchase seeds for many of the gardens' species, as well as gardening accessories. Restaurants include the Dining Room Restaurant, offering fine dining in the Butchart residence, as well as afternoon tea; the Blue Poppy Restaurant, set in the conservatory, which offers cafeteria-style selections; and the Quarry Coffeehouse, which provides quick snacks and beverages.

❷ Begonia Bower
Until 1939 the bower was a free-flight aviary for Mr. Butchart's collection of exotic pigeons, doves, and parrots. Today it showcases hanging baskets of schizanthus, fuchsias, and begonias. The statuary here is *Peace Doves*, installed in 1993.

❸ Sunken Garden
When visitors stand at the lookout high above the Sunken Garden, it may be hard for them to believe that the site was once a limestone quarry that supplied the makings for Portland cement. By 1908 the quarry was exhausted, and, so the story goes, Mrs. Butchart took up the challenge when a friend casually remarked that even she couldn't get anything to grow there. Thus was born the idea of a sunken garden.

Mrs. Butchart transformed the scoured quarry walls by swinging over the side of the precipice in a bosun's chair, carefully tucking ivy clippings into the wall's crevices. She added to this effort by planting a variety of annuals, perennials, and flowering shrubs. By 1910

The Star Pond was once a natatorium for Mr. Butchart's collection of ornamental ducks.

the stately Lombardy poplars were planted and later augmented by white poplars and Persian plums to hide the view of the cement plant. British gardener William Westby was responsible for draining the terrain and hauling in tons of rich topsoil as well as installing the impressive flowerbeds. The deepest section of the abandoned quarry was lined and allowed to fill with water from a natural spring. Later, trout were introduced. The massive rock outcropping protruding up from the quarry was transformed into a promontory rock garden carpeted with trees and flowers from across the globe. The Sunken Garden was completed in 1921.

Riots of flowers await visitors to The Butchart Gardens.

❹ Ross Fountain
Installed in 1964, the Ross Fountain marked the 60th anniversary of The Butchart Gardens. Myriad intricate timing mechanisms and pump systems control the centre jets that reach heights of 24 metres. A fine spray bathes the jet's base at water level, cleverly concealing the rigid piping and pumps. The four-minute segments of jet and spray merriment are variations on a theme, interrupted by a playful water curtain between performances. Come dusk, coloured lights switch on, illuminating the fountain's spray pattern. The lighting accompaniment is purposefully unsynchronized, allowing for a broad and constantly interesting variety of effects.

❺ Fireworks Viewing
Begun in 1978 by the great-grandson of the Butcharts, pyrotechnics dance across the skies every Saturday night in July and August during 30-minute shows choreographed to music.

❻ Rose Garden
A former kitchen vegetable patch, at its peak from June through mid-August the Rose Garden bursts with more than 3000 spectacular and fragrant blooms. Constructed during 1929-30, the gardens were designed by Butler Sturtevant, a Seattle landscape architect, and adapted by Mrs. Butchart, with installation overseen by Bob Ballantyne, the Butcharts' chief gardener from 1928 to 1958. Plantings are marked with their country of origin as well as the year the variety was selected by the American Rose Society. Each year, new prize-winning roses are added.

Formal in its sensibility, the setting features arches of old-fashioned climbing roses, as well as tiered beds planted with purple, blue, and white Pacific giant delphiniums encircling an oval lawn. A sparkling gazing ball mirrors the floral abundance. The pretty wrought-iron wishing well came from Florence, Italy, and coins tossed in are donated to the local children's hospital.

❼ Fountain of the Three Sturgeons
Cast in Florence, Italy, the magnificent bronze fountain was crafted by Sirio Tofanari, known for his powerful depictions of animals in motion. This spiralling trio of gracefully arched sturgeons provides a focus at the end of the Main Lawn.

❽ The Japanese Garden
The Japanese Garden was the Butcharts' first major horticultural endeavour, inspired by their memorable trips to Asia and the wonderfully peaceful gardens they visited there. In 1906, Mrs. Butchart enlisted the help of Isaburo Kishida, a noted landscape artist, to design and install a traditional Japanese garden, situated

The Butchart Gardens

The Fountain of Three Sturgeons was cast in Florence, Italy.

10 Italian Garden

It was Sir Henry Thornton, president of the Canadian National Railway, who suggested to the Butcharts that the tennis court adjacent to the residence might make an excellent site for an Italian garden. Samuel McClure, the Butcharts' architect, was asked to lay out the garden's overall design, as he was also responsible for the extension and renovation of the residence.

In 1926 the Italian Garden began taking shape. Sheltered on two sides by the home, the north end of the garden was planted with Lawson cypress. Trellised arches cut into the cypress walls gave entrance from the Star Pond. A cross-shaped lily pond, surrounded by oblong flower beds, provides the restful focal point for the garden. At one end of the pond rises the winged Roman god Mercury, while in the centre of the pond is a sculpture of a dolphin and young girl.

11 Piazza

Dedicated to all the children and animals that visit Butchart Gardens, the bronze boar Tacca lounges upon his haunches at the heart of the Piazza. A replica of the statue that stands next to the famed Straw Market in Florence, Italy, Tacca's burnished snout bears the mark of thousands of visitors who rub his upturned nose for luck.

The Butchart Gardens
Box 4010
Victoria BC V8X 3X4
Open every day at 9 am, except Christmas and New Year's Day, when it opens at 1 pm
250-652-5256 (recorded information)
250-652-4422 (office)
www.butchartgardens.com

between the house and Butchart Cove. Chinese workers, borrowed from the Butcharts' nearby factory, implemented Kishida's vision, which included a magnificent red lacquer torii gate, flanked by grand copper beeches, which are among the oldest trees in the gardens. It took nearly four years to complete the first phase of the Japanese Garden.

During 1961, significant improvements were added to the garden. Japanese lanterns were strung, petite footbridges were placed over gurgling rivulets, and carvings were carefully installed among the plantings. Of particular note is the chuckling Buddha sculpted of clay by Kenneth Bloomfield. The two weeping hemlocks commemorate 50 years of Ross stewardship of the gardens.

9 Star Pond

Designed by Mr. Butchart in 1931, this formal water feature was originally a natatorium for Mr. Butchart's collection of ornamental ducks. The duck house is still visible at the far side of the pond.

South Vancouver Island

A sculpture of a killer whale announces the entrance to the small community of Port Renfrew.

Two main routes provide easy access to the South Vancouver Island region, which encompasses the entire southern tip of Vancouver Island outside Victoria. Highway 17, also called the Pat Bay Highway, is familiar to many as it is the road that leads out of the BC Ferries' Swartz Bay terminal and is the most expeditious way to Victoria. This busy thoroughfare bisects South Vancouver Island's Saanich Peninsula and offers easy access to the area's many diversions. Westward from Victoria, Highway 14, also called the West Coast Road, ventures into the Western Communities and the Sooke region, and from there all the way to the small west coast town of Port Renfrew.

Sidney is the comely seaside village-cum-urban centre of the Saanich Peninsula. The municipality bustles with the comings and goings of BC Ferries and of Victoria International Airport, only five minutes to the southwest.

Readers love Sidney for its many fine bookstores, and the small museums here are a delight. Within minutes, however, the townscape gives way to rolling countryside dotted

South Island Recommendations

- Without question, plan a visit to The Butchart Gardens, 23 hectares of incredible horticultural wonders.
- Dawdle through lovely seaside Sidney and its many, many bookstores, but be sure to make time to check out the Sidney Marine Museum, the Marine Ecology Station, and the British Columbia Aviation Museum.
- Relax in tidy Oak Bay. Have tea and do some shopping in the pretty neighbourhood, considered by many to be Victoria's most British-looking hamlet.
- Take an afternoon to explore Fort Rodd Hill and Fisgard Lighthouse National Historic Sites.
- Venture into the Sooke area to discover artisan studios, great natural recreation sites, and excellent dining.
- Drive the historic West Coast Road from Sooke to Port Renfrew for a taste of the wild Pacific Coast. Allow time for a walk along fascinating Botanical Beach.

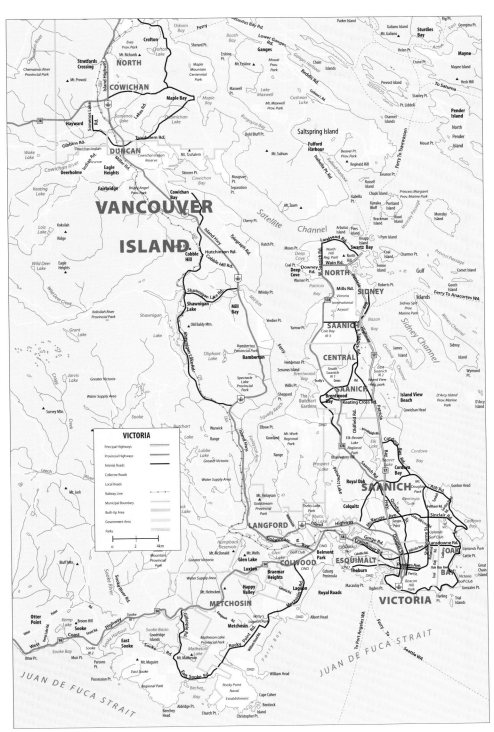

Honour stands are common sights along Vancouver Island roads.

with farms and meadows. Tiny communities, parks, forests, lakes, and ocean inlets are the most common sights of this lovely landscape, and The Butchart Gardens spreads over 23 glorious hectares not far from Brentwood Bay.

Farther south, the Greater Victoria communities of Oak Bay, Esquimalt, and View Royal beckon with their own distinct personalities. Oak Bay in particular is ever so charming and very English, with Tudor-style storefronts and homes, great pubs, and traditional afternoon teas. The Scenic Marine Drive skirting the area rewards motorists with stunning views and great diversions.

Across the Johnson Street Bridge from Victoria is "Strategic Esquimalt," as Esquimalt Harbour shelters Canada's Pacific naval fleet. The CFB Esquimalt Naval and Military Museum here is top of the line. West of Esquimalt, the road leads into the Western Communities of Colwood, Langford, Metchosin, and the Highlands.

Sooke and its environs offer easygoing relaxation with splendid parks and recreational opportunities. In addition,

there is an exciting art scene with a self-guided studio tour, and some of the continent's finest dining. From Sooke, Highway 14 becomes the scenic West Coast Road, a winding, seashore-hugging route to Port Renfrew. Natural wonders such as the fascinating tide pools at Botanical Beach or the 47 kilometre wilderness trek of the Juan de Fuca Marine Trail are just two of the many attractions of this farthest southwestern corner of Vancouver Island.

Saanich Peninsula
Saanich Peninsula Chamber of Commerce
PO Box 2014
Sidney BC V8L 3S3
250-656-0525
Visitor Centre: 10382 Pat Bay Highway (Highway 17)
Population: 37,670
The Saanich Peninsula boasts the blessings of quiet country life as well as the salubrious conviences of urban life, along with a bounty of parks offering beach waterfront strolls, scenic vistas, and rural rambles. Fruit and flower stands follow the age-old honour system, tempting visitors and residents alike to add a little something special

to the day. Always exceptional is The Butchart Gardens, located near Brentwood Bay. And don't overlook Heritage Acres, its park setting dotted with restored buildings and antique farming equipment. The neighbourhood of Cordova Bay, set above Haro Strait and looking off to stunning views of Mt. Baker, showcases the Saanich Peninsula's bucolic beauty — and a fine collection of shops at Mattick's Farm.

Saanich Historical Artifacts Society / Heritage Acres
7321 Lochside Drive; east side of Highway 17 at Island View Road
250-652-5522
www.horizon.bc.ca/~shas
Open daily in summer; morning hours only, October to June
Admission charged
This 12 hectare site, criss-

West Coast Road

Highway 14, also called the West Coast Road, delivers a superb scenic experience as it winds along the southwest shoreline of Vancouver Island from Sooke to Port Renfrew. Lush rain forest and rocky cliffs, lighthouses and spectacular beaches are its rewards, in addition to many, many options for hikes, from short casual strolls to full-day treks and sojourns for expert campers. Wildlife lovers will not be disappointed. Bird-watchers can take in Whiffen Spit, a natural breakwater between the Strait of Juan de Fuca and Sooke Harbour, and those seeking sightings of black bears will have ample opportunity.

Victoria Butterfly Gardens house some 35 species of butterflies.

Scenic Marine Drive

Easily one of Vancouver Island's prettiest tour routes, the Scenic Marine Drive skirts the coastline south and east of Victoria proper. The route begins on Dallas Road at the Odgen Point Breakwater, a nice place for a morning walk to watch boats and ships enter and exit the Inner Harbour.

Farther along Dallas Road at Douglas Street, Beacon Hill Park offers more ambling possibilities. A green space since the 1860s, the park is Victoria's most beloved patch of greenery. Here, too, is the marker for Mile Zero of the Trans-Canada Highway.

At Clover Point, just east of Beacon Hill Park, kite flyers take advantage of the perpetual breezes, and a paved footpath and staircases lead down to the beach where parasailers and windsurfers flock. Motoring east along Dallas Road, which goes through a couple of name changes before it becomes Beach Drive, there are glimpses of stunning waterfront and cliffside homes, as well as lovely vistas over the Strait of Juan de Fuca.

Soon Beach Drive takes a swing through the Victoria Golf Club, the city's oldest course. Oak Bay, the surrounding neighborhood, is Victoria's most "British," with several fine places to stop for a spot of tea.

Continuing on Beach Drive, Willows Beach, known for its sandy strand, beckons for a stroll. Back on Beach Drive, the Scenic Marine Drive dips through the Upland Estates, once the site of the Hudson's Bay Company sheep farm and now one of Victoria's most exclusive neighborhoods. Stop at Cattle Point to peer out towards the Discovery Islands, then drive on past Cadboro Bay (the road undergoes more name changes) and through Mt. Douglas Park to Cordova Bay. Here, motorists can opt to return to Victoria (south on Highway 17) or take in the Saanich Peninsula up to Sidney by turning north on Highway 17.

crossed by forest trails and graced with a lake and small pond, provides a natural setting for working artifacts from earlier eras including a mini-railroad, a sawmill and planer mill, plus plows and grain threshers.

Saanich Pioneer Museum

7910 East Saanich Road; north of Mt. Newton Cross Road
250-656-2572
Open Monday and Saturday,
10 am-2 pm
Donations accepted
Stop here to peruse archival photographs and memorabilia of Saanich Peninsula's olden days.

Victoria Butterfly Gardens

1461 Benvenuto Avenue; corner of Saanich and Keating Cross roads
250-652-3822
877-722-0272
www.butterflygardens.com
Open daily in summer; variable winter hours
Admission charged
Conveniently located on the main route to The Butchart Gardens, this all-enclosed, 3600 square metre tropical setting is alive with 35 species of butterflies — literally dozens of colourful butterflies fluttering to and fro. See gigantic blue morphos as well as delicate glasswings, and observe the butterfly life cycle, from egg to cocoon, in a special incubation chamber. Brightly coloured goldfish and koi swim in the gurgling creeks, and more than 50 birds — cockatiels, canaries, budgies, zebra finch, and doves — flit here and there throughout the gardens.

Swan Lake / Christmas Hill Nature Sanctuary

Swan Lake Road; 0.5 kilometres east of Highway 17 on McKenzie Avenue, turn right on Rainbow Road, left on Ralph Street, then right onto Swan Lake Road
250-479-0211
www.swanlake.bc.ca
Open year-round
Admission charged

Short walking trails wind through this 47 hectare site of meadow and lake. Head to Christmas Hill to see 11 hectares of Garry oak, and venture around the lake for bird-watching plus glimpses of water-loving wildlife.

University of Victoria

McKenzie Avenue at Gordon Head Road; 4.5 kilometres east of Highway 17
250-721-7211
www.uvic.ca
Maltwood Art Gallery:
250-721-8298
University Centre Auditorium:
250-721-8299

Phoenix Theatre: 250-721-8000
Cincenta Films: 250-721-8365

Some 17,500 students enjoy their studies on this 160 hectare campus set among gardens and forests. Finnerty Gardens alone is well worth the trip. So are the university's cultural assets: the Maltwood Art Gallery features ever-changing art exhibits, including pieces from the late Katherine Maltwood's collection; Cinecenta shows new, classic, and cult movies; Phoenix Theatre presents excellent theatre productions; and the University Centre Auditorium is a popular venue for large concerts.

Horticulture Centre of the Pacific

505 Quayle Road
250-479-6162
Open year-round
Admission charged

With more than 20 demonstration gardens, the centre can guarantee that visitors will see something in bloom any time of the year. Meandering paths take in the seasonal blooming of snowdrops, daffodils, crocuses, rhododendrons, irises, roses, fuchsias, and lilies.

Brentwood Bay

Saanich Peninsula Chamber of Commerce
PO Box 2014
Sidney BC V8L 3S3
250-656-0525
Population: 3200

Still retaining a hint of its rustic origins around its wharves, Brentwood Bay takes its moniker from Brentwood, Essex, in Great Britain. Municipal home to The Butchart Gardens, Brentwood Bay is also the southern terminus of the Brentwood Bay-Mill Bay Ferry (250-386-3431), which means that the town sees daytrippers and recreationalists venturing across the Saanich Inlet.

Galloping Goose and Peninsula Trails

A ribbon of green stretching from Sidney to Sooke, the Galloping Goose and Peninsula Trails stitch together 100 kilometres of greenspace. They are also the first installment of the 18,000 kilometre Trans Canada Trail, a shared-use route across Canada. Built upon abandoned railbeds and private, provincial, and federal lands, the trail is shared by hikers, cyclists, equestrians, and cross-country skiers.

Inaugurated in 1989, the Galloping Goose Trail is named for the raucous little railcars that transported passengers between Sooke and Victoria during the 1920s. Parts of the Peninsula Trail follow what were once the routes of the Victoria & Sidney and the Canadian National railways. Divided into three sections — West, East, and North — the Galloping Goose and Peninsula Trails are a mixture of paved and unpaved routes, with some sections following existing roads. For joggers, rollerbladers, hikers, and cyclists who only want to experience a portion of the trail system, BC Transit buses equipped with bike racks intersect the trail system at several locations. Call BC Transit at 250-382-6161 or key into www.transitbc.com

for more information.

The West section, the original route of the Galloping Goose, accesses several parks including Sooke Potholes Provincial Park and Matheson Lake Regional Park. Leechtown, the far western point of the trail, was the site of a gold mining community in the 1860s. Many Victoria bicycle commuters use the East leg; some 2000 residents travel the system each day to get to and from work. The North section reaches up the Saanich Peninsula, incorporating Lochside Trail and Lochside Drive and passing many kilometres of country farm and field.

The Butchart Gardens

800 Benvenuto Avenue
250-652-4422
www.butchartgardens.com
Open daily
Admission charged
(See the feature on pages 68 - 73.) This former estate and quarry overlooking Tod Inlet has been transformed into 23 hectares of marvellous gardens, attracting more than a million visitors a year. It is easily one of the world's top horticultural attractions. See The Butchart Gardens box, page 68.

The Centre of the Universe

5057 West Saanich Road; on
Little Saanich Mountain,
eastern side of Highway 17A
250-363-8262
www.nrc.ca/iha
Open daily, April-October;
closed Mondays during winter;
open for Saturday night
stargazing, April-October
Admission charged
Atop Little Saanich Mountain, this astronomy interpretive centre gives great views of Victoria and the universe. It features a 1.82 metre telescope that was once the world's

largest — back in 1918 — and was used to map the size, structure, and spin of our own backyard, the Milky Way Galaxy. Don't miss Saturday night star parties during the summer.

Peninsula Country Market

Saanich Fairgrounds
1528 Stelly's Cross Road
250-652-3314
Saturday mornings, June-October
Admission free
Stop here to load up on fresh fruits and vegetables, arts, and crafts.

Fort Rodd Hill & Fisgard Lighthouse National Historic Sites

Fisgard Lighthouse is the oldest operating lighthouse on the west coast.

From the late 1800s to the 1950s, soldiers at this complex of military lookouts and artillery positions stood watch over Victoria and Esquimalt harbours, protecting Canada's western coast. The "Victoria-Esquimalt Fortress" was a strategic link in Britain's worldwide defense system, and over time it expanded

to become the fortified compound seen today. Fort Rodd Hill has been well preserved, with many original structures intact, and consequently represents one of the best examples of this type of stronghold. Visitors may embark on a self-guided walking tour that takes in more than 20 locations around

the fortification, from battery sites to commander's post.

At the end of the causeway rises Fisgard Lighthouse, the oldest operating lighthouse on Canada's West Coast. Built when Vancouver Island was still a Crown Colony, the structure is now completely restored to its 1859 condition. Its stately architecture is engaging, and inside it houses a range of educational displays. Proclaimed a national historic site in 1960, it is still a working sentry for sailors, the landmark to locate Esquimalt Harbour and, along with Race Rocks Lighthouse to the southeast, the safety marks for the Royal Road Anchorage.

Fort Rodd Hill & Fisgard Lighthouse National Historic Sites
603 Fort Rodd Hill Road;
take Highway 1A to Highway 14 to Ocean Boulevard
Victoria BC V9C 2W8
250-478-5849

Sidney

*Saanich Peninsula Chamber
of Commerce
PO Box 2014
Sidney BC V8L 3S3
250-656-0525
Visitor Centres: 10382 Pat Bay
Highway, western side of
Highway 17 between BC Ferries
terminal and town centre; also
at 5th Street and Ocean
Avenue in Sidney
Population: 10,790*

Blessed with a village-like ambience, Sidney is considered downtown on the Saanich Peninsula. Founded in the 1890s as the terminus of the Victoria and Sidney Railway, the town's namesake was Frederick Sidney of the Royal Navy. Although farming has been, and still is, a mainstay of the local economy, numerous retirees, as well as tourists arriving aboard the Washington State Ferries that dock here, have helped make Sidney far more than simply a market centre.

A stroll down Beacon Avenue reveals a sophisticated and playful art scene, evident in the collection of Nathan Scott outdoor sculptures; the bounty of cafes, bakeries, boutiques; and especially the wonderful bookstores — nine within a four-block radius offering new, used, rare, and specialty books. Sidney's popular Summer Market, held Thursday evenings from the end of May through August, transforms the main street into a pedestrian-only country market with some 150 vendors displaying wares and fresh produce. Don't overlook the Port of Sidney's relaxed marina atmosphere, stretching pleasantly along a waterfront park promenade.

Downtown Sidney features several Nathan Scott outdoor sculptures.

Sidney Marine Museum

*9801 Seaport Place; at Sidney
wharf
250-656-1322
www.town.sidney.bc.ca/museum/
Open daily in summer; variable
winter hours
Donations accepted*

Cetaceans take centre stage here with fascinating displays covering whales from humpbacks to killer whales. Other exhibits feature ocean evolution, marine ecology, and seals, sea lions, and sea otters. Especially interesting are the marine skeletons and historical photographs.

Sidney Historical Museum

*2423 Beacon Avenue; lower
level of post office
250-655-6355
www.town.sidney.bc.ca/museum/
Open daily in summer; variable
winter hours
Donations accepted*

Step into Sidney's olden days with displays of pioneer artifacts ranging from dolls to farm equipment.

Tanners Books

*2436 Beacon Avenue
250-656-2345*

This store is one of the main sources of books, maps and information on local and regional attractions and history. Not to be missed.

Marine Ecology Station

*9835 Seaport Place; at Port of
Sidney marina
250-655-1555
http://mareco.org
Open daily
Admission charged*

Come here to delve into Vancouver Island's undersea world, as numerous aquarium exhibits depict British Columbia's diverse marine habitats. Dedicated to increasing marine awareness at all levels, the station is equipped with special mini-aquariums outfitted with microscopes that offer visitors in-your-face views of tiny sea creatures. The touch tanks present truly hands-on biology lessons for kids, and youngsters will enjoy guiding the remote-operated underwater submarine.

British Columbia Aviation Museum

*1910 Norseman Road; at
Victoria International Airport
southeast corner*

Sidney's waterfront park promenade offers pleasant strolling.

250-655-3300
www.bcam.net
Open daily
Admission charged

Exploring the history of air flight in Canada, displays of more than 30 aircraft — replicas as well as restored flying wonders — and lots of aeronautical paraphernalia will fascinate aviation buffs. Look for the Gibson Twin plane built by William Gibson of Victoria; its original bested the Wright brothers' 36 metre flight record set in 1903 by nearly 25 metres before encountering an oak tree. Also on display is the only remaining example of an Eastman Sea Rover, once used for mining exploration in northern BC.

Greater Victoria Municipalities: Oak Bay, Esquimalt, and View Royal

Tourism Victoria InfoCentre
812 Wharf Street
Victoria BC V8W 1T3
250-953-2033
www.tourismvictoria.com

Oak Bay

This tony municipality sits east of Victoria, with its main access and shopping area on Oak Bay Avenue. To enter here, say some folks, is to part the "Tweed Curtain" and arrive in what is considered Victoria's most British neighbourhood. Oak Bay Village's tidy rows of shops accent the Avenue, which is lined with dogwood trees and side streets featuring Tudor-style homes. Quaint shops cosy up next to pubs, which snuggle up to boutiques and cafes. Close at hand are parks, always prettily trimmed, and, yes, beaches that are mellow and impeccably maintained. Don't miss the

Seagulls and a harbour seal relax in the sun.

Oak Bay Marina, with its salt tang and resident seals, or Cattle Point, which offers breathtaking views across the Strait of Juan de Fuca. In Oak Bay one can rest assured of finding refined living and high tea done the proper way. There's even the Oak Bay Tea Party held annually on Willows Beach.

Esquimalt
Population 17,000
A short drive across the Johnson Street Bridge from Victoria sits Esquimalt. Called "Strategic Esquimalt," the harbour shelters Canada's Pacific naval fleet today, and before that the British Royal Navy had a permanent base here beginning in 1865. Today's town is largely centred around military life, as this is the second largest Canadian Forces naval base and dock-yards after Halifax, Nova Scotia. Thousands of service personnel are stationed here, attending to the extensive dockyards and administration

needed to support frigates, destroyers, marine coastal patrol vessels, and a recently welcomed submarine and crew.

CFB Esquimalt Naval and Military Museum
CFB Esquimalt; inside gates off Admirals Road
250-363-4312
www.navalandmilitarymuseum.org
Open Monday to Friday; bus tours mid-June to mid-August
Chart Canadian West Coast naval history here at historic HMCS Naden, with displays in several heritage buildings designed by early Victoria architect John Teague. Exhibits include re-creations of a World War II shipboard wheelhouse, communications room, and mess hall.

View Royal
Population: 7587
Named for its expansive scenic overlook, this community's first landowner was Dr. J.S. Helmcken, who purchased 100 hectares of farmland from the Hudson's Bay Company.

Craigflower Manor and Schoolhouse
Corner of Craigflower and Admirals roads
250-383-4627
www.heritage.gov.bc.ca
Grounds open to public
Donations accepted
Kenneth McKenzie built this Georgian-style manor over-looking Victoria's Gorge in 1853, on lands acquired by the Hudson's Bay Company from the Esquimalt First Nation. Across the bridge is the Craigflower Schoolhouse, BC's oldest, which sits atop a 2500-year-old Kosapsom village site.

Western Communities: Colwood, Langford, Metchosin, and Highlands
West Shore Chamber of Commerce
2830 Aldwynd Road
Langford BC V9B 3S7
250-478-1130
www.westshore.bc.ca
Still in recent memory are the days when what is now known as the Western Communities were rolling farmland and

Craigflower Manor was built in 1853 on land acquired from the Esquimalt First Nation.

forest. To be sure, much survives of those sylvan days — rural farmland, lakes, parks, and wilderness areas — though in large measure today's Colwood, Langford, and Metchosin have evolved into bustling municipalities.

Fort Rodd Hill and Fisgard Lighthouse National Historic Sites
603 Fort Rodd Hill Road; turn south off Highway 1A to hwy 14 onto Ocean Boulevard, three kilometres from Colwood Interchange
250-478-5849
Open daily
Admission charged

Occupying nearly 19 hectares along shoreline rising up to fields interspersed with stands of Garry oak, arbutus, and Douglas fir, the Fort Rodd Hill site preserves military batteries built in the 1870s to protect Esquimalt Harbour and its navy base. The picturesque lighthouse rising from a rocky escarpment dates from 1859 and is British Columbia's oldest. See the Fort Rodd Hill and Fisgard Lighthouse National Historic Sites box on page 85.

Colwood
Population: 14,524
In the mid-1800s, the Puget Sound Agricultural Company (an offshoot of the Hudson's Bay Company) established one of several large farms here to supply Fort Victoria. Incorporated since 1985, Colwood is now a pleasant residential community.

Hatley Park National Historic Site
Royal Roads University; off Sooke Road 0.5 kilometres past Colwood Corners
250-391-2660 (Friends of Hatley Park)
www.royalroads.ca/per/garden
Admission free
Grand by any standard, Hatley Castle, situated on the campus of Royal Roads University, evokes the sense of a regal Scottish country estate. The home was built in 1908 by James Dunsmuir, wealthy industrialist, BC premier from 1900 to 1902, lieutenant governor from 1906 to 1909, and scion of coal king Robert Dunsmuir, who constructed Victoria's Craigdarroch Castle. Visitors may contact Friends of Hatley Castle for tours.

Goldstream Provincial Park

Barely 19 kilometres north of Victoria, Goldstream Provincial Park is one of Vancouver Island's most cherished nature and recreational areas. Within its 395 hectares tower 600-year-old Douglas fir, stands of western red cedar flourish, and arbutus trees display their distinctive reddish trunks and peeling bark.

From October to December the park becomes especially popular. Pacific salmon are returning home after their three- to four-year ocean sojourn, and Goldstream River becomes choked with fish —

so much so that the clear water turns bright red with swarms of salmon struggling up-current to spawn and then die where they were hatched. In the trees above the waters, legions of bald eagles anticipating easy prey perch and preen in between swoops into the throng for a meal.
Goldstream Provincial Park
Highway 1; 18.5 kilometres from Victoria city centre
250-391-2300 or 800-689-9025 (reservations)
395 hectares / 173 campsites and sanitation facilities

Langford

Population: 18,060
E.E. Langford of the Puget Sound Agricultural Company lent his name to the town, once a farming outpost with good access to Colwood Corners and the West Coast Highway. Today, location still favours Langford as it holds several popular discount shopping stores such as Wal-Mart, Costco, and Home Depot.

Metchosin

Population: 4670
Struggling to maintain a small-town feel amid Greater Victoria's expansion, the town's centre still houses a small cafe, country store, and crafts store.

Metchosin School Museum / Pioneer Implements Museum

4475 Happy Valley Road; at Metchosin Road
250-478-3451
Open Saturday and Sunday afternoons, April-October
Donations accepted
Opened in 1872, the Metchosin School was British Columbia's first school built after the province joined Confederation in 1871. The adjoining Pioneer Implements Museum showcases settlement memorabilia.

Highlands

This rural residential pocket north of Victoria looks across Finlayson Arm to the Malahat Drive, the route up-Island to Duncan, Nanaimo, and beyond.

All Fun Recreation Park

2207 Millstream Road
250-474-3184
Open June to September
Admission charged

With 16 waterslides and a whitewater river run, plus driving range, mini-golf, and bumper boats, it's a great place for families.

Sooke Harbour House

The Sooke Harbour House

Consistently proclaimed one of the world's best country inns, the Sooke Harbour House is indeed a treat. Styled as a French country auberge, it not only features tiptop accommodations, but its five-star restaurant also presents the finest in regional cuisine.

Frederique and Sinclair Philip and family have drawn together a superb team of talent — from hosts and hostesses to farmers and gardeners to chefs and wait-staff — dedicated to the high art of hospitality. Sooke Harbour House's 28 individu-ally designed and decorated rooms all have fireplaces and marvellous views of the ocean. Guests may choose from an interesting collection of milieus, from "The Artist's Study" to the "Edible Blossom Room," the "Mermaid Room," or the "Phycologist's Study" — for those interested in seaweed. Clearly, creativity abounds at this hospitality haven.

One glimpse of the menu shows how true this is. It changes daily and focuses on fresh local organic seafood, meat, and produce, always presented with imagination and flair. The property's own herb and edible flower gardens provide many of the exceptional flavours to the extraordinary culinary creations. The garden thrives with some 400 varieties of herbs, greens, vegetables, edible flowers, and trees.

Sooke Harbour House
1528 Whiffen Spit Road
Sooke BC V0S 1N0
250-642-3421
www.sookeharbourhouse.com

Whiffen Spit Park affords gentle views of tranquil Sooke Harbour.

Caleb Pike Homestead

Millstream Road; 6.6 kilometres north of Highway 1
Open during the summer
Admission charged
Stop here to see the one-time home of Caleb Pike, a Hudson's Bay Company sheep and cattle rancher.

Sooke

Sooke Regional Museum and Visitor Information Centre
2070 Phillips Road
Sooke BC V0S 1N0
250-642-6351
www.sookemuseum.bc.ca
Population: 11,620
Although the area was noted in 1790 by Spanish explorer Manuel Quimper, well-situated Sooke Harbour and the town of Sooke truly became noteworthy during the rough-and-tumble gold mining days of 1864. That was the year many a fortune seeker arrived, searching tirelessly along the banks of the Sooke and Leach rivers for a gilded future. Sadly, the sands and shorelines relinquished only some $100,000 worth of the glimmering metal before the boom burst.

Salmon fishing was the next great economic boon for the area, and interestingly it was an adaptation of the traditional First Nations' fishing weir that spawned the industry. Sooke's location along salmon migration routes encouraged the commercial development of immense versions of weirs — some fishing traps measured a kilometre in length, their webbing secured to 45-metre-tall pilings sunk into the seabed.

Sooke Arts

A good way to experience the Sooke art scene is through the Sooke Studio Tours Arts Collective, which offers a self-guided excursion taking in six artist studios: Exhibit Room III, showcasing the handmade felt of Sheila Beech; Aviars Logins, featuring wood turning; Blue Raven, displaying the First Nations artwork of Carey, Edith, and Victor Newman; stained glass works at Shards Glass; pottery at Orveas Bay-Otter Point Gallery; and South Shore Gallery, exhibiting South Vancouver Island paintings, sculpture, glass, and pottery.

The Sooke Community Arts Council, a non-profit society dedicated to support and development of local artists, musicians, and performers, counts more than 40 members. Spanning the spectrum from handpainted birds at Bobbie's Birds to The Bellowing Blacksmith, where master smithy Sandy Sydham demonstrates this age-old craft, Sooke-area artisans welcome visitors by appointment.

Sooke Community Arts Council
PO Box 46
Sooke BC V0S 1N0
250-642-6411

Logging, and more recently tourism, also evolved as two of the region's financial foundations. Add to this a robust fine arts mini-industry; Sooke is recognized as one of Western Canada's more sophisticated residential enclaves for artists, musicians, and performers. Sooke's philharmonic orchestra is conducted by Norman Nelson, retired concertmaster of the Vancouver Symphony Orchestra and co-founder of Great Britain's noted Academy of St. Martin-in-the-Fields. The Sooke Harbour House is one of North America's most celebrated restaurants, consistently lauded by top gourmands. And the annual Sooke Fine Arts Festival is one of British Columbia's largest, drawing hundreds of artists.

Sooke Region Museum and Art Gallery

Also houses Info Centre
2070 Phillips Road; Sooke side of Sooke River Bridge on Highway 14
250-642-6351
Open daily; closed winter Mondays
Donations accepted
Step into quaint, turn-of-the-century Moss Cottage and be transported back in time as costumed actors welcome guests to "their" simple home. Learn about "bed pigs" and such during the playful tours through the tiny rooms filled with household memorabilia. Next door, in the visitor centre, displays and artifacts tell of the T'Sou-ke First Nation's history in the area, in addition to that of the many pioneers and gold miners who ventured here.

First Nations symbols and motifs decorate many Island buildings.

Point No Point

Restaurant and Seaside Resort
1505 West Coast
250-646-2020
Early hydrographers surveying this stretch of coastline dubbed the place Point No Point because of the curious topography that from one viewpoint reveals a definite headland, but from another viewpoint nearby shows no landmass. Visitors seldom miss the point, though; the 400-metre-long headland provides a constant show of tumultuous waves and, during the spring and autumn, sightings of migrating gray whales.

Jordan River

Population: 284
Primarily a small logging community, Jordan River is also home to the Jordan River Surf Club. Indeed, the place is esteemed among the surfing community as one of Canada's top venues. Wave riders slide high here on the hefty surf off the river's mouth.

Port Renfrew

Population: 400
Literally the end of the road, Port Renfrew is the terminus for the West Coast Road (Highway 14), the restricted logging roads from Cowichan Lake and Shawnigan Lake, and the ends (or for some the beginnings) of both the Pacific Rim National Park West Coast

All compass directions point to pleasurable activities on Vancouver Island.

Trail and the Juan de Fuca Marine Trail.

Founded as a steamer landing, Port San Juan was its first name. Postal confusion with the American San Juan Islands forced residents to rename their home Port Renfrew, honouring Lord Renfrew, who once hatched a plan to locate Scottish crofters here. The Port Renfrew Hotel and Pub at the government wharf hosts weathered hikers to casual beachcombers. Four kilometres from Port Renfrew along a secondary road is Botanical Beach, one of Vancouver Island's natural treasures.

Of special interest to tree aficionados is the Red Creek Fir, located approximately 17 kilometres from Port Renfrew. With a circumference of four metres and height of 73 metres, the 700- to 1000-year-old tree is the largest standing Douglas fir in Canada.

Juan de Fuca Marine Trail

Primarily experienced hikers head here to tackle the challenging 47 kilometre Juan de Fuca Marine Trail from China Beach to Botanical Beach. Hiking the entire length of the trail takes three to four days, but day hikers can also access the system at several points. Note that the Juan de Fuca Marine Trail is a wilderness trek and very susceptible to changing weather conditions. Hikers should come prepared: obtain information on current trail conditions before leaving, and notify friends or relatives of specific plans and return date.

China Beach Provincial Park
37 kilometres west of Sooke off Highway 14
An ideal beach for picnics, this park also has old-growth rainforest hikes. China Beach is the trailhead for the Juan de Fuca Marine Trail. A 45-minute hike from China Beach leads to Mystic Beach, with interesting sandstone cliffs and shallow caves.

Sombrio Beach
57 kilometres west of Sooke off Highway 14
The sandy and stone beach is an easy walk from the parking lot and is great for beachcombing and surf watching.

Parkinson Creek
66 kilometres west of Sooke off Highway 14
Mature rain forest and wilderness trails make this a popular starting point for hikes to either Sombrio Beach or Botanical Beach, both day hikes from Parkinson Creek.

Botanical Beach Provincial Park
76 kilometres west of Sooke; at the end of Highway 14
Vancouver Island's best spot for observing tide pools. Tides below 1.2 metres are the best for viewing these tiny intertidal ecosystems. Several trails — Botany Bay, Botanical Loop, and portions of Mill Bay — are suitable for younger and older hikers alike.

Botanical Beach outside Port Renfrew is one of Vancouver Island's best places to see tide pools.

South Island Festivals & Events

FEBRUARY-APRIL
Sooke Philharmonic Chamber Players
Holy Trinity Church, Sooke
Springtime chamber music recitals.

MAY
Esquimalt Lantern Festival
West Bay Walkway and West Bay Marina
A parade of hundreds of handcrafted lanterns along the West Bay Walkway to the West Bay Marina, then dancing till midnight.

JUNE
Oak Bay Tea Party
Willows Beach, Oak Bay
The biggest party of the year in Oak Bay, this annual event includes food, entertainment and a midway.
Buccaneer Days
Archie Browning Sports Centre, Esquimalt
Esquimalt's community festival includes a parade, kids' games and a midway all weekend.

JULY
Sooke Festival of the Performing Arts
Sooke
A month of orchestral concerts and stage shows.

AUGUST
Sooke Fine Arts Show
Sooke
Vancouver Island's largest juried art show with hundreds of works on display.

SEPTEMBER
Saanich Fall Fair
Saanich Fairground, Saanich Peninsula
Western Canada's oldest continuous agricultural fair, plus a midway and food court.
Sooke Fall Fair
Sooke
Legendary autumn fair with flowers, vegetables, baking contests, and agricultural exhibits.

OCTOBER
Salmon Run
Goldstream Provincial Park
Every autumn, witness the cycle of life as Pacific salmon forge their way up the streams of the Pacific Northwest to spawn and die.

DECEMBER
Moss Cottage Christmas & Snowman Building
Sooke Regional Museum, Sooke
Carolling and traditional foods, along with a snowman-building contest for kids 2 to 10 years old.

DECEMBER-FEBRUARY
Eagle Extravaganza
Goldstream Provincial Park
More than 200 bald eagles congregate here to feast on the dying salmon.

Visit a Vancouver Island farmer's market for a bounty of fresh flowers and vegetables.

South Island Tee Time

Victoria Golf Club
1110 Beach Drive
Oak Bay, BC
250-598-4322
Eighteen holes

**Cedar Hill Municipal
Golf Course**
1400 Derby Road; off Cedar
Hill Road
Victoria, BC
250-595-3103
Eighteen holes

Mt. Douglas Golf Course
4225 Blenkinsop Road
Victoria, BC
250-477-8314
Nine holes

Uplands Golf Course
3300 Cadboro Bay Road
Victoria, BC
250-592-1818
Eighteen holes

Gorge Vale Golf Club
1005 Craigflower Road
Esquimalt, BC
250-386-3401
Eighteen holes

Royal Oak Golf Course
540 Marsett Place; off Elk Lake
Drive
Saanich, BC
250-658-1433
Nine holes

**Glen Meadows Golf and
Country Club**
1050 McTavish Road
North Saanich, BC
250-656-3921
Eighteen holes; curling and
tennis in winter

Ardmore Golf Course
930 Ardmore Drive; off West
Saanich Road
North Saanich
250-656-4621
Nine holes

Sunshine Hills Golf Course
7081 Central Saanich Road; at
Highway 17
Central Saanich, BC
250-652-5215
Eighteen holes

**Royal Colwood Golf and
Country Club**
629 Goldstream Avenue
Colwood, BC
250-478-8331
www.royalcolwood.org
Eighteen holes

Olympic View Golf Club
643 Latoria Road
250-474-3671
Metchosin, BC
www.olympicviewgolf.com
Eighteen holes

**Metchosin Golf and
Country Club**
4100 Metchosin Road
Metchosin, BC
250-478-3266
Nine holes

**Broome Hill Golf and
Country Club**
2197 Otter Point Road
Sooke, BC
250-642-6344
Nine holes

South Island Parks & Recreation

Thetis Lake Regional Park
Exit 10, the Highway 1A/14 exit off Highway 1; 1.5 kilometres along Highway 1A to Six Mile Road, then right
250-478-3344
635 hectares / private campground next to park
A great place for picnicking and freshwater swimming, the three adjoining lakes of Thetis Lake Park are also popular with canoeists and kayakers.

Island View Beach Regional Park
Island View Road: 10 kilometres from downtown Victoria off Highway 17
40 hectares / day use
Primarily a long rocky shoreline, Island View is fun for beachcombers and a favourite of photographers and artists.

McDonald Provincial Park
Highway 17 near Swartz Bay ferry terminal
14 hectares / 28 campsites
Woodsy, this park is good for picnics and short camp outings.

Gonzales Hill Regional Park
Denison Road
1.8 hectares / day use
Come here for great views from the site of a 1914 weather station.

Capital Regional District (CRD) Parks
250-478-3344 or 250-474-7275
8100 hectares / day use and campsites
CRD Parks oversees 25 parks, protecting sites from the Gulf Islands to southern Vancouver Island. Over 4000 hectares of the total area are contained in the Sooke Hills Wilderness. In all, there are some 300 kilometres of hiking trails.

Sidney Spit Provincial Marine Park
Sidney Island; three kilometres east of Sidney
250-391-2300
400 hectares / 20 campsites
Located on Sidney Island, just offshore from Sidney via private ferry. There are great beaches and swimming here, along with bird-watching, hiking trails, and a chance to spot fallow deer, introduced from England in the early 1900s.

John Dean Provincial Park
Dean Park Road; turn west off Highway 17A at McTavish, turn south onto East Saanich Road and proceed two kilometres to Dean Park Road
155 hectares / day use
Mt. Newton is the destination here, offering great views of the Saanich Peninsula and the Gulf Islands.

Elk / Beaver Lake Regional Park
Sayward Road
250-478-3344
www.crd.bc.ca/parks
411 hectares / no camping
Beaches, windsurfing, rowing, fishing, hiking, and horseback riding make this a popular summertime destination.

Gowlland Tod Provincial Park
Three vehicle access points:
Tod Inlet: Turn south off Benvenuto Road onto Wallace Drive before The Butchart Gardens entrance
McKenzie Bight: Turn west off Wallace Drive onto Willis Point Road, then south onto Durrance Road
Caleb Pike: North off Highway 1 onto Millstream Road, then west onto Caleb Pike Road
250-391-2300
1221 hectares / day use
This large park protects a portion of the Saanich Inlet. The northern section encompasses the west bank of Tod Inlet, while to the south rises the Gowlland Range, reaching 430 metres above Finlayson Arm. A network of hiking trails, old logging roads, and horse trails traverses the park.

Mt. Work Regional Park
Highway 17A to Wallace Drive, then turn onto Willis Point Road
536 hectares / day use
An 11 kilometre hiking trail leads to the summit of 446-metre-high Mt. Work. Also here is the Mt. Work-Harland Special Recreation Area, 210 hectares of multi-use trail available to mountain bikers.

Lone Tree Hill Regional Park
Millstream Road; eight kilometres north of Highway 1
31 hectares / day use
Overlooking Finlayson Arm, this is a good place to spot eagles and red-tailed hawks.

Mill Hill Regional Park
Millstream Road to Atkins Road, south of Highway 1
50 hectares / day use
Hiking trails track through meadows and forest, reaching the summit of Mill Hill overlooking Esquimalt Harbour.

Goldstream Provincial Park
Highway 1; 18.5 kilometres from Victoria city centre
250-391-2300 or
800-689-9025 (reservations)
395 hectares / 173 campsites and sanitation facilities
Only minutes from the city, the park boasts stands of ancient Douglas fir, a salmon spawning river, waterfalls, and many hiking trails. The trek up Mt. Finlayson is challenging but rewarding.

South Island Parks & Recreation

Galloping Goose Regional Trail
Various access points; parking areas at Atkins Avenue in View Royal, Aldean Avenue at Colwood, Luxton Fairgrounds on Sooke Road, Rocky Point Road in Metchosin, and at Roche Cove Regional Park
This 60 kilometre trail begins at View Royal, then proceeds to Langford, Colwood, Metchosin, and Sooke, before ending in the Sooke Hills. Following an abandoned Canadian National Railway line, it is beloved by cyclists, hikers, and equestrians.

Witty's Lagoon Regional Park
Metchosin Road; seven kilometres from Highway 14
250-474-2454
56.5 hectares / day use
Water is the central theme of this ecosystem, which is adjacent to the Strait of Juan de Fuca and contains creeks, waterfalls, a beach, and the lagoon. Perfect for hiking, beachcombing, and bird-watching, particularly great blue herons. Good place to see seals too.

Mt. Douglas Park
Cordova Bay Road
10 hectares / day use
Summit Lookout sports views of the surrounding landscape. The park's lower section features a relaxing beach.

Roche Cove Regional Park
Gillespie Road; three kilometres south of Highway 14
250-478-3344
11 hectares / day use
This saltwater cove of the Sooke Basin is favoured by swimmers for its warmth and shallow water. It's not far from the Galloping Goose Trail and makes a nice place to rest after hiking.

Matheson Lake Regional Park
Matheson Lake Park Road; turn south off Highway 14 onto Happy Valley Road, then west onto Rocky Point Road and proceed to Matheson Lake Park Road
162 hectares / day use
Matheson Lake is a popular place in the summer. The lake is ideal for a cool dip, or take a canoe or kayak out to the lake's island for a peaceful picnic spot.

East Sooke Regional Park
Three entrances: From Highway 14, turn south onto Gillespie Road, then west onto East Sooke Road to entrances at Anderson Cove and Pike Road, or east onto East Sooke Road and then south on Becher Bay Road to Aylard Farm
250-478-3344
1442 hectares / day use
More than 50 kilometres of hiking trails lead past pocket beaches and along rocky coves, taking in ocean views, beaches, wide expanses of meadow, and lovely forests. Bird-watching and beachcombing are popular here.

Sooke Potholes Provincial Park
Sooke River Road; off Highway 14, 22.5 kilometres west of Colwood
7 hectares / day use
Formed by the rushing waters of the Sooke River, the swimming here is great — and mighty popular with locals.

Whiffen Spit Park
Whiffen Spit Road; 27 kilometres west of Colwood
1200 metre spit
Only a minute or so past downtown Sooke, this wide expanse of sandbar and shore grass stretching out into Sooke Harbour is a wonderful place for bird-watchers, as well as for folks simply looking for a walk.

French Beach Provincial Park
Highway 14; 46 kilometres west of Colwood
250-391-2300
www.discovercamping.ca
59 hectares / 69 campsites
A playground and picnic tables make French Beach ideal for family outings. The pebbly beach, mixed with sandy spots here and there, will keep sandcastle builders occupied for hours. Stroll west down the beach to find tide pools. Offshore, migrating whales are sometimes sighted.

Pacific Rim National Park Reserve
Encompasses Long Beach, the Broken Group Islands, and the West Coast Trail
Box 280, 2185 Ocean Terrace Road
Ucluelet BC V0R 3A0
250-726-7721
Long Beach Information Centre (seasonal)
250-726-4212
Pachena Information Centre (seasonal)
250-728-3234
Port Renfrew Information Centre (seasonal)
250-647-5434
http://parkscan.harbour.com/pacrim/
49,962 hectares / campsites and wilderness camping
This world-renowned reserve is divided into three sections: Long Beach, Broken Group Islands, and the West Coast Trail. See the Pacific Rim National Park Reserve box.

Tide Pools: Amazing Water Worlds

Tide pools offer fascinating glimpses into Vancouver Island's intertidal ecosystem.

Pooling in the fissures and natural depressions of Vancouver Island's rocky coastline is the amazing marine world of tide pools. These tiny pools, constantly re-energized with oxygen and nutrients from rising and receding tidal flows, are the permanent home to a host of fascinating life forms.

Tide pools are part of the Island's intertidal environmental zone. This is the narrow strip where the two mighty forces of water and land come together to create an extraordinary set of ecosystems. Inundated by surf and wave, or sheltered by cove and cranny, the habitats are governed by their exposure to air and water, a world that is constantly changing and rife with unpredictability. The plants and animals dwelling here have adapted in sometimes unbelievable, and usually brilliantly hued, ways. Some are mobile, while others are fixed permanently to one place.

Botanical Beach outside Port Renfrew is one of Vancouver Island's best places to see tide pools. Sculpted by waves and tidal flow, these shallow ponds cupped in the soft sandstone support a colourful array of marine creatures: spiny purple sea urchins, chitons, starfish, and green sea anemones. To see tide pools at their best — or at all — plan to visit at low tide.

Shells of many kinds, most often broken into bits and pieces, are strewn along the beaches and mudflats of intertidal zones. The shells are commonly those of clams and mussels, as well as the circular, pyramid-shaped ones of limpets. Whelks and periwinkles are also often found, as are the disk-shaped sand dollars. Be aware that shell collecting is prohibited in many areas to protect the balance of biological material present at these locations. Respect the animals and plants of tide pools as well; resist the temptation to rearrange their realm by moving or prodding plants and animals.

Eelgrass
Seen submerged or partially floating in calm waters, this plant releases "pollen rafts" that travel by wave and wind and eventually find other eelgrass to fertilize. First Nations people harvested the white rhizomes for food.

Red Fringe
A common algae with wide reddish leaves, it connects itself to eelgrass, appearing to be part of the plant.

Sea Palm
Growing on surf-swept rocks, this tough yet flexible brownish seaweed stands upright with drooping, drenched fronds.

Sea Sac
Light green and up to 10 centimetres high, these fleshy-feeling water-filled sacs release a fine mist when gently squeezed. The gas bladder at the sac's tip keeps it upright.

Sea Staghorn
Called also "deadman's fingers," the dark green branches of the staghorn grow up to 30 centimetres long. Permanent tide pools are its environment.

Tidepool Coral
Also known as "coralline algae," the bright pink, rigid branches reach about eight centimetres in length. Shallow tide pools in rocky

Tide Pools: Amazing Water Worlds

Tide pools are formed in natural rock depressions.

environments exposed to heavy surf are their favourite locales.

Sea Anemone

Looking like flowers with undulating petals, these animals are in fact carnivorous. The short tentacles release a poison that induces paralysis in prey, which is then drawn into the anemone's wide mouth. Sea anemones can detach themselves from the rock and move, though they tend to remain fixed in a location if food resources are plentiful. Sea anemones come in many varieties, and colouration ranges from white to pink and red to green. The most common and largest is the green sea anemone that may span 30 centimetres in diameter.

Nudibranch

The semi-translucent branching gill of this animal gives it its name, which means "naked lungs." It's also known as a "sea slug" because its soft body does not have a protective shell. Apparently protection is unnecessary, as not many predators find nudibranchs acceptable eating; they retain the stinging cells from their diet of sea anemones within their fragile-looking bodies.

Chitons

Oval and oblong, this mollusc grows to a length of five to seven centimetres and prefers tight spaces, co-habitating with mussels and barnacles. One species, the gumboot, can reach a length of 30 centimetres and is intensely dark red.

Blue Mussel

These bivalves establish immense colonies, with their legions of dark purple shells protruding from tide-drenched rocks. Inside its shell, the flesh is deep orange to yellow in colour.

Goose Barnacle

Appearing in clusters on exposed, water-refreshed rocks, these creatures have flexible but tough stalks and rake-like feet that snag food from the passing tide.

Starfish

Sea stars are their other name, and there are more than 2000 species across the globe. Vancouver Island's waters support about three dozen varieties. Starfish have the ability to regenerate a severed limb; some types sport up to 24 arms.

Periwinkle

Just above the high tide mark is the place to spot these little snails. They only like a splash of surf and can drown in water too deep for them.

Sea Urchins

While sea urchins primarily inhabit colder and darker offshore waters, they sometimes travel into tide pools seeking food. Sometimes called porcupines of the sea, sea urchins rely on their long spines to deter predators. Like their relatives, sea cucumbers and sea stars, sea urchins have a hard outer body. Their outer skeleton is called a "test" and is made up of as many as ten fused plates that encircle it like the slices of an orange. Tests grow to 7 to 10 centimetres in diameter. Sea urchins use their beak-like mouths to scrape algae from rocks.

The Southern Gulf Islands

Gabriola Island, the most northerly of the Gulf Islands, is home to artisans and superb natural beauty.

Although there are some 200 Gulf Islands sprinkled across the Strait of Georgia east of Vancouver Island, only a handful are populated and accessible via ferry. The most populated and the most popular are Saltspring, North and South Pender, Galiano, Mayne, and Saturna

islands, which can all be reached by ferry from Swartz Bay on Vancouver Island or from Tsawwassen on the BC mainland. Lying just off the Saanich Peninsula, well within the rain shadow of Vancouver Island, these five southern Gulf Islands enjoy Canada's most temperate weather — in fact, they experience more sunshine and frost-free days than any other place in the nation.

Not surprisingly, then, these islands account for the bulk of the nearly 14,000 permanent residents of the Gulf Islands, a number that has grown by nearly 30 percent over the last decade. People from across the globe and from all walks of life have chosen the

Gulf Islands as their home. Consequently, the islands' lifestyle is both rural and

robust, benefiting immensely from the eclectic mix of artists and musicians, farmers and

Gulf Islands Recommendations

- Devote a day to visiting Saltspring Island's many arts and crafts studios; the self-guided studio tour lists 35 stops.
- Mosey along Pender Island's "Gallery Row," the island's highest concentration of artisans and their studios.
- Play a round at Pender Island's 18-pole disc golf park, designed for Frisbee golfers.
- Cycle Galiano Island's eastern shores, riddled with old logging trails and country

lanes, as well as sheltered beaches and coves.
- Hike to Mayne Island's Halliday Viewpoint at Mt. Parke Regional Park for spectacular Gulf Islands panoramas.
- Stop at the base of Mt. Warburton Pike for winery tours and wine tastings at Saturna Island Vineyard.
- Explore Gabriola Island's varied arts scene, and don't miss the Malaspina Galleries, actually natural sandstone rock formations.

Quaint houses dot the landscape of Saltspring Island.

Gardens on Saltspring Island

fishers, retirees and many, many tourists.

Gabriola is the most developed and most northerly of the northern Gulf Islands and is easily accessible from Nanaimo. Visitors will find

Gulf Islands Tee Time

Blackburn Meadows Golf Club
289 Blackburn Road; eight kilometres from Fulford Harbour
Saltspring Island, BC
250-537-1707
Nine holes

Salt Spring Island Golf and Country Club
805 Lower Ganges Road
Saltspring Island, BC
250-537-2121
Nine holes

Pender Island Golf and Country Club
2305 Otter Bay Road
Pender Island, BC
250-629-6659
Nine holes

Galiano Golf and Country Club
24 St Andrews Road
Galiano Island, BC
250-539-5533
Nine holes

all the amenities, including restaurants and pubs, a golf course, and definitely superlative natural attractions on this 59-square-kilometre isle. There are also three provincial parks — Drumbeg, Gabriola Sands, and Sandwell — set within Gabriola's coastline. For paddlers and cyclists, Thetis Island provides an ideal natural retreat. Kuper Island is the homeland of the Penelakut First Nation, and therefore only invited guests are encouraged to visit.

Long inhabited on a seasonal basis by First Nations people, the Gulf Islands are situated within the Strait of Georgia, not in a gulf at all. It was the first Europeans, visiting in the late 1700s and early 1800s, who applied that inaccurate designation, and in due course they also mapped and named many of the islands, their geographic features, and the surrounding waters. Consider only two Spanish explorers, Dionisio Alcala Galiano and Juan Francisco de la Bodega y Quadra, and the *Saturnina*, a Spanish vessel, to trace the origins of three island names.

Sir George Henry Richards, British surveyor, borrowed names from his patrons and crew as well during his 1854-63 exploration of the islands; aboard his flagship, HMS *Plumper*, were shipmates Daniel Pender and Richard Charles Mayne.

Saltspring Island
Saltspring Tourist Information Centre
121 Lower Ganges Road
Saltspring Island BC V8K 2T1
250-537-4223
www.saltspringtoday.com
Visitor Centre: 121 Lower Ganges Road
Population: 9247
The largest and most populated of the Gulf Islands, some 43 kilometres long by 14 kilometres at its widest point, Saltspring Island acquired its moniker in recognition of the numerous briny pools and springs on the isle's north end. But don't imagine a wasteland; the island also supports thick forests and pastoral meadows, pebbly beaches and rugged highland mounts. Indeed, Mt. Bruce (709 metres), Mt. Tuam (630 metres), and Mt. Maxwell (595 metres) are the

Catholic Church, Fulford Harbour

An outdoor market at Ganges showcases the island's bounty.

Gulf Island's tallest mountains. And St. Mary Lake at Saltspring Island's northern end is the largest of the Gulf Islands' lakes.

Known as Admiral Island from 1859 to 1905 in honour of Rear-Admiral R.L. Baynes, Saltspring Island was a traditional homeland of both the Wsanec people of the Saanich Peninsula and the Cowichan people from across Sansum Narrows. The first settlers were African-Americans from San Francisco, expatriates seeking Canada's freedoms. Other early settlers included more Americans, affluent English gentry, Australians, and Hawaiians brought here by the Hudson's Bay Company. Later, many Japanese came to Saltspring Island as fishers and labourers.

Saltspring still produces an agricultural bounty. The island is well known for its rich variety of specialty farms, producing everything from free-range chicken to edible tulips, plus dozens of varieties of apples, garlic, cheese, herbs, and even tofu.

Moreover, Saltspring Island is renowned for its flourishing artistic scene. Dozens of artists and craftspeople, including weavers, potters, painters,

photographers, writers, and poets, call the island home. Understandably, fairs and events, galleries, and studios are plentiful, offering some of the best island diversions. Sandwich this all in between recreational opportunities from sailing to cycling, scenic drives to picnics, beachcombing to bird-watching and the result is a superb vacation spot.

Fulford Harbour

Island idyllic describes Fulford Harbour, though it can also be busy since it's the main ferry entry point from Swartz Bay and other islands. Tiny houses hug the forested hills that slip down towards the timber-edged inlet, and in town a grocery store and gas station, Rose's Café, the post office, harbour marina, and several gift shops cater to the needs of locals and visitors. For drinks, head down the road a ways to the Fulford Inn's friendly pub.

St. Paul's Roman Catholic Church

Overlooking Fulford Harbour, just beyond Beaver Point Road Diminutive and darling, this church was constructed in the early 1880s of lumber, and was later sheathed in stone in the 1950s. While primarily

built of wood harvested locally, other materials were hauled in via oxen-drawn "stoneboats," land-going barges which transported supplies arriving at Saltspring's Burgoyne Bay from Cowichan Bay. In the tiny cemetery are grave markers — called "Kanaka" stones — commemorating several of Saltspring's early Hawaiian settlers. *Kanaka* is a Hawaiian word for "man" and was an early slang sobriquet for these immigrants working for the Hudson's Bay Company.

Ganges

Population: 1133
Named after a British Royal Navy ship that patrolled these waters from 1857 to 1860, the town of Ganges is the Gulf Island's largest community with a bustling marina, supermarkets and pharmacies, cafes and restaurants galore, and many, many shops, boutiques, and galleries specializing in local arts.

ArtSpring

100 Jackson Avenue
250-537-2102
www.artspring.ca
Admission charged
New to Ganges is this 265-seat theatre and gallery, the

Ganges' bustling marina welcomes visitors to Saltspring Island.

Off the Pender Islands

centrepiece of the island's art scene. Theatrical productions and musical events are regularly held here, as well as artists' shows.

Gulf Islands Spinning Mill

351 Rainbow Road
250-537-4342
www.gulfislands.com/spinningmill
Open daily; tours by appointment
Admission free

Yarns, rovings, and batts flow from this tiny mill, where visitors can witness the process of wool carding, spinning, and felting. The mill processes fibres of several types including mohair, llama, and alpaca.

Vesuvius Bay

It was here that Saltspring's first settlers, African-Americans arriving from the United States, made their home. Nowadays the settlement serves as the entry and exit point for BC Ferries plying the Stuart Channel. Vesuvius Beach, accessible from Langley Road down a set of wooden steps, is regarded as one of Saltspring Island's best spots to view dramatic sunsets.

Long Harbour

The third BC Ferries terminal on the island. Ships arrive here from the mainland and outer Gulf Islands.

Pender Islands

Pender Islands Visitor Information
2332 Otter Bay Road, RR1
Pender Islands BC V0N 2M1
250-629-6541
Population: 2200

Known as quiet resort islands, the 34 square kilometres of North and South Pender Islands offer more than 20 access points to lovely, secluded beaches. Once separate landmasses linked by a land neck called the "Indian Portage," the two islands were cleaved by a 1911 canal and later rejoined by a highway bridge in 1955. Yet the island is still deeply geographically divided by Browning and Bedwell harbours. An overwhelming majority of residents live on

Henry Wright Bullock

Arriving at Saltspring Island in 1892, Henry Wright Bullock became known as the "Squire of Saltspring." Indeed, he thought of himself as English gentry, and he had the wealth to back up the claim. Purchasing a 90 hectare property, Bullock built an elegant residence, complete with the island's first indoor plumbing and gas-generated power.

A bit of a dandy, Bullock doted on his own appearance, as well as that of his island neighbours. He gave women acquaintances white gloves and pretty earrings, even encouraging them to have their ears pierced to better display the fancy frippery. Eton-style suits were acquired for local lads to wear at church. Strict dress codes were set for Bullock's elaborate luncheons and dinner parties.

In time, Bullock and his estate became fodder for legends. One tale tells of his farm's prodigious produce — corn that stood five metres high, and Bing cherries "so big they had to be individually wrapped." Notwithstanding Bullock's eccentricities, he is also remembered as a generous benefactor to the church and local causes.

Saltspring Island Studio Tour

Saltspring Island's artistic community is among the most varied in the Gulf Islands — perhaps even more so than Vancouver Island's. The island's self-guided studio tour is rewarding, yet potentially expensive. Visitors to the 35 listed properties / studios will find irresistible wares, gifts, and fine art set amid the special environments in which they were made — not to mention only a handshake away from the creative artists and artisans who crafted them. Helpful roadside signs, bearing a silhouetted black sheep and studio number, point the way to each property.

Also of note is the Ganges Saturday Market held at Centennial Park from April to October. The island tradition features more than 50 creative vendors who "make it, bake it, or grow it."

For more information about Saltspring Island's studio tour, pick up a map at the Ganges tourist office or contact:

Saltspring Island Studio Tour
250-537-9865
www.saltspring.com/studiotour

Meg Buckley Pottery
Meg Buckley
2200 Fulford-Ganges Road
250-653-4391
Functional everyday stoneware and porcelain pottery.

Seven Ravens Woodworks
Michael Nickels
1641 Fulford-Ganges Road
250-653-9565
Furniture and household items manufactured from wood taken from the 40 acre eco-forest.

Belle's Post Home Couture
Susy Mallin

150 Frazier Road
250-653-4416
Original versions of household items such as lamps, vases, and frames crafted from forged metal.

Gwen Butcher
161 Cranberry Road
250-537-2003
Original watercolours of West Coast themes, plus prints and cards.

Seagull Art Studio Gallery
Bert Small
131 Forest Hill Place
250-537-4643
Watercolours and wood objects, plus 3D stained glass creations.

French Country Fabric Creations
Darlene Lane
109 Broadwell Road
250-537-9865
French Provencal cottons and Portuguese laces are used to make table linens, handbags, and accessories.

Pacific Basketry
Lorna Cammaert
190 Broadwell Road
250-538-0033
Natural handcrafted baskets of cedar, honeysuckle, willow, reed, and kelp.

Islandweaver
Diane Mortensen
240 Monteith Drive
250-538-0040
Handwoven fashions, table and home accessories.

Studio on Duck Bay
Dawn Morrell
165 Mountain Park Drive
250-537-9115
Original watercolours and acrylic paintings, plus prints and cards.

Cocoon
Sarah Mathieson
324 Sunset Drive

250-537-8791
Fabric creations, fashions and home accessories.

Johnstone-Rob Studios
Donna Johnstone
353 West Eagle Drive
250-537-5654
Quilts, clothing, sleepware, and artwork made of natural fabrics and polar fleece.

Rose Hill Craft Studio
Sandy Robley
1325 Sunset Drive
250-537-2082
Candles and farm-crafted items such as sheepskins.

Blue Horse Folk Art Gallery
Paul Burke and Anna Gustafson
175 North View Drive
250-537-0754
Raku ceramics as well as folk-art animals and paintings.

North Beach Studio
Ronald Smith and Helen Ormiston Smith
1671 North Beach Road
250-537-1890
Ceramics and contemporary paintings.

Two Danes
Freddy and Bente Taupe
150 Le Page Road
250-537-4393
Garden sculpture and wrought-iron objects, in addition to candles.

September Moon Pottery
Rita Alexander
148 Trincomali Heights
No phone
Functional stoneware and tiles.

Bob McKay and J.D. Evans Gallery
Bob MacKay and J.D. Evans
201 Grantville Street
250-537-9862
Turned wood bowls, pepper-mills, lamps, etc.

Saltspring Island Studio Tour

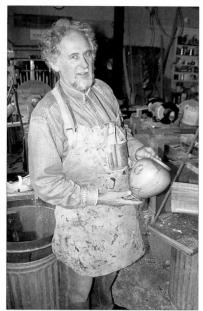

Saltspring Island artisans are eager to display their handiwork.

Coco Loco
Lou Ellis and Steven Stairs
117 Robinson Road
250-537-5075
Organic cotton duvet covers and sheets.

Chickadee Pine
Roger Warren
125 Churchill Road
250-537-9606
Handcrafted pine furniture.

Serendipity Studio
Margaret Threlfall
112 Robinson Road
250-537-4535
Original watercolours, plus wool and raw fleece.

Cedar Lane Studio
Osman Phillips
210 Cedar Lane
250-537-5667
West Coast photography, available in prints and greeting cards.

Cedar Mountain Studios

Don and Suzanne Zacharias
250-537-5776
180 Thomas Road
Fabric purses and wooden gifts / accessories.

Bigfoot Herbs
P. Anne Barnes
104 Eagleridge Drive
250-537-4466
Organic herbs, salad vinegars, and bathwaters.

Amy Buchwald Glass
Amy Buchwald
104 Peregrine Way
250-538-0351
Kilnworked and torchworked glass plates, bowls, platters, and *objets d'art.*

Stoneridge Pottery & Flowers by Arrangement
Gary and Beth Cherneff
520 Long Harbour Road
250-537-9252
Pots of raku, terra cotta, stoneware, and porcelain, plus fresh flowers.

The Tangled Web
Pat Barnes
771 Long Harbour Road
250-537-9199
Women's polar fleece jackets, vests, and pullovers with original appliqued designs.

Renée at Play
Renée Kreeft
872 Long Harbour Road
250-537-9631
Original felted mohair wall-hangings and pottery bowls, plates, and platters.

Soul Vibrations Instruments
Geoff Fishleigh
337 Beddis Road
250-537-1032
Musical instruments and meditation chimes.

Katepwa Garden Studio
Joan Warren
120 Cottonwood Road
250-537-9722
Porcelain and stoneware, plus quilted fabric tableware.

Antonio Alonso Woodwork
Antonio Alonso
145 Cottonwood Road
250-537-5659
Functional and decorative turned wood bowls, vases, and platters.

Mosaic Tile Works
Ruth Murray
185 Arnell Way
250-537-1196
Pots, wrought-iron tables, picture frames, etc., decorated with mosaic tile designs.

The Old Island Stamp Company
Steve and Trudy Mueller
109 Meyer Road
250-653-9091
Handmade rubber art stamps and supplies.

Sunshine Rock Farm
Henri and Tangachee Goebl
201 Bulman Road
250-653-9573
Jams, chutneys, vinegars, and healing creams made from organically grown fruits and vegetables.

Woodland Studio
Peter and Gail Eyles
261 Demetri Way
250-653-4526
Toy boats, suncatchers, frames, paintings, and cards.

Everlasting Summer
Marcia Jeanne
194 McLennan Drive
250-653-9418
Fresh and dried flowers, pots, statuary, plus a rose nursery and heritage rose garden.

BC Ferries service the Gulf Islands.

North Pender, largely around Magic Lake. It was here in the late 1960s that strident controversy erupting over Gulf Islands real estate development led to the creation of the Islands Trust, an elected representative body that governs the Gulf Islands, much like a municipal council.

These days the Penders are home to many artists and writers who prefer their peaceful, away-from-it-all ambience. The islands have long had a reputation as an escape: notorious gangsters Legs Diamond and Machine Gun Kelly went underground here for a spell during the days of Prohibition. There are no villages per se on the Pender Islands, though there are a greater concentration of houses and services at the older settlements of Port Washington and Hope Bay.

Port Washington

Situated on Grimmer Bay, this small community with government wharf showcases some historic buildings such as the Port Washington General Store and the Old Orchard Farm.

Hope Bay

Between Port Washington and Hope Bay along the Port Washington Road sits "Gallery Row," the island's highest concentration of artisans and their studios. Works of all sorts can be found, from oil paintings to Bohemian glass to handspun woollens. Hope Bay, unfortunately, lost most of its historic buildings in a 1998 fire.

Saltspring Island Farms & Nurseries

Owing to a blessed horticultural environment and a long agricultural heritage, Saltspring Island is a market basket brimming with right-at-the-source shopping opportunities. As the following are first and foremost working farms, rather than strictly retail outlets, it is best to call ahead before visiting.

Fraser's Thimble Farms
175 Arbutus Road
250-537-5788
Plant nursery and gardening supplies.

Northend Farm
2521 North End Road
250-537-4442
Lamb, fruits, and vegetables.

Bullock Lake Farm
360 Upper Ganges Road
250-537-4895
Knitwear, spinning and knitting supplies.

Willowcrest Farm
112 Robinson Road
250-537-4535
Wool and fleece.

Island Valley Farm
111 Leisure Lane
250-537-8882
Flowers and vegetables.

Moonstruck Cheese
1306 Beddis Road
250-537-4987
Cheeses.

Schwartzentruber Farm
143 Andrew Place
250-653-9529
Poultry.

Apple Luscious Organic Orchard
110 Heidi Road
250-653-2007
Organic apples.

Parkside Gardens
251 Demetri Way
250-653-4917
Irises and other water-loving plants.

Everlasting Summer
194 McLennan Drive
250-653-9418
Fresh and dried flowers, plus a rose and herb nursery.

Stowel Lake Farm
190 Reynolds Road
250-653-4303
Fresh fruits and vegetables.

Falcon Farm
455 Musgrave Road
250-653-9070
Fresh vegetables and beef, bedding plants, and pickles.

Cusheon Creek Nursery
175 Stewart Road
250-537-9334
Plant nursery and gardening supplies.

Byron Farm
536 Beaver Point Road
250-653-4450
Saltspring Island lamb and beef.

Salt Spring Seeds
355 Blackburn Road
250-537-5269
Seeds.

Duck Creek Farm
134 Tripp Road
250-537-5942
Apples, garlic, and fresh vegetables.

Pender Island Disc Golf Park
North Pender Island; off Schooner Way near Magic Lake
No phone
Admission free
This four hectare park is Pender Island's 18-pole disc golf park, designed for Frisbee golfers. It's free, but bring your own

De Courcy Island

Located between Vancouver Island and the southern tip of Gabriola Island, De Courcy Island shelters a mysterious past. In 1929 the island became a home for the Aquarian Foundation and its charismatic leader known as Brother XII.

A retired sea captain whose real name was Edward Arthur Wilson, Brother XII was also a zealous devotee of Madame Blavatsky, a British theosophist. In time, Wilson garnered a following of disciples, and eventually he founded a colony of believers, first on Vancouver Island, and later on De Courcy. Legend has it that Brother XII secreted vast quantities of gold at De Courcy and that along with his mistress, Madame Zee, he meted out discipline with a touch of cruelty. Some disgruntled followers claimed the two-some created a veritable "hell on earth" for their ad-herents. Brother XII eventu-ally moved his colony to the northern tip of Valdes Island, then fled to Europe where he died (though some claim his death was faked).

For years boaters avoided De Courcy's shores, fearing all sorts of calamities from gunfire to abduction. Nowadays, the island is a popular marine park.

equipment. The front nine poles are a par 27, the back nine are 29.

Driftwood Centre / Browning Harbour
This is the islands' main commercial centre, with a marina, grocery store, bank, laundromat, pub, plus accommodations and camping.

Bedwell Harbour
Bedwell Harbour offers a full-service destination resort and marina. It is also a summer-time Canadian Customs port of entry for air and sea craft. Medicine Beach, at the north end of Bedwell Harbour, was once the site of an ancient First Nations settlement.

Church of the Good Shepherd
Gowlland Point Road; brief walk from Bedwell Harbour
An Anglican house of worship, this charming wooden church was constructed in 1938 by Pender Island parishioners.

Galiano Island
Galiano Island Visitor's Association
PO Box 73
Galiano Island BC V0N 1P0
250-539-2233
www.galianoisland.com
Population: 1000
With an area of nearly 100 square kilometres, Galiano is the second largest of the Gulf Islands and the driest, receiving less than 60 centimetres of

Hastings House

Likened to "an English country estate dropped into the Canadian wilderness," Hastings House is indeed a bastion of Old World charm in the embrace of forest and seashore, meadow and garden. Situated on 10 hectares overlooking Ganges Harbour, the one-time home of prominent naval architect Warren Hastings resembles an 11th-century Sussex-style manor house and is now the centrepiece of the Gulf Islands most exclusive hotel and restaurant. It has garnered accolades by the dozens, deservedly, and is one of only six Canadian members of the prestigious Relais et Châteaux hotel association.

In all there are 18 guest suites ensconced in the manor house, plus six other out-buildings — four century-old but lovingly restored estate buildings, and two newly constructed facilities. Guests, many of them on return visits, can opt to cuddle in the former barn; in The Post, the island's original Hudson's Bay Post; or even in the Churchill Cottage, once the estate manager's home, now a three-bedroom woodland retreat. All rooms come with amenities galore and, of course, top-drawer service.

Each night Hastings House is also the setting for some of the area's most memorable cuisine: five-course meals prepared by Swiss-born chef Marcel Kauer. Menus change daily, taking advantage of the market's freshest Saltspring Island lamb and seafood, herbs, vegetables, and fruits.
Hastings House
160 Upper Ganges Road
Saltspring Island BC V8K 2S2
250-537-2362
800- 661-9255
www.hastingshouse.com

rainfall annually. Named for the Spanish explorer Dionisio Alcala Galiano, the island is narrow and long, stretching for 25 kilometres. Its eastern shores are riddled with old logging trails and country lanes, in addition to sheltered beaches and coves — in all, perfect for campers, day hikers, and kayakers. Cycling is also popular, as is just taking it easy. Galiano's quiet pace encourages vacationers to enjoy a simpler life. Check out the superb Montague Harbour Provincial Marine Park with three white-shell beaches, or venture to the top of 660 metre Mt. Galiano for wonderful views of Active Pass.

Sturdies Bay

Located on the island's eastern end, this is downtown Galiano Island with a ferry terminal, lodge and restaurant, plus shops selling gifts and sundries.

D'Arcy Island

Situated less than two kilometres off Sidney Island, tiny D'Arcy Island is now a marine park. During the late 1800s and early 1900s, however, the mote of land held a leper colony, home to dozens of unfortunate souls banished here as quarantine against the frightful disease. D'Arcy inhabitants lived in makeshift shelters and relied on the arrival of a supply ship every three months for provisions. In 1924 the colony was relocated to Bentinck Island, 16 kilometres south of Victoria.

Fruit farms dot Saltspring Island.

Gulf Islands Festivals & Events

MAY
Pender Island Invitation Disc Tournament
Pender Island Disc Golf Park, Pender Island
Frisbee golf at its finest with more than 100 competitors.

JUNE
Sea Capers
Various venues, Saltspring Island
Eclectic get-together with sandcastle building contests, a driftwood contest, and a treasure hunt.

JUNE TO SEPTEMBER
ArtCraft
Ganges, Saltspring Island
Annual summertime show and sales featuring more than 200 Gulf Islands artists.

JULY
North Galiano Jamboree
North End Community Hall, Galiano Island
Traditional island get-together with food and music.

Festival of the Arts
ArtSpring, Saltspring Island
Annual celebration of the island's local arts.
Lamb Barbeque
Winter Cove Provincial Marine Park, Saturna Island
Saturna Island's Canada Day barbeque has been a popular event for decades.

AUGUST
Pender Island Fall Fair
Pender Island
Annual autumn celebration with food and entertainment.
Fulford Day
Drummond Park, Saltspring Island
A full day of games and food and music.
Galiano Wine Festival
Lion's Hall, Galiano Island
Annual celebration of the vine, with wine tastings and awards.

SEPTEMBER
Saltspring Island Fall Fair
Farmers Institute Grounds
The island's main event, with artisans, contests, games, food, and entertainment.

Gabriola Island

Mayne Island

Mayne Island Community
Chamber of Commerce
PO Box 2
Mayne Island BC V0N 2J0
250-539-2715
www.mayneislandchamber.ca
Population: 900

Totalling 23 square kilometres, Mayne is a quiet place with an interesting and colourful past, visible in its historic farmhouses, churches, and shops. Named for Richard Charles Mayne, a lieutenant aboard HMS *Plumper*, which explored the area in the 1850s, the island boomed with the 1858 Fraser River Gold Rush. Miners Bay is named for the intrepid souls who congregated here, halfway in their journey from Vancouver Island to the golden prospects of the Fraser River.

Agricultural homesteads began flourishing on Mayne Island around the turn of the century; apple orchards were successful as was tomato growing. Indeed, farmer Richard Hill was known as the "Tomato King," operating huge greenhouses in which horse-drawn wagons were used to harvest the produce.

Village Bay

The BC Ferries terminal is in Village Bay, as are several late 1800s to 1930s buildings. Archaeological evidence suggests that First Nations peoples have been dwelling in this area for more than 4500 years.

Miners Bay

Mayne Island's commercial centre, overlooking Active Pass, figured prominently during the heady days of gold discovery at the Fraser River in 1858. Mayne Island's location midway between Vancouver Island and the mouth of the BC mainland's Fraser River made it a convenient stopover for wild-eyed fortune seekers braving the Strait of Georgia crossing.

Mayne Island Museum
Off Fernhill Road
Open summer weekends
Located in a one-time jailhouse, artifacts and curios provide a glimpse into the island's early days. They include fossils that are 70 million years old, First Nations tools, and wreckage from the 1872 sinking of the *Zephyr*. The first prisoner here was Henry Freer, arrested for larceny in connection with his hair-growing and freckle-removing elixirs.

St. Mary Magdalene Church
Overlooking Miners Bay
Erected in 1898, the church's sandstone baptismal font weighs in at 160 kilograms and was brought by rowboat from Saturna Island in 1900. The cemetery holds many early Gulf Islands pioneers.

James Island

Across Cordova Channel, off the Saanich Peninsula, James Island, at 315 hectares, holds some 11 kilometres of fine sand beach, some say the best in all of the Gulf Islands. At the turn of the century, access to the island was a privilege of the prestigious James Island Club, wealthy Victoria residents who enjoyed the retreat's private hunting and horse racing. James Island today is still exclusive, a privately owned island complete with a Jack Nicklaus-designed golf course.

In 1913, however, James Island was far less salubrious. In that year, Canadian Explosives Ltd. purchased the property, erected a factory, and began producing the new explosive TNT. It was James Island operations which produced the TNT that was aboard the French vessel *Mont Blanc* when it exploded in Halifax Harbour in 1917, killing 1654 people.

At its peak production, the James Island plant employed 800 workers, and the island supported a self-contained community. In 1962 the town was dismantled, and many of the homes were barged to other islands. The munitions operations were finally closed in 1979.

Active Pass Light Station
Georgina Point Heritage Park
First installed in 1885, this beacon will be familiar to ferry riders who pass it while travelling between Swartz Bay and Tsawwassen.

Centennial Well
Horton Bay Road
Enjoy a splash of cold, clear, clean water, watched over by a statue of a bewhiskered angel placed here in 1967 to commemorate Canada's centennial.

Saturna Island
Saturna Island Tourism Association
Box 50, Saturna Island BC V0N 2Y0
250-539-5577
www.saturnatourism.bc.ca
Population: 326
Considering that nearly half of Saturna's 31 square kilometres is designated parkland and protected area in the new Gulf Islands National Park, it's little wonder that the island still gets its share of off-the-beaten-track

Gulf Islands Parks & Recreation

Gulf Islands National Park
Pacific Marine Heritage Legacy / Parks Canada
2nd Floor, 711 Broughton Street Victoria BC V8W 1E2
888-812-7778 or 250-363-8569
www.harbour.com/parkscan/pmhl
23 square kilometres / campsites and wilderness camping
Scattered throughout the southern Gulf Islands is this newest BC park-in-progress, managed by the federal-provincial Pacific Marine Heritage Legacy in cooperation with Parks Canada. To date, 21 island parklands have already been purchased, including Tumbo, Georgeson and Russell islands, 11 square kilometres of Saturna, as well as portions of Mayne, Prevost, and the Pender islands.

Princess Margaret Marine Park
Portland Island; eight kilometres northeast of Sidney
250-391-2300
194 hectares / primitive camping
Northwest of Sidney and accessible via water taxi, this island park features great hiking trails, sandy beaches, and rocky shoreline exposed at low tide. Hawaiian farm workers planted apple orchards, which can still be seen on the island. Divers favour the location for its access to the MV *G.B. Church*, a 53-metre-long freighter scuttled here in 1991.

Saltspring Island
Ruckle Provincial Park
Beaver Point Road; 8.5 kilometres from Fulford Harbour
250-391-2300
486 hectares / 70 campsites
The 1876 home of the Ruckle family stands near the entrance to this largest of the Gulf Islands' provincial parks. Within the park is a working sheep farm, forested trails, open meadows, and the shoreline above Swanson Channel, a good place to watch passing ferries.

Drummond Park
Fulford Harbour; at the west side of the head of the harbour / day use
Although a good place for a picnic, the main reason many visit this spot is to marvel at the beautiful petroglyph of a seal at the park's entrance.

Mt. Maxwell Provincial Park
Cranberry Road; nine kilometres off Fulford-Ganges Road
199 hectares / day use
Here rises Mt. Maxwell. Its highest point, Baynes Peak (595 metres), is the Gulf Islands' third highest peak and provides great views of Fulford Harbour.

Pender Islands
South Otter Bay Protected Area
Shingle Bay Road; from the ferry, travel to South Otter Bay Road, then left on Shingle Bay Road
215 hectares / day use
This wildlife habitat offers good shoreline hikes, as well as old-growth forest trails.

Prior Centennial Provincial Park
Canal Road
250-391-2300
www.discoverccamping.ca
16 hectares / 17 campsites
Hamilton and Medicine beaches are good for walks, and there are nice wooded areas too.

Mt. Norman Regional Park
Canal Road; turn on Ainslie Point Road
Named for William Henry Norman, paymaster of HMS *Ganges* in 1841, the payoff here is cresting the hill at 271 metres and scanning the marvellous views of the Penders. The hike takes about 45 minutes one-way.

Beaumont Provincial Marine Park
North side of Bedwell Harbour; boat or hike from Ainslie Point Road
250-391-2300
58 hectares / 11 campsites
Popular with boaters and kayakers, this park also attracts hikers, as Mt. Norman can be reached via a trail from here.

seekers, even though they need to take at least two ferries to get here. They will be well satisfied with Saturna's old-timey character, its wonderful sandy beaches, and its great hiking. Saturna has five peaks higher than 300 metres and 60 kilometres of hilly road.

Lyall Harbour
Containing the BC Ferries dock and the government wharf, this is Saturna commercial central with a general store, community hall, and mitre-shaped St. Christopher's Church.

Saturna Island Vineyards
8 Quarry Road; turn off East Point Road at Harris Road
877-818-3388 or 250-539-5139
www.saturnavineyards.com
Stop here at the base of Mt. Warburton Pike for tastings of this vineyard's varietal wines, a delicious toast to their interesting winery tour.

Gulf Islands Parks & Recreation

Galiano Island
Bellhouse Provincial Park
South side of Sturdies Bay at Burrill Point
2 hectares / day use
Overlooking Active Pass, the rocky peninsula is favoured by shore fishers spincasting for salmon.
Galiano Bluffs Park
Off Bluff Drive; approximately two kilometres from the intersection with Georgeson Bay Road
173 hectares / day use
At some 120 metres above Active Pass, lookouts from this park offer great places from which to watch BC Ferries and ships, plus views of eagles, and of sea lions in the spring and autumn.
Montague Harbour Provincial Marine Park
Montague Park Road; eight kilometres from ferry terminal via Sturdies Bay Road, then Georgeson Bay Road and Montague Harbour Road
250-391-2300 or 800- 689-9025 reservations
www.discovercamping.ca
97 hectares / 25 vehicle campsites and 15 walk-in
British Columbia's first marine park, Montague Harbour is also the one-time site of a Coast Salish settlement. Forest walks and boating are the most popular activities.

Bodega Ridge Nature Reserve
Northwest end of island via Cottage Way
250-539-2677 (Bodega Resort)
150 hectares / day use
The four kilometre ridge rises from sea cliffs to Galiano Island's 328 metre summit; hiking trails meander through grassy meadows and stands of old-growth Douglas fir.
Dionisio Point Provincial Park
Northwest end of Galiano Island
Acquired from forestry giant MacMillan Bloedel, this nature retreat features shoreline hikes and sandy beaches. Race Point Lighthouse stands above Coon Bay.

Mayne Island
Mt. Parke Regional Park
End of Montrose Road
40 hectares / day use
The trek to the Halliday Viewpoint takes about 45 minutes, and at 245 metres above sea level offers commanding panoramas.

Saturna Island
Mt. Warburton Pike
South of Lyall Harbour
At 490 metres this is Saturna Island's highest point, offering great views.
Winter Cove Provincial Marine Park
Winter Cove Road
91 hectares / day use
Boaters favour the park for its wide anchorage, as do picnickers who like the beach, grassy meadows, and forested walks.
East Point Regional Park
Eastern tip of Saturna Island
2.5 hectares / day use
The Gulf Islands' easternmost point is a favourite spot for naturalists, who enjoy watching its many seabirds. During the summer, killer whales can be spotted offshore.

Gabriola Island
Gabriola Sands Provincial Park
Between Taylor Bay and Pilot Bay
6 hectares / day use
Great beaches for swimming and sunning, plus picnic facilities. Near the park are the Malaspina Galleries, distinctive sandstone formations.
Sandwell Provincial Park
Turn north off North Road onto Barratt Road, left onto Bond Road, and then left on Strand
12 hectares / day use
Follow the one kilometre trail from the parking area to a pebble and sand beach, good for sunning and picnics.

Drumbeg Provincial Park
Southwestern end of Gabriola Island
20 hectares / day use
Beachcombing, swimming, and fishing are the draws at this park.

Gabriola Island

Gabriola Chamber of Commerce
PO Box 249
Gabriola Island BC V0R 1X0
250-247-9332
www.GabriolaIsland.org
Visitor Centre: Folklife Village Mall
Population: 3412

Gabriola is the most developed and most northerly of the northern Gulf Islands, and is easily accessible from Nanaimo. Residents and visitors alike enjoy its many amenities, including restaurants and pubs, a golf course, and certainly its artistic, ultural, and natural attractions that enliven the 59-square-kilometre isle.

Pioneers first came to Gabriola in the 1850s, workers from Naniamo mines seeking places to live and raise their families. A sandstone quarry started operations in 1887, supplying stone for Victoria and Vancouver building projects and three-ton milling stones for wood pulping. Irish and Scots, in addition to many Portuguese, began farms to supply the growing population of the area.

Today, creative folks — artists of all sorts, authors, potters, and weavers — thrive here, and many welcome visitors at their galleries, giving Gabriola the nickname "Isle of the Arts." The Gabriola Community Arts Council lists nearly 40 members, representing dozens of artists and artisans working in a variety of mediums, from fine art drawings done in a Renaissance style to handwoven clothing. Fogo Folk Art is not to be missed. This studio is as whimsical and fun as they come, with some of the most unusual folk art creations to be found anywhere. Look for the annual studio tour at Thanksgiving, which includes several studios not usually open to the public. Stop by the Folklife Village Mall to browse and to see the building; it was formerly the Folk Life Pavillion from Vancouver's Expo '86, transported to Gabriola Island and reassembled.

As for nature, eagles and seabirds nest on Gabriola's high jagged bluffs, and three provincial parks — Drumbeg, Gabriola Sands, and Sandwell — sit within the island's shores. Not to be missed are the Malaspina Galleries, intriguing eroded sandstone sea caves, 70 metres long, with a spectacular overhang resembling a thunderous cresting wave. Cyclists love the ring road for its easy pace and scenery. Scuba divers descend into Gabriola Passage in search of Pacific octopus, as well as the sunken HMCS *Saskatchewan*.

Ferries to Gabriola Island depart from Nanaimo; call BC Ferries for a schedule, or visit www.bcferries.com.

Gabriola Historical & Museum Society
505 South Road; between RMCP headquarters and the Farmers Market
250-247-9987
Open Monday to Friday, 10 am-4 pm
Admission charged

Stop by to learn more about the history of Gabriola Island through artifacts and archival photographs.

United Church and Petroglyphs
South Road near Degnen Bay

One of the Gulf Islands' most extensive petroglyph sites is located behind the United Church. North of the church is a path that leads to bedrock panels featuring more than 50 ancient figures carved in the naked rock, from mythological creatures to geometric shapes.

Thetis Island

Population: 341

For paddlers and cyclists, Thetis Island provides a nice escape. There are warm waters in the summer for kayakers and quiet roads for two-wheelers, though Pilkey Point Road's 15 percent grade up Moore Hill is challenging, to say the least. Motorists won't find their cars of much use, as most of the island's shops and stores are within walking distance of the ferry landing. A popular place to visit is the Nugget and Pot of Gold Coffee Roasting Company for treats and 26 different varieties of roasted coffee beans.

Thetis and Kuper islands were once one. A turn-of-the-century canal dredging separated the two. The name Thetis comes from the 36-gun frigate *Thetis*, under the command of Captain Augustus Kuper, which was based at Esquimalt from 1851 to 1853.

Ferries for Thetis Island leave from Chemainus.

Kuper Island

Population: 271

Kuper Island is the homeland of the Penelakut First Nation, and therefore only invited guests are encouraged to visit.

South Central Vancouver Island

South Central Vancouver Island's hamlet of Cowichan Bay features homes and businesses built upon pilings.

Acclaimed as "The Warm Land," South Central Vancouver Island's Cowichan and Chemainus valleys enjoy a moderate climate with some 1800 hours of sunshine annually. Add to this natural warmth the gracious hospitality of a diverse population that includes artisans, farmers and ranchers, First Nations people, seafarers, and retirees. Embracing the seaside and upland terrain from the Malahat down into Mill Bay and as far north as Ladysmith, the region also has abundant pastoral scenery.

Generally speaking, South Central Vancouver Island can be divided into two broad regions, North Cowichan and South Cowichan. Shawnigan Lake, Cobble Hill, and Mill Bay are the south's town centres, set amid rolling farmland, forest, wineries, and coastal shoreline. Cowichan Bay, a bit farther north, is a picture-perfect seaside hamlet a waterfront of boardwalks, moorings, landings, and homes built upon pilings above the ever ebbing and flowing tides.

Duncan is the Cowichan Valley's principal town, noted especially for its unequalled collection of totems, which

South Central Island Recommendations

- Follow the Wine Route to discover Vancouver Island's robust vineyards; allow time for stops for fresh produce and cheeses.
- Stroll Duncan's streets to see its many outstanding totem poles, and experience the Quw'utsun' Cultural and Conference Centre.
- Enjoy the Cowichan Bay estuary and the seaside hamlet of Cowichan Bay; plan time to see the Cowichan Bay Maritime Centre.
- Spend a day or two relaxing in the Cowichan Lake area, perfect for water activities and outdoor adventure.
- Definitely see the famous Chemainus murals, Canada's largest outdoor art gallery.
- Plan a picnic outing to the BC Forest Discovery Centre; enjoy the easy walking trails and the forestry heritage recreations.
- Stroll through Ladysmith's pretty downtown; then go for a dip at nearby Transfer Beach Park, with some of the Island's warmest waters.

has given the community its nickname, "City of Totems." The area has long been a First Nations homeland, and the Quw'utsun' Cultural and Conference Centre is now the welcoming hand extended to visitors wishing to better understand and experience their culture. To Duncan's east the Cowichan Lake District, with its string of shoreline communities along Cowichan Lake, offers relaxing nature escapes and access to Vancouver Island backcountry.

North Cowichan encompasses the communities of Maple Bay, Genoa Bay, Crofton, and Chemainus. Seaside serenity and small-town charm stroll arm-in-arm here. In particular, Chemainus, known worldwide for numerous huge murals gracing its buildings, never fails to entertain and inspire. The same can be said of pretty Ladysmith, itself unique, astride the 49th parallel and brimming with historic heritage.

Malahat Summit Viewpoint
Highway 1; 30 kilometres north of Victoria
Note: This viewpoint is only accessible to northbound traffic.
Look for the Salish Bear totem marking 352 metres above the Saanich Inlet, eastern Vancouver Island's only inlet. The panorama is refreshing: trailing headlands merge with the deep blue waters of the Strait of Georgia, the Gulf Islands huddle in the distance, and farther still rise the Coast Mountains of BC's mainland.

First hacked through the wilderness in the 1860s, the Malahat Drive section of Highway 1 between Goldstream Provincial Park and the Cowichan Valley functioned for years as a roadway to move cattle and supplies between Victoria and up-Island communities.

Gulf Islands Viewpoint
Highway 1; 33 kilometres north of Victoria
Take this roadside exit for a view across Saanich Inlet towards the southern Gulf Islands and the American San Juan Islands. On clear days,

The Aerie

The Aerie excels at outstanding accommodations and cuisine.

From a commanding perch high atop the Malahat, overlooking Finlayson Arm and the Strait of Georgia beyond, The Aerie, as it name implies, delivers views, in addition to hospitality of the highest calibre. A member of the distinguished Relais et Chateaux association, as well as the recipient of four diamonds from the CAA, four stars from Mobil, plus a host of other prestigious awards, the Mediterranean-style villa complex rewards guests wccccccccsith outstanding accommodations and cuisine.

Surrounded by four hectares of grounds and gardens, its 23 rooms and suites are sumptuous private escapes resplendent with fine furnishings, antiques, and Persian silk carpets. Most include Jacuzzis, fireplaces, and private decks. As well, there is an award-winning restaurant with a spectacular wine list, and a top-flight wellness and beauty centre bursting with rejuvenating options from massage to sea salt scrubs. Relaxation knows no better retreat.

It is the realization of a dream for owner Maria Schuster, who began building The Aerie in 1984. From Austria originally, and an experienced luxury resort proprietor in the Bahamas, Schuster was beguiled by Vancouver Island's loveliness and set about to create a haven of pampering. With The Aerie's opening in 1991, the vision became a reality and today the resort is one of Vancouver Island's best sanctuaries for the soul.

The Aerie Resort
PO Box 108
Malahat BC V0R 2L0
250-743-7115
www.aerie.bc.ca

View from the summit of the Malahat over Saanich Inlet

Washington State's Mt. Baker, at 3285 metres in elevation, can be seen rising across the Strait of Georgia.

South Cowichan: Shawnigan Lake, Cobble Hill, and Mill Bay

South Cowichan Chamber of Commerce
Travel Info Centre at Mill Bay Centre
RR1
Mill Bay BC V0R 2P0
250-743-3566
Population: 11,600
Only 20 minutes south from Duncan and 40 minutes north of Victoria, this collection of communities epitomizes the semi-rural lifestyle sought by many wishing access to big city services, but with the slower pace of the country. Parks are numerous, as are farms, wineries, and artisan studios. The towns are blissfully small and friendly, but with their own distinct personalities: Shawnigan Lake is much loved by vacationers and outdoor enthusiasts; Cobble Hill sits amid rolling farmland, and local farmers are among Vancouver Island's largest milk producers; Mill Bay is seaside serene with a lovely marina and wharf.

Shawnigan Lake
Population: 1020
Primarily a summer recreation and vacation cottage area, an increasing number of folks are calling this a permanent address. The attractive locale, forested woods, and undulating meadows and fields are also seeing their share of development. Shawnigan Lake itself, with its well-kept beaches, is the fair-weather focus of the community, the spot for canoeing, water-skiing, swimming, and fishing. Nearby is the Kinsol Trestle, the largest wooden structure on the Island, and slated to become a portion of the Trans Canada Trail.

Shawnigan Lake Museum
Southwest of four-way stop in centre of community; intersection of Shawnigan Lake-Mill Bay Road and Shawnigan Lake Road
250-743-3566
Open afternoons, July-August
Admission charged
Located in the old fire hall, this is the place to learn about the area's founding as interpreted through artifacts and memorabilia.

Cobble Hill
Population: 3000
This tiny village offers some shops and basic services, the essentials for folks living in the surrounding wooded areas dotted with farms and orchards. During the 1940s, the limestone quarry here laid the foundation for the local economy. Nowadays folks like to hike up Cobble Hill for panoramic views stretching from the Saanich Peninsula to Cowichan Bay.

The community of Cowichan Bay curls along the Cowichan River estuary.

Merridale Ciderworks
1230 Merridale Road
Cobble Hill BC V0R 1L0
250-743-4293
www.merridalecider.com
This is Vancouver Island's only cidery and BC's first to brew English-style "scrumpy." Guests are encouraged to amble through the lovely apple orchards; chat with cider crafters; see the apple mills, presses, and fermentation casks; and sample the robust result.

Mill Bay
Population: 953
This pretty seaside community is growing, expanding its marina and shopping services, but it has always been popular with boaters using the public boat ramp to access the calm bay. Nearby Satellite Channel is popular with seals, which laze about the docks and floats. Mill Bay is northern terminus for the Brentwood Bay-Mill Bay ferry, providing transport

across the Saanich Inlet to Brentwood Bay. Note: This is BC Ferries' smallest, taking only 16 cars and 134 passengers. Call BC Ferries, 888-724-5223.

Cowichan Bay
Cowichan Tourism Association
25 Canada Avenue
Duncan BC V9L 1T3
250-715-0709
www.cowichan.bc.ca
Population: 2679
Curled along the Cowichan River estuary, this delightful little village and marina stretch out along nearly a kilometre of shoreline, offering a limited though good collection of restaurants, cafes, pubs, and some accommodations farther outside the village centre. Sportfishing excursions are popular, and several charter operations are available. Cowichan Bay also has the distinction of consistently offering some of Vancouver Island's best sunsets, marvellously coloured bay and

mountain views catching the fading light of dusk.
Wooden Boat Society and Cowichan Bay Maritime Centre
Cowichan Bay village centre
250-746-4955
www.classicboats.org
Open daily, April-September
Donations accepted
Quintessentially maritime, the society works to preserve traditional boat crafting skills through workshops and small-boat building courses. Explore the centre's interesting exhibits to see incredibly intricate model ships and a fascinating collection of outboard motors, from their early 20th-century inception to modern times.
South Cowichan Lawn Tennis Club
Cowichan Bay and Tzouhalem roads
250-746-7282
Lawn courts open to public
Admission charged
After prestigious Wimbleton, this is the British

Duncan, "City of Totems."

Commonwealth's oldest tennis club. The BC Heritage Site hosts the Annual Grass-Court Championships, one each in June, July, and August.

Duncan

Duncan / Cowichan Bay Visitor Info Centre

381A Trans-Canada Highway
Duncan BC V9L 3R5
250-746-4636
www.duncancc.bc.ca
Population: 4583

Duncan is the commercial and social centre for the Cowichan Valley and therefore has grown into a small but busy city to serve the region's 75,000 residents. Consequently, Duncan offers extensive services and several worthwhile diversions. Topping the list is an impressive collection of 80 totem poles, located mainly downtown and along the highway. Together they stake Duncan's claim to fame as the "City of Totems."

It all started in 1985, when six local carvers were invited to begin creating the town's first totem poles. The Totem Pole Project was envisioned as a cooperative venture involving primarily Cowichan artisans to celebrate this unique and ancient art form, but over the years the endeavour has embraced the work of many craftspeople. Take the downtown walking tour (follow the yellow footprints or pick up a map from the Info Centre) to view more than three dozen totems, some traditional and some with more modern sensibilities. Additional totems are located at the impressive Quw'utsun' Cultural and Conference Centre, where visitors experience an in-depth look at this First Nations culture.

Note too the numerous historical buildings gracing Duncan's downtown, many dating from the turn of the

---

Cowican Valley's Delectable and Distinctive Roadside Treats

The Cowichan Valley's long agricultural heritage means that travellers can come across an abundance of farm gates, staffed by friendly owners and operators eager to share the fruits of their labours, whether that be fresh vegetables and flowers, preserves, herbs, cheeses, or free-range poultry. Look too for summertime farmers' markets at Duncan and Mill Bay.

Abbott's Choice Fine Cheeses
1282 Cherry Road
Cobble Hill BC V0R 1L0
250-715-0563
A specialty producer of varietal cheeses such as Camembert, chevre, Brie, and cheddar curd, Abbott's creations come highly recommended; their products are proudly served in many of the area's finer restaurants, as well as proffered by the best

shops. Traditional curing techniques and the best ingredients ensure the quality of these European-style full-flavoured cheeses.

Beech Lake Farm
1385 Carlton Drive
Cobble Hill BC V0R 1L0
250-743-9869
Stop here to procure organically grown fruits and vegetables, free-range eggs, preserves, and specialty meats.

Westcott Farm
6691 Westcott Road; just north of BC Forest Discovery Centre
Duncan BC V9L 1T3
250-748-5698
Raised here are choice black Welsh Mountain sheep, whose wool is crafted into a variety of products, especially felt hats. Also available are locally raised poultry, lamb, and turkeys, in addition to honeys and jams.

Community Farm Store
3633 Glenora Road
Duncan BC V9L 1T3
250-748-6227
A bastion of wholesome foods, especially produce, this is a complete grocery store dedicated to organically created products. The on-site bakery prepares great breads and pastries using all natural ingredients.

Neel Creek Ranch
4275 Howie Road
Duncan BC V9L 1T3
250-746-0708
www.aplacas-iaoc.com
This working llama and alpaca ranch maintains a herd of more than 400 of these South American animals. Their fleece is crafted into a number of products: sweaters, scarves, hats, socks, and mittens, in addition to felt and yarn.

The Cowichan Valley "Un Petite Provence"

The Cowichan Valley has long been known for its excellent growing conditions and, as a result, its abundance of fresh produce. Now there are increasing numbers of boutique farms and vineyards supplying delectable comestibles: asparagus, salad greens, cheeses, lamb, pastured poultry, balsamic vinegar, plus fine wines and cheeses. Enthusiastic growers hope to one day earn the Cowichan Valley the honour of being designated British Columbia's first "appellation," a term bestowed by French connoisseurs to a region known for superior food and wine.

Of special interest, too, is Canada's only orchard dedicated to cider making. The Merridale Ciderworks grows several types of apples to produce honest English ciders. Their "scrumpy" is dry, a solid pub cider. The wildflower honey-sweetened "Cyser" is based upon a 400-year-old Elizabethan England recipe. For even more discerning palates, the Normandy Select Dry Cider is sparkly and champagne-like, aged for over a year.

In fact, the Vancouver Island Wine Route begins at Merridale Ciderworks, before heading north to a cluster of vineyards situated near Duncan. One final vineyard is farther north at Nanaimo.

Known for their outstanding varietal, Cherry Point Vineyards, between Cobble Hill and Cowichan Bay, merrily follows Merridale. Next up, Glenterra Vineyards, a new vineyard and already winning awards with its pinot gris. Then it's on to the venerable Venturi-Schulze Vineyards and the nearby Blue Grouse Vineyards on either side of Highway 1 near Cowichan Bay. Blue Grouse Vineyards bottles exceptional fresh and fruity traditional German-style wines. About 15 minutes later, near Duncan's southern limits, is Vignetti Zanatta Vineyards. The Zanatta family has been fermenting wine on their Glenora farm for more than 40 years and recently began offering the fruits of their labours to wine enthusiasts. West of Duncan is the Godfrey Brownell Vineyards, and to the north is Alderlea Vineyards. From there it's 30 minutes north to Nanaimo and the Chateau Wolff Vineyard, the Island's northernmost vineyard, known for its highly acclaimed pinot noir.

Winery /Cidery Tours

Merridale Ciderworks Corp.
1230 Merridale Road
Cobble Hill BC V0R 1L0
250-743-4293
www.merridalecider.com
Cherry Point Vineyards
840 Cherry Point Road, RR3
Cobble Hill BC V0R 1L0
250-743-1272
www.cherrypointvineyards.com
Glenterra Vineyards
3897 Cobble Hill Road
Cobble Hill BC V0R 1L0
250-743-2330
Venturi Schulze Vineyards
4325 Trans-Canada Highway, RR1
Cobble Hill BC V0R 1L0
250-743-5630

www.venturischulze.com
Blue Grouse Vineyards & Winery
4365 Blue Grouse Road
Duncan BC V9L 6M3
250-743-3834
www.bluegrousevineyards.com
Vigneti Zanatta Vineyard
5093 Marshall Road
Lake Cowichan BC V9L 1T3
250-748-2338
www.zanatta.bc.ca
Godfrey Brownell Vineyards
4911 Marshall Road
Duncan BC V9L 6T3
250-748-4889
www.gbvineyards.com
Alderlea Vineyards
1751 Stamp Road, RR1
Duncan BC V9L 5W2
250-746-7122
Chateau Wolff Vineyard
2534 Maxey Road
Nanaimo BC V9S 5V6
250-753-9669

Vancouver Island's wine route takes in several vineyards.

The Quw'utsun' Cultural Centre extends a welcoming hand to visitors wishing to experience First Nations culture.

Duncan's train station also houses the Cowichan Valley Museum and the Cowichan Historical Society.

century. The 1913 post office is a designated heritage site, as is the train station. Duncan also sports the world's largest hockey stick, hanging from the community centre on Highway 1. Originally on display at Expo 86 in Vancouver, it would reach 63 metres high if it was stood on end.

Quw'utsun' Cultural and Conference Centre
200 Cowichan Way; turn left off Highway 1 after the Silver Bridge crossing the Cowichan River
250-746-8119 or 877-746-8119
www.quwutsun.ca

Open daily
Admission charged
The Cowichan Valley is the traditional homeland of the Quw'utsun' people; their descendents number upwards of 3000, living primarily in Duncan and six adjacent reserve communities. The Quw'utsun' Cultural and Conference Centre is the welcoming hand extended to visitors wishing to better understand and experience their culture. Numerous exhibit facilities display artifacts and aspects of their heritage, including: the

Great Deeds multimedia presentation; the Circle of Children, an area for kids' workshops that introduce the making of traditional crafts; and the World's Largest Carving House, where master woodcarvers demonstrate their skills.

Elders are available to answer questions, and the restaurant offers traditional food such as smoked salmon. In the gift shop are excellent collections of native-themed books and souvenirs, arts and crafts, and jewellery, in addition to genuine hand-knitted Cowichan sweaters.

Cowichan Valley Museum / Cowichan Historical Society
120 Canada Avenue; in the Duncan train station
250-746-6612
Open Monday to Saturday in summer; Wednesday to Saturday in winter
Admission charged
Tucked into Duncan's charming turn-of-the-century train station, numerous exhibits and artifact-filled period settings chronicle the area's history from the arrival

113

Totem Poles

Woodcarving, especially the carving of totem poles, is a highly developed skill among Pacific Northwest First Nations people. For millennia since as early as 5000 BC the original inhabitants of the area painstakingly rendered the materials at hand notably western red and yellow cedars into fascinating depictions of their vibrant culture and the world in which they lived.

Essentially, a totem pole is the visual representation of the ceremonial privileges and identity of its owner. Figures and symbols on the pole are often transformational spirit-animals, mythical beings that could change shapes: at times wondrous animals, and at other times humans with mystical powers. First Nations family groups or clans claimed these figures as family ancestors and incorporated them on a pole as a depiction of family history, as a record of encounters with the supernatural beings, or in some cases as a way to display certain rights to sources of wealth or trading relationships. In a broad sense, totem poles might be seen as family crests, a clan's coat-of-arms. Totem poles were carved to commemorate a great person or great event, and occasionally to teach lessons. Yet the full meaning of a totem pole is very personal, and only the pole's owner and its carver can truly describe its full symbology and significance.

The renaissance of totem pole carving began with the reliable access to iron tools that came with European contact. Prior to this time, First Nations' use of metal had been limited, but with the arrival of Spanish, British, and Russian traders, an abundance of metal tools created a flourishing woodcarving craft. The upper classes of First Nations villages commissioned totem poles with verve, each chief attempting to garner more praise and grandeur with his ceremonial potlatch feasts. The massive free-standing poles came into fashion, as did shorter versions, greeting figures, decorative houseboards, and mortuary poles. From the mid to late 1800s, totem pole carving reached its most prolific pace as coastal Pacific Northwest First Nations carvers improved their techniques and codified poles' traditional renderings.

The ceremonial art form declined rapidly, however. The scourge of smallpox and later measles decimated indigenous populations. Further, missionaries, mistaking the poles for symbols of pagan worship, discouraged their construction as native conversion to Christianity increased. Finally, the government's repressive laws forbidding First Nations' potlatches and their massive gift giving diminished the need for totem poles.

For nearly five decades, until the end of World War II, totem pole carving virtually

Totem poles are often crafted to commemorate a great person or event.

ceased among First Nations. A revival occurred in the early 1950s as commercial businesses and government entities looked to totem poles as unique expressions of the area and began commissioning totem poles for office buildings, stores, and various celebrations. Tourist-oriented versions of poles emerged too, as public appreciation for the cultural icons evolved. Today, all across Vancouver Island, from Victoria's Thunderbird Park to Duncan the "City of Totems" to any number of civic parks and gardens, bank lobbies, hotel lounges, department stores, and restaurants, totem poles are poignant reminders of the past, and present expressions of marvellous ingenuity and creativity.

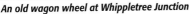

An old wagon wheel at Whippletree Junction

The Old Farm Market outside Duncan

Whippletree Junction

of the HMS *Hecate* in 1862 to the growth years of the 1950s. The Alderlea General Store introduces visitors to shopping selections of the day, and the King's Daughters' Hospital / Medical Room reveals the fright-inducing medical equipment of earlier days pneumonia jackets, forceps, calipers, surgical instruments, and such. Historic archives and photos round out the experience.

BC Forest Discovery Centre
2892 Drinkwater Road; two kilometres north of Duncan
250-715-1113
www.bcforestmuseum.com
Open daily, May-September
Admission charged
Education and activity combine on this 40 hectare site near Somenos Lake, where visitors engage the history of BC forestry through extensive indoor informational displays and outdoor exhibits, including a working sawmill and restored planer mill. A 1920s-era narrow-gauge steam locomotive chugs guests around the grounds during the summer, passing by a forest ranger station, fire lookout tower, and logging camp, through patches of old-growth forest, and even over Somenos Lake via a tiny trestle. Easy walking trails through the forest and plenty of picnic areas round out this great family-oriented destination.

Whippletree Junction
Seven kilometres south of Duncan
Open daily
Admission free
Whippletree Junction is a collection of interesting shops housed in a re-created early

1900s village. Fourteen restored buildings were gathered here from Duncan's old Chinatown and other sites in the area.

Old Farm Market
Four kilometres south of Duncan
Open daily
Admission free
Shoppers from all over the area pull into this popular roadside market to peruse and purchase fresh local vegetables and seasonal fruits. Arts and crafts complement the offerings.

Cowichan Lake District: Lake Cowichan, Honeymoon Bay, Youbou, Mesachie Lake, and Caycuse

Cowichan Lake District Tourism Info Centre
PO Box 824
125C South Shore Road
Lake Cowichan BC V0R 2G0
250-749-3244
Population: 6000
Known by the First Nation peoples as *Kaatza* or "big lake," Cowichan Lake is indeed the second largest lake on Vancouver Island, and its tiny shoreline communities provide access to the back-country wilds of South

Central Vancouver Island. Lake Cowichan is the largest town, with a range of services for visitors. It is certainly worth stopping here to visit the delightful Kaatza Station Museum, situated in a one-time Esquimalt and Nanaimo Railway station. From Lake Cowichan, travellers can tackle the 75 kilometre trip around the lake to take in the waterside hamlets of Honeymoon Bay, Mesachie Lake, Caycuse, and Youbou. Remote and remarkable Caramanah Walbran Provincial Park shelters some of the province's largest spruce trees.

Lake Cowichan
Population: 3086
Cosied up to Cowichan Lake, Vancouver Island's second largest lake at 32 kilometres by 3 kilometres, the community of Lake Cowichan is the region's principal town and the starting point for both the North Shore and South Shore roads, which travel 75 kilometres around the lake. Services are plentiful here, and fishing, boating, and water-skiing are popular pastimes for local residents and the many weekenders and campers coming in from the Cowichan Valley area.
Kaatza Station Museum
125 South Shore Road;
Saywell Park
250-749-6142
Open daily, May-September;
weekdays, October-April
Admission charged
In what was once a 1913 Esquimalt and Nanaimo Railway station, the Kaatza Station Museum showcases both a 1929 Westcan #7 and a 1927 #12 Shay locomotive outside, while indoors there is an extensive array of artifacts and

A sunflower welcomes a new day in the Cowichan Valley.

period setting exhibits outlining the logging legacy of the Lake Cowichan area. See re-creations of a typical pioneer home, a general store and post office, plus a mining tunnel.

Youbou
This north shore community, 15 kilometres from Lake Cowichan, is still rebounding after the 2001 closure of the TimberWest sawmill. Intrepid motorists take advantage of the town's services, the last chance for accommodation, meals, and gas before tackling the 108 kilometres of logging road to Bamfield on Vancouver Island's west coast.

Mesachie Lake
Only seven kilometres from Lake Cowichan on the south shore of the lake, this village is

home to the Cowichan Lake Research Station, founded in 1929 to foster coastal tree production and operated by the BC Ministry of Forests. Mesachie Lake is also the access point to the logging road leading to Port Renfrew on Vancouver Island's west coast. Note: This route is open to non-logging traffic only during non-working hours.

Honeymoon Bay
The tiny community of Honeymoon Bay sits 12 kilometres from Lake Cowichan and offers a pleasant escape; its post office, market, and pub provide ample services for vacationers.

A historic train recalls South Central Vancouver Island's logging legacy.

Honeymoon Bay Wildflower
Ecological Reserve
Highway 18; 15 kilometres
beyond Lake Cowichan
Come April, Honeymoon
Bay Wildflower Ecological
Reserve sprouts Vancouver
Island's largest concentration
of pink Easter lilies. Situated
on the flood plain of Sutton
Creek, the 7.5 hectare site
protects the lilies, in addition
to two dozen other wildflowers
such as wild ginger, white
trillium, and smooth wood
violets.

Caycuse

Caycuse, 26 kilometres past
Lake Cowichan, is said to be
the longest-operating logging
camp in Canada, and perhaps
even in all of North America.
A downturn in the logging
business has made Caycuse
a quieter place these days.

North Cowichan: Maple Bay/Genoa Bay, Crofton, and Chemainus
District of North Cowichan
PO Box 278
7030 Trans Canada Avenue
Duncan BC V9L 3X4
250-715-0709
www.northcowichan.bc.ca
Population:
Seaside ambience is one
theme that connects the small
communities of the North
Cowichan area. And charm.
Cosy Maple Bay and Genoa
Bay are snug shelters for
boaters and kayakers. They
also offer great beaches for
swimmers, and scuba divers
like the area's close-in diving
sites. A one-time mining
town, Crofton, farther north,
is now home to the Norske
Skog Canada Pulp and Paper
Mill, which offers interesting
tours. Farther north sits cute-
as-can-be Chemainus, known
internationally for the many
murals decorating the town's
buildings.

Maple Bay / Genoa Bay
Duncan Cowichan Visitor
Info Centre
381A Trans-Canada Highway
Duncan BC V9L 3R5
250-746-4636
www.duncancc.bc.ca
Population: 1848
Separated by eight kilometres,
Maple Bay and Genoa Bay are
quiet, small, seaside communities with marinas, pubs, and
cafes. Kayakers, windsurfers,
and divers depart from Maple
Bay for Sansum Narrows
between Saltspring and
Vancouver islands. Hikers
point their compasses towards
Mt. Tzuhalem, Mt. Provost,
and Maple Mountain.

Crofton
Crofton Visitor Centre
PO Box 128
Crofton BC V0R 1R0
250-246-2456
Visitor Centre: 1507 Joan
Avenue
Population: 2700
Crofton is essentially a

company town, though one with a sunny, seaside disposition. Tucked into Osborn Bay, this one-time farmstead boomed into a town in 1902 when lumber baron and mining mogul Henry Croft constructed a smelter here to extract copper and gold from diggings at his Lenora Mine on nearby Mt. Sicker. In its heyday, the mine produced $1000 a day. That was before copper prices plunged in 1908, crushing the prospects for the Crofton smelter. Boom times returned in 1956 with the construction of a pulp mill north of town, now a Norske Skog operation. Ferry service to and from Vesuvius Bay, Saltspring Island, departs from the dock. Call BC Ferries, 888-724-5223, for the sched-ule.

Crofton (Old School) Museum
1507 Joan Avenue
Phone: 250-246-2116
Admission free
Located next to the BC Ferries terminal, this is the old country school, and there are rows of tiny wooden student desks to prove it. These are in addition to exhibits and historic photos telling of the nearby Mt. Sicker Mine and Crofton's refining operations.

Norske Skog Canada Pulp and Paper Mill Tours
Hay and Crofton roads; north of Crofton off Highway 1A
Phone: 250-246-6006
Open weekdays, June-August, 1:30 pm
Admission free
Mill tours take in the pulping processes that produce newsprint, directory paper, and market pulp at this mill, owned by Norway's Norske Skog.

Chemainus
Chemainus Visitor Info Centre
PO Box 575
Chemainus BC V0R 1K0
250-246-3944
www.chemainus.com or www.muraltown.com
Visitor Centre: 9796 Willow Street
Population: 4000
Chemainus is a Canadian success story. A down-and-out town in the early 1980s, hit hard by the closing of the local sawmill, Chemainus became "The Little Town That Did." Launching a unique revitalization program, Chemainus engaged artists

Cowichan Sweaters

When the Scottish settlers of the 1800s came to the Cowichan Valley, they brought with them not only sheep, but also their tradition of carding and spinning wool. It's a skill that Cowichan women quickly mastered, adding their distinct indigenous design to the making of sweaters. Thus was created the Cowichan sweater, appreciated the world over not only as a durable and comfortable garment, but also as a work of art.

The crafting of true Cowichan sweaters is today a cottage industry in the Cowichan Valley, and the business is run by a small cooperative of knitters. Only sheep raised on Vancouver Island breeds such as Dorset, Hampshire, and Suffolk donate their soft fleece to the making of a Cowichan sweater. The colours are kept natural, ranging from cream to black. A Cowichan Valley mill washes, dries, and hand cards the wool. Cowichan weavers then do their magic, spinning the wool into a single strand on a Bulky or Indian Head spinner.

Weavers follow traditional inspiration for design. The wildlife of the area, especially eagles, salmon, whale, and deer, often appears. Some designs are borrowed from historic images, while others are family heirlooms, passed down from mother to daughter. Yet though the motifs may be familiar, they are nonetheless unique as each sweater is handcrafted.

Given the popularity of the Cowichan sweater and its limited supply, imitations have been spun out over the years. Authentic Cowichan sweaters are knitted in the Fair Isle method, "in the round." The garment's only seam is along the top of the shoulder; there are no arm seams. Most garments will have a zipper, and it will be sewn in by hand. The sweater shouldn't look as though it has been cut, and the zipper should not be machine-sewn into place. Finally, if it's the real thing it will show the label "Genuine Cowichan Sweater."
For a catalogue of Cowichan sweaters contact:
Cowichan Knitters Co-operative
200 Cowichan Way
Duncan BC V9L 4T8
250-746-8119
888-331-6363
www.cowichan.org

and commissioned larger-than-life murals and outdoor sculptures to honour the area's history. Now there are three dozen murals plus a dozen sculptures making it Canada's largest outdoor art gallery. Follow the footprints leading about the downtown and old town areas; the works are all well marked and organized in a self-guided walking tour.

Maps are available at the information centre. Or hop aboard a horse-drawn carriage, horse-drawn trolley, or steam-powered mini-train to see the sights during 30-minute narrated tours.

Artistic sensibilities infuse the pretty town. Chemainus retains many historic buildings, all of them gussied up and many housing boutiques, antique shops, and galleries galore. The Chemainus Theatre is renowned for its classic performances, accompanied by fine dining. And right in town is playful Waterwheel Park and interesting exhibits at the Chemainus Valley Museum.

Chemainus is also the location for the ferry to Thetis and Kuper islands; the dock is west of the old town area.

South Central Island Festivals & Events

APRIL
Birdhouse Building Competition
Duncan
Annual festival for avid avian lovers who create handcrafted nests.

MAY
Wooden Boat Festival
Maple Bay
Annual gathering of wooden boat enthusiasts for sailings and shows.

JUNE
Vancouver Island Paddlefest & Kayak Conference
Ladysmith Harbour
Celebration of Pacific Coast paddlesports enthusiasts with competitions and displays.
Cowichan Bay Boat Festival
Cowichan Bay
A day of nautical events, entertainment, and food.
Chemainus Daze
Chemainus Waterwheel Park and downtown
Parade and children's activities, food, and entertainment.

JULY
Islands Folk Festival
Duncan, Providence Farm
Longstanding annual country fair with entertainment and food.

AUGUST
Ladysmith Celebration Days
Transfer Beach Park, Ladysmith
Soapbox derby and logger sports, plus barbecues, entertainment, and fireworks.

SEPTEMBER
Vancouver Island Wine Festival
Duncan area
Annual wine celebration with winery tours and tastings.
OCTOBER
Salmon and Mushroom Festival
Lake Cowichan
Annual celebration of migrating salmon, and the harvesting of wild mushrooms.

NOVEMBER-DECEMBER
Trim-A-Tree
Ladysmith
Delightful spectacle of wonderfully and whimsically decorated Christmas trees.

DECEMBER
Chemainus Christmas Carol Ship
Chemainus
Annual sailing to Ladysmith and back aboard a holiday-decorated and illuminated ferry.
Carols Afloat
Maple Bay
Marvel at the flotilla of decorated and illuminated boats sailing in Maple Bay.

South Central Island Tee Time

Arbutus Ridge Golf and Country Club
3515 Telegraph Road
Cobble Hill, BC
250-743-5000
www.golfbc.com
Eighteen holes
Cowichan Golf and Country Club
4955 Trans-Canada Highway
Duncan, BC
250-746-5333
www.connected-sales.com
Eighteen holes
Duncan Meadows Golf Course
6507 North Road
Duncan, BC
250-746-8993
877-746-8993
www.duncanmeadows.com
Eighteen holes
March Meadows Golf Course
Honeymoon Bay
250-749-6241
Home of Canada's famous female golfer, Dawn Coe-Jones
Fun Pacific 9 Hole Par 3 Golf
2591 Beverly Street
Duncan, BC
250-746-4441
Nine holes; also mini-golf
Mt. Breton Golf Club
2816 Henry Road
Chemainus, BC
250-246-9322
Eighteen holes

Picturesque Ladysmith has been likened to an early-day San Francisco.

Chemainus Theatre
9737 Chemainus Road; at Victoria Street
250-246-9820 or 800-565-7738
www.chemainustheatre.bc.ca
Open daily
Admission charged
Excellent theatre productions featuring professional guest artists from across North America, plus fine Vancouver Island cuisine served buffet-style at the Playbill Dining Room, ensure the live performances are both delicious and dramatic hits with local residents and visitors alike. The plays staged here are not only popular classics such as George Bernard Shaw's *Candida* or *Barefoot in the Park* by Neil Simon, but also musicals and new plays. Be sure to make reservations.

Chemainus Valley Museum
Waterwheel Park
250-246-2445
Open daily
Admission charged
Numerous archives and artifacts amid charming displays relate the history of Chemainus and the surrounding region. Of particular note is the "Age of Steam" exhibit, and the

original models of the Chemainus murals.

Chemainus Mill / Weyerhaeuser
2860 Victoria Street
Chemainus, BC
250-246-9793
Open Tuesday and Thursday, May-September, 12:30 pm-2 pm
Admission free
Explore the inner workings of an operating sawmill equipped with state-of-the-art technology.

Ladysmith

Ladysmith Chamber of Commerce
PO Box 598
Ladysmith BC V9G 1A4
250-245-2112
www.ladysmithcofc.com
Visitor Information Centre: 26 Gatacre Street
Population: 6700
Although originally named Oyster Harbour for its profuse oyster beds, Ladysmith was renamed by James Dunsmuir in honour of Ladysmith, South Africa, which was saved from a Boer War siege by British forces in 1900. Dunsmuir even named streets after generals of the 1899-1902 war.

Incorporated in 1904, the town held dormitories for miners' families and functioned as a shipping port for the Extension coal mines to the north. In 1913, Ladysmith became the focus of a bitter labour dispute over safety issues, and in the 1930s the mines closed. Subsequently, residents of Ladysmith turned to logging and fishing for their livelihood.

The community today is anything but unruly; it was once celebrated as one of Canada's 10 prettiest towns. Indeed, charmingly restored historic buildings (many from the Extension mines near Nanaimo) step up steep slopes and line hilly streets, giving Ladysmith a resemblance to an early-day San Francisco. Strolling is a good way to experience the town, and a map for the Ladysmith Heritage Walk is available at the Chamber of Commerce office. The town sits astride the 49th parallel, which marks the United States / Canada border across North America until the border line swings south, allowing all of Vancouver Island to remain within Canada.

Opt to spend some time at nearby Transfer Beach Park, Ladysmith's fun-loving outdoor living room with a sandy beach (and warm swimming), playground for kids, kayak rentals, and oceanside amphitheatre, where many local celebrations are staged.

Black Nugget Museum
12 Gatacre Street
250-245-4846
Open daily, June-September,
12 pm-4 pm; Admission

This museum, housed in a hotel, includes the original hotel bar in a restored barroom, along with memorabilia from pioneer days.

The Bungy Zone Adrenalin Centre
35 River Road; five kilometres north of Ladysmith
250-753-5867 or 800-668-7771
www.bungyzone.com
Open daily, February-Nov.
Admission charged
Set at the Nanaimo River

Gorge, the Bungy Zone Adrenline Centre is Canada's only legal bridge jump facility. Participants can plunge 43 metres, attached to the bridge only by a springy bungy cord tied round their ankles. A variation is the "Ultimate Swing," a 140-metre-long hurl through the canyon. Clothing-optional enthusiasts might take note of the annual February fete: Naked Bungy Weekend.

South Central Island Parks & Recreation

Memory Island Provincial Park
South end of Shawnigan Lake
One hectare / day use
With boat access only, this park is good for fishing and picnics.

West Shawnigan Lake Provincial Park
Northwest side of Shawnigan Lake; six kilometres from Highway 1 on West Shawnigan Lake Road
Nine hectares / day use
Swimming areas and nice picnic spots make this a local favourite.

Spectacle Lake Provincial Park
Spectacle Lake Road at the top of Malahat Drive; one kilometre north of Shawnigan Lake south turnoff
65 hectares / day use
Come here for hiking and biking trails, swimming, and nice picnic areas.

Bamberton Provincial Park
Mill Bay Road; 36 kilometres north of Victoria, north end of Malahat Drive
250-391-2300 or 800-689-9025 (reservations)
www.discovercamping.ca
28 hectares / 50 campsites
Nice place for swimming and camping.

Cowichan River Provincial Park
Three access points:
Skutz Falls Road; off Highway 18
Riverbottom Road: off Highway 18, take Cowichan Lake Road to Stoltz Road, then Riverbottom Road
Robertson Road; south of Duncan, turn off Highway 1 on Miller Road, then take Glenora and Vaux roads to Robertson
250-391-2300 or 800-689-9025 (reservations)
914 hectares / 43 campsites
Straddling one of Vancouver Island's best fishing rivers, this park protects a significant portion of the Cowichan River. The Cowichan River Footpath runs for 20 kilometres from Glenora to Skutz Falls. Hiking the entire length takes about seven hours. Marie Canyon and Stoltz Pool are two popular park destinations.

Cowichan River Footpath
Entrance at Cowichan Fish and Game Association; eight kilometres from Allenby Road turnoff
Starting just west of Duncan, this 20 kilometre path leads to Skutz Falls.

Chemainus River Provincial Park
Hillcrest Road; 6.5 kilometres west of Highway 1
93 hectares / camping allowed
Good swimming, fishing, and hiking make this a popular spot.

Roberts Memorial Provincial Park
Cedar / Yellow Point Road; three kilometres north of Yellow Point
14 hectares / day use
A nice restful oceanside spot, it's a good place for picnicking and swimming.

Hemer Provincial Park
Hemer Road, on Holden Lake; heed signs off Cedar / Yellow Point Road
93 hectares / day use
Good spot for easy hiking and horseback riding.

Gordon Bay Provincial Park
14 kilometres beyond Lake Cowichan, past Honeymoon Bay
250-391-2300 or 800-689-9025 (reservations)
www.discovercamping.ca
51 hectares / 126 campsites
A sandy freshwater beach is the draw for vacationing families, and there are also many opportunities for fishing, boating, and hiking.

Chemainus Murals

Known worldwide, little Chemainus is hailed as Canada's largest outdoor gallery with nearly three dozen larger-than-life, professionally painted murals depicting the area's history. Additionally, there are 12 sculptures situated about town.

Murals

1. Steam Donkey at Work (1982)
Frank Lewis, Nancy Lagana
Portrays a logging crew with a steam donkey hauling felled logs from the woods.

2. Thirty-three Metre Collage (1982)
Frank Lewis, Nancy Lagana, Paul Marcano
Several historic scenes such as Chemainus Wharf, and Engine #21 rolling logs into a log dump.

3. Steam Train On Bridge Over Chemainus River (1982)
Paul Marcano
Billowing smoke trails Locomotive #4 as it puffs over the Chemainus River with a heavy load of timber.

4. The Hong Hing Waterfront Store (1982)
Paul Marcano
From 1915 to 1950, Hong Hing operated a successful laundry and general store in Chemainus.

5. Fallers Undercutting a Fir (1982)
Thomas Robertson
Tree fallers working as a team tackle a giant Douglas fir.

6. Arrival of the Reindeer in Horseshoe Bay (1983)
Sandy Clark, Lea Goward
Pictured is the arrival of the HMS *Reindeer*, greeted by a First Nation princess.

7. Logging with Oxen (1983)
Harold Lyon
Honours the mighty oxen that largely powered the logging business around the turn of

The murals of Chemainus chronicle the area's history.

the century.

8. Chemainus 1891 (1983)
David Maclagan
Known as Horseshoe Bay back in 1891, the town that would become Chemainus is portrayed.

9. Camp 2 on a Sunday (1983)
David J. More
Loggers of 1902 enjoy a Sunday afternoon at Camp 2.

10. Company Store (1983)
Dan Sawatzky
Depicts the early 1900s interior of the Victoria Lumber & Manufacturing Company store.

11. Temporary Homes (1983)
David White
In 1912, when new roads were being built north of Chemainus, workers lived in these typical construction crew quarters.

12. Native Heritage (1983)
Paul Ygartua
Honours the First Nations legacy of the area with powerful portraits of notable past and present people.

13. Billy Thomas (1984)
Sandy Clark
Billy Thomas was the first white male born in Chemainus. The year was 1874, and Billy lived until the age of 102.

14. HMS Forward (1984)
Harry Heine
Depicts the HMS *Forward*, one

of the British Royal Navy ships sent to search for a group of murderers during an 1864 incident.

15. Chemainus Tug Boat (1984)
Mark and Harry Heine
Proudly depicts the 1909 tug of the Victoria Lumber & Manufacturing Company.

16. Chinese Bull Gang (1984)
Ernest Marza
A 23-member-strong "Chinese Bull Gang" manoeuvres massive timber towards a waiting logging ship.

17. First Schoolhouse, 1883 (1986)
Kiff Holland
Shows the first public school in Chemainus, built in 1883 next to the Esquimalt and Nanaimo Railway station.

18. Julia Askew (1986)
Elizabeth Smily
Honours the 1871 birth of Julia Askew, the first child of European ancestry born in the Chemainus Valley.

19. Mill Street in 1948 (1986)
Mike Svob
Among buildings depicted in this 1948 view of Chemanius are the library, post office, and company store.

20. World In Motion (1986)
Alan Wylie
A Shriner band in colourful

Chemainus Murals

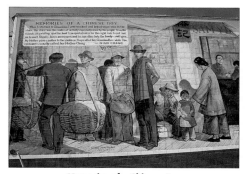

Memories of a Chinese Boy

Native Heritage honours the area's First Nations.

red uniforms keeps this 1883-1939 parade compilation stepping lively.

21. Chemainus Harbour 1910 (1987)
Colin Williams
Chemainus is lovingly captured in this 1910 panoramic view of the town's harbour.

22. Mural under reconstruction due to wall damage.

23. Chemainus Hospital (1988)
Doug Driediger
Built in 1899, the Chemainus Hospital served the medical needs of folks from Nanaimo to Victoria.

24. Second Chemainus Sawmill (1988)
Bruce Rickett
Pictured is the 1879 Chemainus sawmill, the second one built on the same site.

25. Waiting for the Whistle (1989)
Robert Dafford
Interior depictions of the Chemainus sawmill, which operated from 1925 to 1982.

26. Chemainus, The War Years 1915 (1989)
Susan Tooke Crichton
Commemorates the members of the 67th Battalion, shown waiting for the train that would take them from home and into war.

27. The Spirit of Christmas (1991)
Dan and Peter Sawatzky
Pays tribute to the original Chemainus Festival of Murals.

28. Climax Engine Number Three (1991)
Dan Sawatzky
Long-time train engineer Sam Alexander is portrayed at the controls of railway Engine No. 3 of the Victoria Lumber & Manufacturing Company.

29. The Winning Float (1991)
Joyce Kamikura
Shows the winning parade float of June 30, 1939, at the Victoria Lumber & Manufacturing Company.

30. The Lone Scout (1991)
Stanley Taniwa
Honours Edward Shige Yoshida, who started the 2nd Chemainus Boy Scouts, the first all-Japanese-Canadian troop.

31. Lumber Barons (1992)
Constance Greig-Manning
Recalls the lumber bosses who owned and operated the Chemainus sawmill from 1889 to 1945.

32. Telephone Exchange (1992)
Cim MacDonald
Shows the quaint Victorian residence that served as the Chemainus telephone exchange for 30 community telephones.

33. Memories of a Chinese Boy (1996)
Cheng-Shu-Ren (Arthur)
Pays homage to the town's Chinese heritage by depicting travellers of the early 1900s waiting at Sam Yee's store.

Sculpture
In Search of Snipes (1986)
Glenn Spicer
Charlie Abbot The Hermit (1992)
Glenn Spicer
Sea Captain (1991)
Glenn Spicer
Spool Donkey (1983)
Elmar Schultes
Spirit of the Earth (1998)
Daniel Kline
The Waterwheel (1967)
Karl Schutz
Three Generations (1985)
Sandy Clarke
The Older Generation (1989)
Barry Shaw-Rimmington
H.R. MacMillan (2000)
Cheng Shu-Ren (Arthur)
For more information about the Chemainus murals contact:
Chemainus Festival of Murals Society
PO Box 1311
Chemainus BC V0R 1K0
250-246-4701
www.muraltown.com

Central Vancouver Island

The wonderful beaches of Central Vancouver Island encourage relaxation.

Tucked into Vancouver Island's sheltered east-coast midsection is a collection of small to large communities plus offshore islands presenting sensational coastline, beaches, Coast Range vistas, forested bluffs, secret coves, and peaceful flowered meadows. Central Vancouver Island is the Island's playground, wonderful any time of year with a profusion of out-of-doors pursuits.

Nanaimo is Vancouver Island's second largest city, the region's commercial hub, and a critical transportation link. The Trans-Canada Highway sweeps through Nanaimo, and drivers can carry on to the mainland via the Duke Point and Departure Bay ferry terminals. But why not stay right here? Urban amenities are plentiful and easily accessible in the "Harbour City." The city proper offers a splendid arts and cultural milieu amid a heritage backdrop. Venture into the Old City Quarter, into Pioneer Plaza, and along Commercial Street to experience Nanaimo's heritage architecture. Galleries and boutiques offer a range of gift and souvenir items, and restaurants and cafes are close at hand. Offshore from Nanaimo is Gabriola Island, the "Queen of the Gulf Islands," with a wide variety of natural diversions.

Oceanside, anchored by the resort towns of Qualicum Beach and Parksville, is seaside enchantment with beaches to beachcomb and oodles of shops and galleries to peruse. Both resort locales exude relaxing ambience and excel at welcoming vacationers with good restaurants and accommodations. Nearby, the waters off Nanoose Peninsula are a boater's paradise.

Arrowsmith / Coombs Country is, well ... countryside, with charming roadside markets and pretty pastureland. To the north, Lighthouse Country begins, a string of seaside towns steeped in maritime lifestyle. On the western horizon, 1812 metre Mt. Arrowsmith is the centrepiece of the Mt. Arrowsmith Biosphere Reserve, one of two such UNESCO-designated sites on Vancouver Island.

Nanaimo

Tourism Nanaimo
Beban House, 2290 Bowen Road
Nanaimo BC V9T 3K7
250-756-0106
800-663-7337
www.tourismnanaimo.com
Population: 76,173

With six deep-sea docks and the key ferry terminals of Duke Point and Departure Bay, Nanaimo is Vancouver Island's commercial import / export epicentre and amply deserves its moniker of "Harbour City." Overlooking the Strait of Georgia, with Mt. Benson for its western backdrop, the harbour bustles as barges, tugs, yachts, freighters, ferryboats, fishing fleets, and floatplanes hustle in and out, giving the city a busy, energetic air.

The Nanaimo area is no stranger to the comings and goings of people. The name Nanaimo is a corruption of *Snuneymuxw*, the "great and mighty people," a reference to those who lived for millennia along the Nanaimo River. The Hudson's Bay Company established a coal mining operation here in 1852, using

Nanaimo is also known as the "Harbour City."

as labourers the Snuneymuxw, as well as imported Chinese workers. Indeed, Nanaimo sheltered a large Chinese community, but a controversial fire ravaged the downtown settlement in 1960.

While the Trans-Canada Highway zips through the city, skirting Naniamo's suburban development fringes, the city centre offers a vibrant arts and cultural scene in a heritage setting. Venture into the Old City Quarter, into Pioneer Plaza, and along Commercial Street to experience Nanaimo's heritage architecture; several

history walks highlight themes of city development from coal mining to shipping. Galleries and artist studios, gift shops and boutiques offer First Nations arts and crafts, plus works by other local artists in addition to pottery and sculpture, fashions and fine jewellery. Restaurants and cafes are plentiful. And don't miss a chance to amble along the Harbourfront Walkway, a wonderful four kilometre network of public walkways beginning in Departure Bay and ending in the heart of downtown.

Central Island Recommendations

- Venture into Nanaimo's Old City Quarter, into Pioneer Plaza, and along Commercial Street to view the city's heritage architecture.
- Experience the Nanaimo District Museum, a small but satisfying venue of fascinating historic installations.
- Come summer, head to the Bastion, the site of the Noon Gun ceremony, in which Bastion guardsmen, garbed in period attire, fire a fully restored 19th-century cannon.

- Drive the scenic Oceanside Route, the original coastal Highway 19A from Nanoose Bay in the south to Deep Bay in the north.
- Luxuriate at "Canada's Riviera," the 19-kilometre stretch of sandy beach at Parksville.
- Explore Craig Heritage Park, a collection of historic buildings rescued from the Parksville area.
- Drive the backroads through Arrowsmith / Coombs Coun-

try, a pleasant rural ramble rich with wonderfully eclectic attractions and diversions.
- Relax at Qualicum Beach, enjoying the charming town with its many, many diversions, notably the Milner Gardens & Woodlands.
- Dawdle through Lighthouse Country, a collection of small communities that epitomize the seaside village lifestyle.

A Look Back In Time

The pleasant and fertile valley on the south side of Englishman River inspired brothers Albert and John Hirst to settle in the area in 1874. In due course they built a two-story log cabin and planted an orchard in the protected vale.

Over time the Hirsts grew prosperous and took their place among the community's leading citizens and businessmen. Their hotel, the Seaview, was the area's first, and John and his wife ran it, in addition to the store and telegraph office. The year 1885 saw another property added to the Hirst empire, the Rod and Gun Hotel, which became a popular community gathering place.

The First Nations peoples named the settlement Pentelch, and early white settlers simply called it "The River," noting its proximity to the Englishman River. Later it was No Bridge Junction when the Esquimalt and Nanaimo Railway made its first stop in 1910. Today, it is Parksville.

The name stems from Nelson Parks, the area's first postmaster, who was appointed April 2, 1886. Parks and his wife had come to the valley in 1884, living on the Hirst property and working at the farm, before starting their own spread. The first post office was a shack adjacent to Parks' plantings, and signs often directed folks: "Out in field. Go to the west fence and holler." When mail arrived for people living on nearby Lasqueti Island, Parks ignited a beach bonfire to signal that someone had to make the six kilometre row across the channel to fetch the post.

There was no road to Nanaimo until 1886. Prior to this time, mail, travellers, and supplies came by paddle steamer from Victoria, disembarked at Beaver Creek, and from there, astride horses or atop oxen-drawn wagons, lumbered along the rough pioneer roads threading from hamlet to homestead. Stagecoach service arrived shortly after the road was built, connecting the many small communities. Parksville became the halfway point between Nanaimo and Port Alberni, and the Halfway House remained in service until the arrival of the E&N Railway.

Land development began in the late 1880s, and by the early 1900s merchants and entrepreneurs were adding new hotels, golf links, and beach houses. One company, McPherson and Fullerton, focused on the development of the Qualicum Beach townsite, and soon there were stores and a post office, butcher shop, bakery, and garage. A Salvation Army settlement at Coombs brought weekend shoppers and visitors.

The war years slowed Oceanside's growth, though a convalescent home was located in the Qualicum Beach area. Growth returned in the 1950s as vacationers discovered the relaxing diversions the region offered. Travellers continue to favour Oceanside for its attractions, its recreational opportunities, and its relaxing resort ambience. Of late, many retirees have also found Oceanside's temperate weather and urban amenities to their liking.

Robert Dunsmuir Coal Baron

Robert Dunsmuir, a young Scottish engineer, arrived on Vancouver Island in 1851 as an employee of the Hudson's Bay Company. In 1869, Dunsmuir came upon a rich coal deposit at Wellington, near Nanaimo. Two years later he formed a partnership with naval officers in order to exploit the discovery. Coal was hauled to Departure Bay and then shipped as far south as San Francisco. Business expanded, and in 1883 Dunsmuir bought out his last remaining partner. The operation included 150 coal wagons, 16 kilometres of rail-track, five locomotives and more than 500 men.

With the company reincorporated as Robert Dunsmuir and Sons Limited, Dunsmuir's sons Alex and James took on operational duties to further its growth. By 1880, the Wellington mines were churning out nearly 200,000 tonnes of coal. Union Bay fields opened, followed by the mid-1890s unearthing of massive coal deposits at the Extension Mine near Nanaimo. Shipping facilities and worker dormitories were set up at Oyster Harbour, renamed Ladysmith by James Dunsmuir. By 1928, the company Dunsmuir had founded held a virtual monopoly on Vancouver Island coal mining.

The failure of world markets after the 1929 stock market crash drastically reduced demand for coal. It was no longer the fuel of the future. Smaller scale mining operations continued until the 1950s.

Nanaimo District Museum
100 Cameron Road; Piper's
Park near Harbour Park Mall
250-753-1821
Web: ndmuseum@nanaimo.
museum.bc.ca/ndm
Open daily, May-September;
Tuesday to Saturday,
October-April
Admission charged
To stroll through the Nanaimo District Museum is to walk among a small but satisfying assemblage of fascinating installations — "Old Town," "Chinatown Revisited," and replicas of a coal mine and a miner's cottage — which reveal snippets of the city's rich cultural legacy. Of special note is "From Our Elders' Elders," an exhibit created with the assistance of the Snuneymuxw that displays many artifacts repatriated from collections across the globe, in addition to finds from a 2000-year-old village site at Departure Bay. Also accessible to the public is the museum's collection of more than 3000 historical photos.

The Bastion
Bastion and Front Streets
250-753-1821
Open daily, June-September
Admission charged
At one time the Bastion was just that, a fortification attached to the Hudson's Bay Company fort. Over the years it served not only as a fort, but also as an office and store, jail, and meeting house. Today, it is the only remaining example of this kind of defense structure in North America. What it protects today is not only its collection of 1850-80 insignia, guns, military archives, and personal mementos, but also a bit of colourful tradition. Each day during summer, the Bastion is the site of the Noon Gun ceremony, in which Bastion guardsmen garbed in period attire are piped by a bagpiper to a fully restored 19th-century cannon, where, after considerable preparation, a single volley is fired precisely at the stroke of 12 pm. See also the Nanaimo Heritage Walks box.

Nanaimo Heritage Walks
Begins at the Bastion
Self-guided walk; pick up
map at Nanaimo Tourism
Info Centre
This short walk through Naniamo's historic district takes in a number of buildings and sites including the 1896 Nanaimo Courthouse, the 1889 Palace Hotel, and a 1900s-style pharmacy opened in 1985 in the vintage 1909 Dakin Building. See also the Nanaimo Heritage Walks box.

Malaspina University-College
900 5th Street
250-753-3245
www.mala.bc.ca
Admission free
A comely campus situated on 67 hectares that slope down the lower flanks of Mt. Benson, Malaspina University-College is well worth a visit to enjoy its view across Nanaimo Harbour and beyond to the Strait of Georgia.

Nanaimo Art Gallery
At Malaspina University-College
250-755-8790
www.mala.bc.ca/~nag/nag.htm
Open Monday to Saturday
Admission free
and

Nanaimo Art Gallery Downtown
150 Commercial Street
250-754-1750
Open Tuesday to Saturday
Admission free
Nanaimo's public art gallery at Malaspina University-College, along with its downtown extension, presents the work of local and international artists. The permanent collection at Malaspina University-College emphasizes work by contemporary Canadian artists. At the downtown location, works in a variety of media by Vancouver Island and Gulf Islands artists are for sale. The Nanaimo Art Gallery is also responsible for producing the 300 or so street banners that fly from lampposts along city streets from May to September. A guide to the Festival of Banners is available at the Nanaimo Tourism Info Centre.

Vancouver Island Military Museum
Rutherford Village Mall; five
kilometres north of city centre
250-756-2554
Open Monday to Saturday
Admission free
Operated by the Vancouver Island Military Museum Society, the small museum showcases memorabilia relating to Canada's military past, including a Victoria Cross Memorial Room dedicated to the memory of the 94 Canadians who have been awarded the famous medal of valour.

Oceanside
Oceanside Tourism Association
PO Box 374
Qualicum Beach BC V9K 1S9
250-752-2388
888-799-3222
www.oceansidetourism.com
Stretching along Highway 19A between Nanoose Bay and Lighthouse Country, Oceanside was once a country escape for the well-off upper classes of

Nanaimo Heritage Walks

❷ Globe Hotel
25 Front Street
The Globe Hotel has been in continuous operation since 188[?] however the origina[l] 1887 structure hous[es] a Nanaimo marble works. Take note of [?] Second Empire detai[l] such as the mansard roof and arched third-floor dorm[er] The multi-coloured tilework acros[s] the ground floor front is Art Dec[o] from a later remodel.

❶ The Bastion
98 Front Street
Fort Colvile (as the settlement was originally known) was dedicated to exploiting the nearby coalfields, and in 1853 the Hudson's Bay Company constructed a fort to facilitate trade in the area. The Bastion is the only surviving fortified tower of the many built along the coast. Built of hand-hewn logs, it was originally located on the other side of the street. Behind the Bastion is the location where the Princess Royal Pioneers landed in 1854 after a six-month voyage around Cape Horn from Great Britain.

❸ Nanaimo Court House
31-35 Front Street
Noted architect Francis Rattenbury conceived this Richardsonian Romanesque edifice built in 1895. Its rough-dressed ashlar masonry, sandstone facing, and prominent round arched openings are typical of the popular style. The original slate roof with its copper flashing is still in place, as are the ornate leaded stained and painted glass windows.

❹ St. Paul's Anglican Church
100 Chapel Street
St. Paul's Anglican Church sits on land bequeathed by the Hudson's Bay Company in 1859. The grant stipulated that the property would revert to the Company if the church ever ceased operation, and hence this is the third church on this site. The Lord Bishop of London laid the cornerstone for the present concrete structure in 1931. Its Gothic Revival styling is distinguished by stained glass windows and ornamental pre-cast concrete trim.

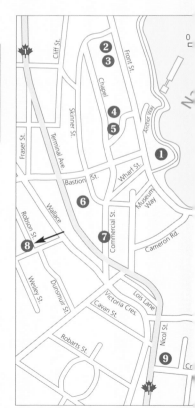

Nanaimo Heritage Walks

⑤ Great National Land Building
5-17 Church Street
The Classic Revival styled Great National Land Building was originally built as the Bank of Commerce in 1914 during Nanaimo's boom years. The design and placement of the building creates a dramatic anchor to the north end of Commercial Street.

⑥ Palace Hotel
275 Skinner Street
Built in 1889, the Palace Hotel was one of the first brick hotels in Nanaimo. An arcaded wooden balcony once ran across the front facade, and two of the second-floor windows were originally doors leading to the balcony. Yet these and other alterations over time haven't totally obscured the Victorian character of the Palace. Renovations in 1985 revealed the swagged, painted wall sign, which was faithfully repainted.

⑦ Commercial Street
Many historic buildings line Commercial Street; in the 1860s it was Nanaimo's principal transportation link, taking coal from Park Head Slope to ships moored at the

foot of Wharf Street. Edwardian is the overall style of the Van Houten Block at 16 Commercial Street (1909), the Hirst Block, later the Dakin Block, at 93-99 Commercial Street (1911) and the Rogers Block at 83-87 Commercial Street. The Hall Block at 37-45 Commercial Street (1925) follows a Classic Revival styling, seen in corbelled brickwork and projecting metal cornice. Dr. G.A.B. Hall was mayor of Nanaimo from 1930 to 1931.

⑧ Esquimalt and Nanaimo Railway Station
321 Selby Street
The first train arrived at Nanaimo in 1886. In attendance were Canada's first prime minister, Sir John A. Macdonald, and the railway's builder, Robert Dunsmuir. Completion of the railway spurred the development of Fitzwilliam Street. The current structure dates from 1920.

⑨ Nanaimo Fire Hall #2
34 Nicol Street
Nanaimo's first fire hall was built at the corner of Wharf and Commercial streets in 1879. A fire destroyed the hall in 1894. Fire Hall #2 was already under construction, however, and when it was completed, the city's fire department moved there.

the 19th century. Nowadays it is far more diverse and popular for family outings and romantic getaways. Little wonder — Oceanside offers miles upon miles of ocean and mountain vistas along sandy beaches. Add to this great golf courses, lush parkland, and charming communities known for their hospitality, fine dining, great arts and crafts shopping, and fun festivals and events.

The Oceanside Route, the original coastal Highway 19A strings together several of the more popular resort areas from Nanoose Bay in the south to Deep Bay in the north. Look for the official Oceanside Route "starfish" signs pointing the way. You can set a leisurely pace, off the beaten track, and take detours to explore the headwaters of the Englishman River, French Creek, and the Big and Little Qualicum Rivers, flowing down from Mt. Arrowsmith and other peaks. The distance from ocean to alpine is only 18 kilometres.

Diving Into Vancouver Island ... Waters

The accolades British Columbia's scuba diving has received explain why this western Canadian destination is increasingly seen as one the world's top locales for the sport. British Columbia was lauded in 2001 by Rodale's *Scuba Diving Magazine*, finishing first in 8 out of 14 categories: Best Destination, Best Value, Healthiest Marine Environment, and on and on.

On Vancouver Island, Nanaimo makes an ideal base from which to explore the area's underwater realm. The city holds the largest fleet of dive charter boats; there are also numerous dive stores and diver-friendly accommodations. Add to this many, many nearby dive locations. Here are some of the favourites:

Dodd Narrows
Consistently rated as one of BC's top ten dive spots, the swift currents of Dodd Narrows deliver marine life galore only five nautical miles southeast of Nanaimo. The sheer vertical drops off the Mudge Island side are home to sea anemone, Puget Sound king crab, cod, and rockfish, plus Orange Cup corals. Steller's sea lions are sometimes encountered during the winter months, and it's a special treat watching them chase salmon in the tidal stream.

HMCS Saskatchewan
Scuttled on June 14, 1997, the 114-metre-long by 12-metre-wide ship has already become a marvellous artificial reef. Urchins, anemones, starfish, wolf eels, and the occasional octopus gather along with dozens of other fish. Dive depths range from 16 metres to over 40 metres, so it's fine for an intermediate dive and excellent for advanced divers with experience and skill.

Breakwater Island
The rocky bench and vertical shelf dropping 26 metres support a range of life including perch and tubeworms clustered in the bull kelp beds. Resident wolf eels are quite camera friendly.

Snake Island
Harbour seals live here, and divers have excellent chances to observe their grace and speed while underwater. Snake Wall, on the west side of the island, extends out 15 metres, then drops away some 60 metres. White plumose anemones, plus boot and cloud sponges are some of the marine life present.

Four Fathom Reef
The top of an underwater pinnacle rising here helps create a renowned spawning locale for rockfish, greenling, lingcod, and spiny pink scallops. The giant Pacific octopus also dwells here, and during the daytime the octopi are often away from their dens and active.

Far to the south, Race Rocks off the coast south of Victoria is a popular dive spot, but the strong currents here make it advisable to book a knowledgeable guide for any outing. Ogden Point Breakwater and Ten Mile Point are also good dive sites, and out from Sidney are two artificial reefs, the *G.B. Church* (1991) and HMCS *MacKenzie* (1995). Heading to the Pacific Rim on the west coast of the Island, diving services are available in Port Alberni, Bamfield, Tofino, and Tahsis. The calm fiords and inlets are the big draw here. Hornby Island, accessible from the east coast, sports year-round diving, offering chances to see wolf eels, octopus, sea lions, and, certainly during the summer, the large six-gill sharks. Farther north, Discovery Pass off Campbell River has strong currents — guides are recommended. HMCS *Columbia*, scuttled off Maud Island in 1996, is a key attraction. Go far north to Port McNeill and Port Hardy for incredible cold-water diving.

Craig Heritage Park is comprised of relocated historic buildings.

Parksville's beaches are among the island's best.

Once a sleepy stop on the Island Highway, this burgeoning resort community and essence of "Canada's Riviera" bears the name of its first postmaster, Nelson Parks, who began shuffling mail here in 1886. Growth over the last 20 years has transformed the village so that it is now home to some of Vancouver Island's most sought after commercial and residential real estate. Indeed, the area's population has increased nearly three-fold in the last two decades, and predictions are that it will double again over the next 15 years.

Blame its popularity on its long stretches of sandy beach, which during ebbing tides can reveal up to a kilometre of shoreline. Crescent-shaped Community Park alone has nearly 7.5 kilometres of beach and tidal flats. On warm, sunny days these wide expanses of sand interspersed with shallow pools are irresistible to vacationing families. The three-week August Parksville Beach Festival is one of the Island's favourite events, especially the annual Canadian Open Sand Sculpture competition.

Craig Heritage Park
1245 East Island Highway; next to Info Centre
250-248-6966 summer;
250-248-3431 winter
Open daily, May-September
Admission charged
A sense of nostalgia is easily evoked at Craig Heritage Park, which features among its collection of historic buildings rescued from the surrounding area such gems as a 1942 fire hall complete with a 1946 fire truck; the Duncan McMillan House, a log construction typical of the region; the log-and-timber French Creek post

Lantzville
Population: 408
This small seaside community is best known for its wintering population of sea lions — as many as 400 in residence some years. Look for them lolling about the nearby Ada Islands off Lantzville's waterfront.

Nanoose Bay
Population: 5000
North of Nanaimo, this peninsula of undulating terrain — forested and developed with homes and cottages, resort enclaves, and an accompanying marina — provides inviting diversions in spite of the fact that the Canadian Forces Maritime Experimental and Test Ranges are located here, and it's not unusual to spy large military vessels on the water. At the test firing range is docked the famous "yellow submarine," used for torpedo practice.

Fairwinds Schooner Cove Resort serves as the launching point for a number of activities such as fishing, sailing, diving, and kayaking. Guided sightseeing trips to Jedediah Island Provincial Marine Park can also be booked. Fairwinds Golf and Country Club is one of the area's premier courses.

Parksville
Parksville Chamber of Commerce
PO Box 99
Parksville BC V9P 2G3
Info Centre: Intersection of Highway 19 and Highway 19A; next to Craig Heritage Centre
250-248-3613
www.chamber.parksville.bc.ca
Population: 10,613

131

Qualicum College Inn

The Qualicum Heritage Inn was once a private boarding school.

Quaint and looking as if it was just transported from the English countryside, the 70-room Qualicum Heritage Inn did indeed begin as a school, specifically a private boarding school for boys.

Ivan Knight founded the institution in 1935 and served as its headmaster until 1970, at which time it was sold, renovated, and reopened as Qualicum College Inn.

While hospitality is the inn's cornerstone today, in its time as a boy's school the "Seven Cs" were the daily dictum: Christianity, Classics, Cricket, Cadet Corps, Cold Baths, Courtesy, and Corporal Punishment. The last of these was meted out by a whipping cane, still close at hand in the inn's lobby.

Indeed, vestiges of the inn's good ol' schooldays are evident throughout the property. Look to the lobby floor at the entrance to see inlaid ceramic tiles depicting the school crest and Latin motto, *Sequere Lucem*, "Seek the Truth." The Old Boys Gallery off the lobby displays class pictures in chronological order from 1935 to 1970. College Pub, at one time the school gymnasium, is dressed for the occasion, decorated with the school's actual trophies and awards, plus vintage sporting equipment. The third and fourth floors, once dormitories, are now comfy guestrooms. Room 341 was the headmaster's room. In 1974 the original building was expanded with the addition of the Oxford Wing, and 1984 saw the completion of the Cambridge Wing and new dining facilities.

Over the years a number of guests and staff have reported various psychic phenomenon — ghosts, if you will — occurring at the inn. Experiences have run the ethereal spectrum from amusement to cautious wariness: the annoying sounds of boys running down the halls, the startling slamming of doors, the inexplicable whimpering of an adolescent boy, lights and TVs turning themselves off and on automatically.

Disturbing or charming? It seems patrons don't mind; the inn has an exceptionally high guest return rate.

Qualicum Heritage Inn
427 College Road
Qualicum Beach BC V9K 2G4
800-663-7306
250-752-9262
www.qualicumheritgaeinn.com

office; and the petite and pretty 1911-1912 Knox United Heritage Church. The tiny chapel is still a popular place for weddings. The park also houses pioneer and native artifacts as well as newspaper and photographic archives.

Paradise Adventure Mini-Golf
375 West Island Highway
250-248-6612
Open daily, March to October
Admission charged
Kids of all ages — from six to 96 — love the two 18-hole mini-golf courses fitted into an extravaganza of fantasy, complete with castles, moats and bumper boats. The house-size Old Woman's Shoe is always popular for that youngster's birthday party.

St. Ann's Anglican Church
Church Road; left off Wembley Road
250-248-3114
Admission free
St. Ann's Anglican Church dates from 1894 and is one of Vancouver Island's oldest pioneer places of worship.

French Creek

French Creek is small but industrious, featuring a large dock, a marina, and a Coast Guard station, as well as a campground and some rental cabins. Fishers will find the place welcoming as there is good fishing from the beach at French Creek's mouth, and a number of fishing charter outfits are based here. Many commercial fishing boats dock here too, and consequently it's an excellent place to buy just-caught seafood right from the crews. The passenger-only ferry to Lasqueti Island leaves from here.

Milner Gardens & Woodland

Milner Gardens & Woodlands shelter one of Vancouver Island's most notable estates.

The former estate of Ray and Veronica Milner outside Qualicum Beach, Milner Gardens & Woodland protects an unparallelled collection of gardens set amid a stand of old-growth Douglas fir. The 28 hectares of woodlands and gardens shelter a heritage home and reward garden lovers with one of Vancouver Island's best historical and horticultural diversions.

Horatio "Ray" Milner purchased the property in 1937 as an island escape from his successful business life. He was the chair and director of several companies, the lead partner in the law firm of Milner and Steer, and a founding director of Canadian Utilities. He and his first wife, Rina, began the gardens. His second wife, Veronica, whom he married after Rina's passing in 1952, transformed the flowerbeds and plantings into an artist's retreat.

Born, reared, and married into the British aristocracy, Veronica Fitzgerald, was the widow of Desmond Fitzgerald, 28th Knight of Glin, County Limerick, Ireland. On her mother's side she could list relatives such as Prime Minister Sir Winston Churchill, the First Duke of Marlborough, and consequently even the late Diana, Princess of Wales. Prince Charles and Princess Diana visited the Milner estate in 1986, as did Queen Elizabeth and Prince Philip, who stayed for three days in 1987.

Veronica Milner viewed her garden as a single living organism, a place of bucolic and beguiling natural beauty and tranquility. Its design follows her artistic sentiments for texture, colour, and form amid myriad seasonal variations — essentially domesticated wildness.

Malaspina University-College acquired the estate in 1996. Its goal is to preserve the property in perpetuity for education and the community's benefit in memory of the Milners. Hence, the institution has undertaken a number of restoration projects to reclaim the garden's glory.

Today's visitor may follow the Forest Trail to wander beneath the canopy of a largely undisturbed old-growth forest of Douglas fir, western red cedar, and grand fir. As visitors emerge from the woodland, groves of heritage rhododendron — nearly 500 varieties — await. Plantings of blue-green hosta and lace-cape hydrangea peek out here and there, as do exotic trees, many of which were acquired by Ray and Veronica on trips abroad. They include Katsura, Davidia, Stewartia, and various maples, birches, beeches, and redwoods.

Farther on, the gardens become more formal with lawns and edge plantings, flowerbeds, and the Food Garden planted with fruits, vines, and root crops. At the centre is the estate house, with marvellous views of the Strait of Georgia and of the Coast Mountains on the BC mainland. Designed and constructed between 1928 and 1931 for General Noel Money, a local sportsman and businessman, the gabled house, festooned with wisteria, features touches drawn from the architecture of Ceylonese tea plantation homes; for example, all bedrooms are master suites with garden access. The covered veranda, which offers garden and ocean views, functions as an outdoor living room, and there is also a swimming pool, pool house, tennis court, and gardener's cottage.

Veronica Milner was an accomplished painter, and she found endless artistic motivation here for her brilliantly coloured oils and pastels, many of which still grace the walls of her one-time home. Indeed, inspiration comes easily here.
Milner Gardens & Woodland
2179 West Island Highway
Qualicum Beach BC V9K 1G1
250-752-6152
www.milnergardens.mala.cb.ca

Lasqueti Island

Population: 300

Paddlers favour lovely Lasqueti Island for its sheltered coves, bays, inlets, and tiny neighbouring isles. Along with the picturesque terrain comes a chance to see turkey vultures and eagles, river otters and seals, and even the occasional whale. Mountain bikers also like the 68-square-kilometre, relatively undeveloped locale for its gravelly backroads and for Squitty Bay Provincial Park at the island's eastern end. False Bay is Lasqueti's town centre, with a marina and general store, plus some accommodations. Foot-passenger-only ferries dock here, arriving from and departing to the French Creek terminal. False Bay is also a gateway to Jedediah Island Provincial Marine Park, accessible from here by private boat or charter.

Arrowsmith / Coombs Country: Errington, Coombs, Mt. Arrowsmith

Parksville Chamber of Commerce
PO Box 99
Parksville BC V9P 2G3
250-248-3613
www.chamber.parksville.bc.ca
Population: 1000

Backroads meander through Arrowsmith / Coombs Country, and the rural rambles reward anyone with a smidgen of

Central Island Parks & Recreation

Morrell Wildlife Sanctuary
Nanaimo Lakes and Dogwood roads, Nanaimo
250-753-5811
111.5 hectares / day use
Features beaver habitat, ponds, and rocky outcroppings with 11.5 kilometres of walking trails and interpretive self-guided walks.

Biggs and Jack Point Parks
Duke Point Ferry Terminal; 4.5 kilometres from Highway 1 / day use
Follow the signs to the Duke Point Ferry Terminal to experience this tiny park with views of the Nanaimo River Estuary, Protection Island, Gabriola Island, and the Northumberland Channel. Jack Point is 2.5 kilometres from the parking lot, over the bluff via stairs and boardwalks.

Petroglyph Provincial Park
Highway 1; three kilometres south of Nanaimo
Two hectares / day use
Local First Nations heritage is clearly evident in the beautifully preserved 10,000-year-old carved images of wildlife seen on the rocks in this park

Maffeo-Sutton Park / Swy-a-lana Lagoon Park
Waterfront; downtown Nanaimo
Swy-a-Lana Lagoon's natural tidal flow creates a marine habitat relished by birdwatchers. Maffeo-Sutton Park, located across a pedestrian bridge, is the site for many local festivities and features playgrounds, picnic spots, a fishing pier, and game fields.

Nanaimo Parkway-Trailway
Between Aulds Road in the north and Chase River in the south, Nanaimo
This 20 kilometre paved network of trails is a dream for cyclists, walkers, and joggers. There are many access points and nature parks along the way including Buttertubs Marsh, Colliery Dam, Bowen Park, and the Harbourfront Walkway.

Newcastle Island Provincial Marine Park
In Nanaimo Harbour; accessible by passenger ferry
336 hectares / 18 campsites
This park has a rich cultural history in addition to its beaches and many walking trails. Over the years, Newcastle Island has been the site of a coal mine, a sandstone quarry, a Japanese herring saltery and cannery, and a resort owned by the Canadian Pacific Steamship Company.

Brant Goose Feeding Area
Highway 19A at Craig's Crossing
As many as 20,000 Brant geese come here in early April.

Mt. Arrowsmith Regional Park
South of Highway 4; 41 kilometres west of Parksville, then 27 kilometres of gravel road
See Oceanside spread out from Nanoose Bay to Deep Bay as you stand atop Mt. Arrowsmith (1817 metres) or Mt. Cokley (1616 metres). Hiking trails lead off into the alpine meadows and along the slopes.

Rathtrevor Beach Provincial Park
Highway 19A; three kilometres south of Parksville, at the mouth of the Englishman River
250-954-4600 or 800-689-9025 (reservations)
www.discovercamping.ca
347 hectares / 175 campsites
Only minutes from Parksville, a spectacular sandy beach, tidal pools, and forest walking trails await visitors. There are more than five kilometres of beach; at low tide it may be nearly a kilometre wide.

curiosity with wonderfully eclectic attractions and diversions, not least of which is the country market complete with rooftop goats. There are also many great opportunities for antiques shopping and studio browsing, as a number of artisans reside here. Plus, look for fun events at the Coombs rodeo grounds, from bronco bustin' to bluegrass festivals.

Errington

Occupying the crossroads of Errington and Grafton roads about two kilometres off Highway 4A, Errington is a small, quiet community with a general store, post office, and cafe.

North Island Wildlife Recovery Centre and Museum of Nature
1240 Leffler Road
250-248-8534
www.islandroots.com/wildlife
Open daily, April-October,

10 am-4 pm
Admission charged
This non-profit society is dedicated to the rehabilitation of injured birds and mammals, and people can adopt a patient — an eagle, an otter, or perhaps even an under-the-weather crow — to help offset the cost of care. Visitors peek in on whatever menagerie is needing care at the time, and they often get a rare look at animals seldom seen up close.

Central Island Parks & Recreation

Top Bridge Park
Highway 19A and Tuan Road, Parksville
250-248-5575 (Arrowsmith Mountain Cycle)
One of only three Mountain Bike Parks in BC. Trails range from easy to expert.

Jedediah Island Provincial Park
250-954-4600
243 hectares / no official campsites
Accessible via watercraft from French Creek or Lasqueti Island, this park was once a privately owned island. It has an old homestead, good sand beaches, and feral goats.

Heritage Forest of Qualicum Beach
East Crescent Road across from Memorial Golf Course, Qualicum Beach
250-752-6951
20 hectares / day use
Once private property, this 20 hectare preserve near downtown Qualicum Beach offers an opportunity to stroll through a rare stand of Vancouver Island east coast Douglas fir. Some of the towering trees date back 600 years.

Horne Lake Caves Provincial Park
(winner of BC's best Outdoor Natural Attractioin in 2002)

Horne Lake Road; take Highway 19 about 60 kilometres north from Nanaimo, then west 12 kilometres to entrance along gravel road
123 hectares / day use
Educational guided and self-guided tours reveal the park's fascinating caves, filled with karst formations and crystalline features. Guided tours include the Triple Cave Adventure, three caves in three hours; High Adventure, a five-hour challenging trek that includes basic rock climbing; and Underground Extreme, which features a rappel down the seven-storey-deep Rainbarrel. Self-exploration outings of the Horne Lake Main and Lower Caves are accessible year-round. None of the caves are lighted, so flashlights are the only source of illumination. Trails are rocky and uneven, and the caves are cool, making them difficult perhaps for the elderly or very young. Call 250-248-7829 for guided excursion reservations, or visit www.hornelake.com.

Spider Lake Provincial Park
Horne Lake Road; west off Highway 19, eight kilometres of gravel road to entrance
65 hectares / day use

Canoeing and swimming are the hallmarks of this park. No motorized watercraft are allowed, and there is a nice sandy beach.

Englishman River Falls Provincial Park
Errington Road; eight kilometres beyond Grafton Avenue
250-954-4600 or 800-689-9025 (reservations)
www.discovercamping.ca
97 hectares / 105 campsites
Close to Parksville and Qualicum Beach, this park features walking and hiking trails, mountain biking, freshwater fishing, and a nice swimming hole. Two spectacular waterfalls are set within the forest.

Little Qualicum Falls Provincial Park
Off Highway 4; 2.5 kilometres west of Highway 4A junction
250-954-4600 or 800-689-9025 (reservations)
440 hectares / 91 campsites
West of Parksville, riverside walking trails and picnic areas here are a treat, as is the playground area for youngsters. Some trails are also wheelchair accessible. Campsites are located where Cameron Lake enters the Little Qualicum River.

The Eagle Flight Cage measures 36 by 12 metres and is 12 metres high, the largest facility of its kind in Canada. Over the years the centre has successfully cared for, rehabilitated, and released hundreds of raptors, as well as many orphaned or injured black bears.

Coombs

Population: 840
The Old Country Market, complete with goats grazing atop its sod roof, says a lot about Coombs' eclectic nature. Founded in the early 1900s, the original community emerged from a Salvation Army program that resettled poor English families onto farmland. The Coombs General Store has been around since 1910. During the early 1960s and into the 1970s, Coombs blossomed with the arrival of new residents eager to experience a back-to-nature, hassle-free lifestyle. The 1980s and 1990s witnessed the arrival of numerous roadside attractions as Coombs became a popular stop for travellers heading to the west coast.

Although the construction of the inland Island Highway bypassed Coombs, travellers still find their way here to enjoy the laid-back atmosphere amidst a bit of carnival. The Coombs Emporium and Frontier Town features many novelty shops and a mini-golf course. Nearby are antique stores, an old-fashioned ice cream parlour, and even a tattoo artist's shop. Fresh vegetables and fruits direct from local orchards and farms ensure the Old Country Market is always busy, even without

St. Ann's Anglican Church is one of Vancouver Island's oldest places of worship.

the attraction of goats prancing across the roof.

Vancouver Island Butterfly World

Highway 4A; one kilometre west of Coombs
250-248-7026
Open daily, March-October
Admission charged
Similar to its sister location, Victoria Butterfly Gardens, Vancouver Island Butterfly World features hundreds of live, free-flying butterflies from across the globe. Exhibits also recount butterfly life from larvae to caterpillar to full-fledged winged wonder.

Little Qualicum Fish Hatchery

Melrose Road; off Highway 4, three kilometres west of Highway 4A
250-752-3231
Open daily
Admission free
From this viewing site it's possible (depending upon the season) to see several types of salmon.

Mt. Arrowsmith

With its profile dominating the skyline, 1812-metre-high Mt. Arrowsmith is the centrepiece of the Mt. Arrowsmith Biosphere Reserve. So designated in November 2000 by

the United Nation's Man and Biosphere Council, the reserve encompasses Mt. Cokely (1616 metres) and Mt. Moriarty as well, and the watersheds flowing into the Strait of Georgia, Nanoose Bay, and the Ballenas / Winchelsea islands archipelago. The reserve, while including parkland and other protected natural area, also takes in the outskirts of Nanaimo and the communities of Parksville and Qualicum Beach — in an attempt to seek a balance between conservation and sustainable resource use.

The Mt. Arrowsmith Biosphere Reserve is one of two on Vancouver Island; the other is the Clayoquot Sound Biosphere Reserve on the west coast. Canada has seven UNESCO biosphere sites, and there are a total of 391 in 94 countries worldwide.

Qualicum Beach

Qualicum Beach Visitor Info Centre

2711 West Island Highway (marked by a totem pole on the beach side of Highway 19A)
Qualicum Beach BC V9K 2C4
250-752-9532
www.qualicum.bc.ca

Population: 7477

Resort and retirement stroll hand-in-hand as pedestrian-friendly Qualicum Beach is popular with both retirees and vacationers. It's the pleasant climate, the expansive sand and gravel beaches, and the quiet pace of the pretty downtown that conspire to make this town charming. Amble the Art Walk and you will come across not only a bounty of galleries, but also boutiques, shops, bookstores, and any number of eateries and cafes. The quaint train station, at mile 101 from Victoria, dates from 1913 and still greets many sightseers arriving on the Esquimalt and Nanaimo Railway. Hanging flower-baskets bursting with petunias line the walkway, as do sculptures and benches, creating a thoroughly salubrious ambience. Notice the absence of chain stores and big-brand mall shops. Enlightened city planners have made sure Qualicum Beach's village centre remains small-town cute and friendly by banning franchises.

The Old School House Gallery and Art Centre
122 Fern Road West; Box 791
250-752-6133
E-mail: tosh@island.net
Open daily, July-September;
Monday to Saturday,
October-June
Admission free
Located in this non-profit cultural enclave are studios and galleries for a number of local sculptors, painters, watercolourists, printmakers, woodcarvers, jewellers, and photographers. Workshops and working demonstrations by the artists create a unique shopping / educational envi-

Central Island Festivals & Events

APRIL
Annual Brant Festival
Various venues
Celebrates the return of 20,000 Brant geese with exhibits, talks, and viewing.

MAY–SEPTEMBER
Errington and Qualicum Beach Farmers' Markets
Errington and Qualicum Beach
Saturday mornings people fill their market baskets with local homemade preserves, honey, and organic produce.

MAY
Hammerfest
Englishman River Falls Provincial Park
Mountain biking competitions, downhill and cross-country; 600 cyclists.
Mt. Arrowsmith Rhododendron Society Garden Tour
Various venues
Visits 12 of the most beautiful mid-Island gardens.

July–August
Bard to Broadway. Enjoy live theatre under a canvas tent.

JULY
Parksville Art in the Street
Memorial Avenue, Parksville
Arts and crafts displays, exhibits, and demonstrations.
Coombs Arts & Crafts Fair
Coombs. Juried show of BC artists including candlemaking, jewellery, and pottery.
Coombs Rodeo
Coombs Rodeo Grounds
Annual Western-style get-together with rodeo events and dances.
St. Mark's Flea Market
Memorial Avenue, Parksville
Giant outdoor flea market with something for everyone.
Grand Prix D'art

Artist race to complete their art work based on qualicum scenes.

AUGUST
French Creek Fishing Festival
French Creek Marina
Family event with several kids' competitions.
Coombs Country Bluegrass Festival
Coombs Rodeo Grounds
Bluegrass musicians and fans gather for down-home tunes.
World Croquet Championship
Parksville Community Park
Beginner to senior events; nine-wicket croquet in teams of three.
Parksville Beach Festival
Parksville Beach
Three weeks of family-oriented activities including an international sand sculpture contest.
Coombs Fall Fair
Coombs Fair Ground
Since 1913, the area's salute to rural summertime living with 4H displays and cooking competitions.
"Just for the Heck of it, No Reason at All" Mid-Summer Nights Parade
Coombs
Starts at the Rodeo Grounds and finishes at the Fair Ground. Check out the "Chicken Chucking Contest," using rubber chickens.

SEPTEMBER
Crabfest
Community Park, Parksville
Annual family feast of whole fresh crab and all the fixins'.

DECEMBER
Carol Ships Night
Deep Bay Marina
Illuminated carol ships sail the harbour.

ronment. Appropriately, the original building was built in 1912 and was where several generations of Qualicum Beach children went to school. After saving it from the wrecker's ball in 1985, the community banded together to renovate the structure and open it again as a learning centre — The Old School House, or simply "TOSH" for short.

Qualicum Beach Historical and Museum Society
587 Beach Road
250-752-5533
Open Tuesday to Sunday, May-September, 10 am-4 pm
Admission charged
Stroll through the Qualicum Beach Museum to explore the development of the area through artifacts and photographs. The name Qualicum, you'll learn, comes from the Pentlatch people's word for chum salmon, *squal-li.* Sometimes, when they're not on travelling exhibition, the Ice Age remains of the Qualicum Beach Walrus, "Rambling Rosie," estimated at 70,000 years old, are on view. Step across to the 1929 powerhouse building to plug into the history of electricity on Vancouver Island: notably an operational Vivian Diesel Engine and exhibits on early hydroelectricity.

Vancouver Island Paleontological Museum
587 Beach Road
250-752-9810
Open Tuesday to Sunday, May-September, 10 am-4 pm
Admission charged
Among the interesting collection of fossils from across Vancouver Island is a replica of "Rambling Rosie," more scientifically known

French Creek features a large dock, marina, and a Coast Guard station.

as *Odebemus romarus,* an example of an adult female walrus some 70,000 years old. Rambling Rosie was unearthed north of Qualicum Beach in 1979 and quickly became famous as one of the world's best-preserved skeletons of an Ice Age walrus.

Milner Gardens & Woodland
2179 West Island Highway
250-752-8573
www.milnergardens.mala.bc.ca
Open Thursday to Sunday, April-October
Admission charged
Easily one of Vancouver Island's most precious gardens, this 28 hectare site was once the home of Ray and Veronica Milner, wealthy philanthropists and passionate gardeners. (Veronica, incidentally, was related to Queen Elizabeth II of England.) The former estate and gardens are now overseen by Malaspina University-College, which is restoring the wondrous rhododendrons and other exotic plantings that the Milners favoured. See the Milner Gardens & Woodland box.

Heritage Forest of Qualicum Beach
East Crescent Road; entrance across from Memorial

Golf Club
Open daily, dawn to dusk
Admission free
Once private property, this 20 hectare preserve near downtown Qualicum Beach offers an opportunity to stroll through a rare stand of Vancouver Island east coast Douglas fir. Some of the towering trees date back 600 years.

Lighthouse Country: Qualicum Bay, Deep Bay, Bowser, and Fanny Bay
Qualicum Beach Visitor Info Centre
2711 West Island Highway
Qualicum Beach BC V9K 2C4
Phone: 250-752-9532
Web: www.qualicum.bc.ca
Between the lighthouse located to the south on Sisters Island and the one on Chrome Island to the north off Denman sit a collection of small communities that epitomize the seaside village lifestyle. Waterborne adventures are easily come by, especially fishing and kayaking.

Deep Bay
Sheltering a tiny fishing resort, Deep Bay will delight fishers.

Qualicum Bay

Not to be confused with Qualicum Beach, the tiny community of Qualicum Bay offers pleasant shorelines and limited services.

Big Qualicum River Fisheries Project

Off Highway 19A, go west just south of Big Qualicum River Bridge
250-757-8412
Open daily, dawn to dusk
Admission free

This hatchery sees some 100,000 salmon return each year, producing millions of spawn. Educational displays along a self-guided walking path tell the story and explain the counting fences, fish ladders, holding ponds, spawning channels, rearing channels, incubation units, and fry-marking units where fish have nose tags inserted so scientists can track their life cycles.

Qualicm Beach's village centre remains small-town charming by banning franchises.

Central Island Tee Time

Fairwinds Golf and Country Club
3730 Fairwinds Drive
Nanoose Bay, BC
888- 781-2777
250-468-7666
Eighteen holes
www.fairwinds.bc.ca

Morningstar International Golf Course
525 Lowry's Road
Qualicum Beach, BC
800-567-1320
250-248-8161
Eighteen holes
www.morningstar.bc.ca

Eaglecrest Golf Club
2035 West Island Highway;
2.5 kilometres south of
Qualicum Beach
Qualicum Beach, BC
800-567-1320
250-752-6311

www.eaglecrest.bc.ca
Eighteen holes

Glengarry Golf Links
1025 Qualicum Road
Qualicum Beach, BC
866-752-8787
250-752-8786
www.glengarrygolf.com
Eighteen holes

Arrowsmith Golf and Country Club
2250 Fowler Road
Qualicum Beach, BC
250-752-9727
www.golfarrowsmith.com
Eighteen holes

Qualicum Beach Memorial Golf Club
115 Crescent Road West
Qualicum Beach, BC
250-752-6312
Nine holes

Bowser

Population: 130
Named for William John Bowser, British Columbia

premier from 1915 to 1916, Bowser and the Bowser Hotel briefly flickered into the limelight in the 1930s, made famous by the pooch that served beer to patrons. Of note too is the Cola Diner at the Kwalikum Beaver Resort, four kilometres south of Bowser. Look for the diner's giant Marilyn Monroe mural, and stop to see a half-century of cola collectibles.

Fanny Bay

Population: 110
Hugging the shores of Baynes Sound, Fanny Bay is famous for its oysters, though its namesake, "Fanny," is a mystery. Her identity is lost in time, perhaps known only to Captain G.H. Richards, who surveyed the area in the 1860s. The Fanny Bay Conservation Area is south of town, offering trails through marshland and tidal mudflats alive with songbirds and shorebirds.

The Pacific Rim

Brady's Beach outside Bamfield typifies the sandy allure of Vancouver Island's west coast.

Stretching along Vancouver Island's western coastline, the Pacific Rim region is almost a world unto itself. Nowhere else on Vancouver Island is the effect of the ocean more prevalent; indeed, it is the very reason to visit. The mighty swells of the Pacific Ocean keep the summers mild and the winters enthrallingly stormy. The Alberni Valley and Port Alberni serve as the gateway to the Pacific Rim. A venerable "Salmon Capital of the World," Port Alberni's outstanding fishing opportunities draw anglers. Each year hundreds of thousands of salmon migrate up the Alberni Inlet and the Somass and Stamp river systems; some chinook tip the scales at over 25 kilograms. Travellers of all interests will like the Alberni Valley's peerless diversions vintage sawmills and trains, excursions along the Alberni Inlet aboard the refitted packet freighters MV *Lady Rose* or MV *Frances Barkley*, and forestry tours, to name a handful.

Farther west, magnificent Pacific Rim National Park Reserve is the destination for nearly all visitors. A spectacular nature preserve of coastal rain forest and offshore islands, the

Pacific Rim Recommendations

- Take in Port Alberni's historical attractions, especially the Alberni Pacific Railway and McLean Mill National Historic Site.
- Hop aboard the MV *Lady Rose* or the MV *Frances Barkley* for exciting excursions into the Alberni Inlet and Barkley Sound.
- Drive out to Sproat Lake to see the Martin Mars Water Bombers, the world's largest aircraft used to fight forest fires.
- Take a forestry tour sponsored by the Alberni Forest Information Centre located in Port Alberni.
- In Ucluelet, take an easy walk on the wild side at the Wild Pacific Trail, a five kilometre loop skirting the rugged cliffs of Amphitrite Point.
- Dawdle a day or two in Tofino, taking in the pretty town and exploring its natural recreation options; the day trip to Hot Springs Cove is one of Vancouver Island's most popular outings.

Pleasure crafts line the docks at Port Alberni's marina.

park is divided into three units: Long Beach, the Broken Group Islands, and the West Coast Trail. Each offers its unique environment and natural pursuits, from hardcore wilderness trekking to easygoing beachcombing.

South of the park sits Ucluelet, at the entrance to Barkley Sound and the Broken Group Islands. Tiny and friendly Ucluelet won't disappoint wildlife enthusiasts; whale watching is a specialty here, and it is one of the best Island locales to witness the 20,000-strong annual migration of Pacific gray whales between Alaska and Mexico's Baja Peninsula. Still farther south, remote and wonderful Bamfield at the mouth of the Alberni Inlet is a kayaker's dream-come-true. Great water and great hospitality are the hallmarks of this Barkley Sound community.

Anchoring the north end of Pacific Rim National Park is the resort town of Tofino, a gateway to Clayoquot Sound, which has been proclaimed a world biosphere reserve and certainly offers an impressive array of outdoor adventures.

Tofino's allure has long been recognized. This eclectic fishing village turned resort community has a seaside ambience that is charming and casual. Yet adventure is close at hand. Tofino is also home to a number of busy tour operators who can arrange whale watching excursions, fishing adventures, sailing sojourns, floatplane excursions, or scuba diving trips.

Port Alberni and the Alberni Valley

Alberni Valley Chamber of Commerce and Visitor Info Centre
RR2, Site 215, C-10
Port Alberni BC V9Y 7L6
250-724-6535
www.avcoc.com
Population: 19,329

Resembling a Norwegian fjord, with forested mountains rising 1000 metres on either side, the Alberni Inlet is a natural saltwater seaway cutting 40 kilometres northeast into Vancouver Island's west coast. The Island's longest inlet, it is 400 metres deep in some places. Originally named the Alberni Canal by Spanish

Cathedral Grove

Ancient Douglas fir

MacMillan Park (Cathedral Grove) sits astride Highway 4 at the end of Cameron Lake, 31 kilometres west of Parksville on the way to Port Alberni. It's hard to miss the road suddenly enters an impressive stand of massive trees, shrouding the terrain with their overarching canopy of branches. Cathedral Grove is an old-growth forest of western red cedar and Douglas fir, with some trees more than 800 years old.

The park was set aside by Harvey Reginald MacMillan, the first provincial chief forester (1912-15) and later founder of the forestry titan MacMillan Bloedel. In 1997 a severe wind whipped through the grove, felling several enormous trees. Now lying in the shadows, the decaying giants foster new forest life. Trails wind through the ecosystem, revealing "nurse logs," where saplings and shrubs sprout from the nutrient-rich felled trees.

Logging booms share Port Alberni's harbour with commercial and recreational fishers.

transport centre.

Logging the surrounding Beaufort Range and lumber milling are still mainstays of the busy town set on rolling hills swooping down to Harbour Quay. Indeed, the logging industry is celebrated here and has sprouted a tourist industry based on the town's heritage. Not only will visitors see logging-themed murals decorating downtown buildings, but curious travellers may also see the inner workings of mills on guided tours, take forestry and logging interpretive excursions, experience the olden days at historic logging mills, ride vintage steam trains, and hop aboard venerable working ships for excursions

explorers in 1791 to honor Lt. Colonel Pedro Alberni, the Canadian government changed its official name to "inlet" in 1931 to better reflect that it was a natural waterway.

In 1862, British Columbia's first industrial sawmill opened here to produce lumber and ship spars, and Port Alberni came of age as the west coast's logging and commercial

Pacific Rim National Park Reserve

Established in 1970, Pacific Rim National Park Reserve was Canada's first Pacific Coast reserve, and the first to include such a fundamental marine element more than 40 percent of the park. Cleaved into three distinct management units Long Beach, the Broken Group Islands, and the West Coast Trail the reserve encompasses a total area of 49,962 hectares. Coastline, islands, islets, and marine waters constitute its remarkably complex environment stretching for some 125 kilometres up Vancouver Island's west coast.

Long Beach

Long Beach is indeed long; nearly 20 kilometres of white-sand beach stretch along the shores of Wickaninnish Bay and Florencia Bay between Ucluelet and Tofino. In all, the unit contains 13,715 hectares, with nearly half the total on

land. Some 450,000 tourists visit annually, the majority coming from May to early October.

At the north end is Grice Bay, with its broad mudflats at low tide. Radar Hill (126 metres) offers excellent views of Meares Island and the Tofino Inlet. Long Beach itself (10 kilometres) and the Green Point Campground occupy the middle section. From the campground, a number of easy walks and hikes can be accessed that explore the rain forest, beach, and shoreline bogs. South of the campground and visible from Combers Beach are rocky outcroppings that are home to resident Steller's sea lions. Long Beach is also the only place on Canada's West Coast where long-board surfers can pursue their sport year-round.

The Wickaninnish Centre at Long Beach's southern end

houses a marine interpretive centre offering a treasure trove of information on the area's natural history. The park information centre is also located here. Guided walks and other activities depart from the centre. Long Beach has day-use areas, a campground, and access for the disabled.

The Broken Group Islands

Comprising more than 100 islets and rocky outcroppings, the Broken Group Islands are scattered across Barkley Sound between Ucluelet and Bamfield, the open Pacific Ocean and Alberni Inlet. Only accessible by watercraft, this is a remote and pristine haven for boaters and experienced kayakers.

In total, the unit contains 10,067 hectares, but only 1350 hectares are land. The largest islands Turtle, Effingham, Turret, Nettle, and Jaques are over 100 hectares in size and

McLean Mill National Historic Site

Alberni Pacific Railway

to Alberni Inlet logging camps and fishing resorts.

Skirted by the Somass River, and with many surrounding lakes, Port Alberni, as well as the Alberni Inlet, is well known for exciting fishing ventures casting for both freshwater and saltwater species. Fishing charters work year-round, plying the local waters for cod, halibut, and especially salmon. Drop by the Alberni Harbour Quay to talk to outfitters.

Also, don't miss the chance to drive out to nearby Sproat Lake, the base for the impressive Martin Mars Water Bombers, the world's largest aircraft used to fight forest fires. Each can haul a whop-

Pacific Rim National Park Reserve

support small forests of cedar, hemlock, and spruce. While the outer reaches of the island group bear the brunt of the Pacific Ocean's currents and tides, the myriad inner islands and channels offer protected waters. Kayaking and ocean canoeing are at their best here and account for nearly three-quarters of the marine traffic. There are rewards aplenty: wildlife watching including bald eagles, whales, and sea lions; natural wonders such as blowholes and rock formations; and cultural discoveries such as aboriginal fish traps and historic sealing sites.

The West Coast Trail

At 77 kilometres, the West Coast Trail, which skirts the rocky headlands and plunges through the rain forest between Bamfield and Port Renfrew, is wilderness hiking at its best. It is challenging, taking on average six days to complete, and should only be undertaken by experienced hikers. Access to the trail is capped at 8000 hikers per season (April to September), and reservations, plus a trail use permit, are required. There are three access points: Pachena Bay, south of Bamfield; Gordon River, outside Port Renfrew; and the Ditidaht First Nation Nitinat Lake Visitor Centre, the trail's midpoint. The latter is primarily for hikers who wish to tackle only half the trail's arduous length. Day-hike-only options from Bamfield include Cape Beale, Pachena Bay, Keeha Beach, Kichha Lake, and Pachena Lighthouse.

The West Coast Trail was hacked from the wild terrain in 1907 as a life-saving route for shipwrecked mariners. More than 50 ships have been dashed to bits against the treacherous coastline. The disastrous 1906 wreck of the *Valencia* was still fresh in mourners' minds when the trail was blazed, and a cabin was built every 10 kilometres, each one fully stocked with provisions. Following a telegraph line that was constructed in the 1890s, the rough trail and rustic cabins offered a way for survivors to reach Cape Beale and safety.

Pacific Rim National Park Reserve

Box 280, 2185 Ocean Terrace Rd.
Ucluelet BC V0R 3A0
250-726-7721
http://parkscan.harbour.com/pacrim/

Long Beach Information Centre (seasonal)

250-726-4212

Pachena Information Centre (seasonal)

250-728-3234

Port Renfrew Information Centre (seasonal)

250-647-5434

Tours of working lumber mills can be arranged at Port Alberni.

See the MV *Lady Rose* and the MV *Frances Barkley* box .
Alberni Valley Museum
Echo Recreation Centre
4255 Wallace Street
250-723-2181
www.alberniheritage.com
Open daily, May-September;
Monday to Saturday,
October-April
Admission charged
Housed in the Alberni Valley

ping 23,000 litres of water, skimming up the payload from a lake in 30 seconds at a speed of 70 knots! A single water drop by the plane can cover 100,000 square metres of terrain. Each aircraft measures 36 metres long, has a 60 metre wingspan, and its tail slices 15 metres above the water's surface. Built during the latter years of World War II as heavy-duty long-range bombers, the "flying boats" were used as troop transports. Only nine were completed, and the two at Sproat Lake are the only remaining examples.

Lady Rose Marine Services
Alberni Harbour Quay
545 Argyle Street
PO Box 188
Port Alberni BC V9Y 7M7
250-723-8313
800-663-7192
www.ladyrosemarine.com
Harbour Quay at the foot of Argyle Street is home port to both the MV *Lady Rose*, a 32 metre passenger / cargo ship, and the MV *Frances Barkley*, a 39 metre former ferry. The ships ply the waters of Alberni Inlet, supplying shoreline communities with food and goods, and ferrying travellers bound for Barkley Sound.

John Meares

A skilled mariner who served in the British Royal Navy and later in the merchant navy, John Meares also had a head for business and adventure.

In 1786, having heard from Captain James Cook's crew of the fabulous wealth that could be made trading sea otter pelts, Meares the entrepreneur sailed for the Pacific Northwest Coast aboard the *Nootka*. Wintering at Alaska's Prince William Sound, he reached China in 1787, profiting handsomely

from his cargo of furs. The following year he founded a trading post at Nootka Sound, cruising the area in search of pelts and claiming the land for England. He also constructed the 40-tonne schooner *North West America*. A year later two of his ships were seized by the Spanish, and Meares returned to England to rouse feelings against Spain. This eventually led to Britain's taking ownership of Vancouver Island.

The Wreck of the Valencia

Bound for Victoria from San Francisco, the American passenger steamer *Valencia* completely missed the entrance to Juan de Fuca Strait. It was January 22, 1906, and a tumultuous storm finally ran her aground off Pachena Point near Bamfield, only 30 metres from shore.

The *Valencia* began taking on water and listing. Lifeboats were launched, but they were dashed against rocks and capsized in the unrelenting surf. Passengers lashed themselves to railings and rigging on the foundering ship so close, yet so far, from shore. Fifteen hours after the ship's grounding, a band of weary souls finally made it to shore, hiked to a telegraph cabin, and raised rescuers in Victoria.

The ships of salvation did arrive, only to find the *Valencia* unapproachable due to the high seas. Rescuers could do nothing but watch in horror as passengers some already dead from hypothermia and others barely alive were washed overboard into the raging waters. Of the 164 passengers and crew aboard the *Valencia*, only 38 survived.

Museum are wonderful collections indigenous to the area not only excellent examples of Nuu-chah-nulth arts and crafts, but also exhibits on the west coast's extensive pioneer history.

The museum's clever visible-storage system of display lends itself to long perusal of the collections' fascinating and varied contents. The informative display cards and indexes let visitors delve into

additional information on individual pieces; the Alberni District Historical Society Archives chronicles an extensive record of companies and local industry as well as historical personalities. Other

The MV *Lady Rose* and the MV *Frances Barkley*

With a marine tradition sailing back over 60 years, the two ships of Lady Rose Marine Services the MV *Lady Rose* and the MV *Frances Barkley* continue the time-honoured duties of serving the commercial transportation and passenger ferry needs of Alberni Inlet and Barkley Sound communities. This is in addition to offering a scenery-filled, slow-paced venture for travellers eager to experience the west coast way of life. Recreational enthusiasts, especially kayakers, favour the reliable vessels for their access to Barkley Sound's 800-square kilometres of superb out-in-the-marine-wild paddling adventures.

Originally christened *Lady Sylvia*, the *Lady Rose* was built in 1937 at A & J Inglis Limited Pointhouse Shipyard in Glasgow, Scotland. The *Lady Sylvia*, 32 metres long with a seven metre beam and two metre draft, was commissioned by the Union Steamship Company to sail the sheltered coastline from Vancouver to Howe Sound. However, before entering service, the ship made a thrill-packed 16,000 kilometre crossing of the Atlantic Ocean, skippered by Captain William Smales. The voyage took nine weeks, and the *Lady Sylvia* became the first diesel-powered, single-propeller vessel to make such a passage. Upon her arrival at Vancouver in July 1937, she

was renamed the *Lady Rose*.

For the next half century the sturdy ship saw duty as a freight and passenger ferry between the Gulf Islands and the Fraser River. During World War II, the *Lady Rose* was even pressed into military service by the Royal Canadian Army Service Corp to ferry army and air force personnel between Port Alberni and Ucluelet.

Today, the *Lady Rose* plies the Alberni Inlet and Barkely Sound, taking local residents and visitors on thrice-weekly sailings (four in July and August) from Port Alberni to Bamfield and waypoints in between. Dockings along the route can include small communities, logging camps, salmon hatcheries, plus fishing and kayaking lodges. Building supplies, groceries, fuel, mail, and equipment account for the ship's freight manifest, and passengers delight in watching the loading and unloading. Departing Port Alberni at 8 am, the ship sidles up to Bamfield's West Dock around noon, allowing day trippers adequate time to explore the town, nearby Brady's Beach, or perhaps the Bamfield Marine Station. Leaving Bamfield in early afternoon, the *Lady Rose* reaches Port Alberni by 5:30 pm.

Additional summer sailings to Ucluelet, Sechart Whaling Station Lodge, and the Broken Group Islands are the routes

of the MV *Frances Barkley*, with mostly kayakers and their gear, in addition to day trippers filling the ship's roster. Commissioned in 1958 as the MS *Rennesoy*, later the MS *Hidle*, the ship served in the Norwegian ferry fleet. Purchased in 1990, the *Hidle* was refitted and sailed from Stavanger, Norway, via the Panama Canal, to Port Alberni. With a length of 39 metres, a beam of eight metres, and draft of three metres, she can carry up to 200 passengers and 100 tons of cargo.

The ship is named for Frances Barkley (1769-1845), the English-born wife of Captain Charles William Barkley, for whom Barkley Sound is named. The couple sailed extensively in their day and spent several months in 1787 exploring the west coast of Vancouver Island. Aboard the *Imperial Eagle* they traded with the local First Nations and bestowed names on the bays, islands, and terrain they encountered. Both Trevor Channel and Hornby Peak were named for Frances Hornby Trevor Barkley.

Lady Rose Marine Services
Alberni Harbour Quay
545 Argyle Street
Box 188
Port Alberni BC V9Y 7M7
250-723-8313
800-663-7192
www.ladyrosemarine.com

permanent installations tell the tale of the West Coast Trail, its history, development, and disasters. Of particular note is the marvellous John Halfyard display; this local resident's folk doll creations are intriguing and wonderfully original.

Alberni Pacific Railway
Kingsway and Argyle Street; near Harbour Quay
250-723-7376
Open daily, May-September; two to three roundtrip train excursions a day
Admission charged

Hop aboard this heritage train for 35-minute rumbles along Port Alberni's industrial waterfront, bound for the McLean Mill National Historic Site. Arrive early for departures so you can spend a moment or two admiring the darling 1912 railway station and, of course, making a close inspection of the mighty Alberni Pacific steam logging locomotive No. 7. Once the conductor hollers "All aboard!" the train chugs out of the station, north along the Alberni Inlet between Fish Harbour Marina and downtown, then climbs into the forest before whistling in to stop at the McLean Mill.

Owned by the City of Port Alberni and operated by the Western Vancouver Island Industrial Heritage Society, the railway was an enlightened community-interest restoration project which reclaimed a piece of the city's heritage by putting that legacy back to work. Its route to, and stop at, the McLean Mill National Historic Site makes for one of Vancouver Island's best historic day trips.

Strung along Bamfield Inlet is the small village of Bamfield.

McLean Mill National Historic Site
Smith Road; from Highway 4, turn right at Beaver Creek Road, then six kilometres to Smith Road
250-723-1376
www.alberniheritage.com
Open daily, May-September
Admission charged

The destination of the Alberni Pacific Railway, the McLean Mill National Historic Site lovingly recaptures a bygone era of Vancouver Island's logging days as it commemorates British Columbia's forest industry. Housed on this 12 hectare site are some 35 period buildings residences, offices, workshops, plus a steam-driven sawmill and millpond that together provide a historically accurate vision of a family-operated lumber business. The McLean Mill Lumber Company, owned and run by Robert Bartlett McLean, his wife Cora, and their three sons, was a successful independent lumber mill business from 1926 to 1965. In spite of the fact that the site lay quiet for nearly three decades before the restoration began, much of its building complex and original equipment is present and in good working order. The

McLean Mill was declared a national historic site in 1989 and has welcomed guests since July 2000.

Of special interest is the sawmill, with its brawny 1890 Wheland Machine Works steam engine still chopping and buzzing through the rough logs hauled in from the millpond. A walk through the nearby second-growth forest offers a look at young alders and red cedar. Plan to attend the Tin Pants Theatre dramatic presentation held at a stage down by the creek. It's old-fashioned, a bit corny, and definitely lots of fun as young thespians recount in song the history of the Alberni Valley and the McLean Mill.

Alberni Forest Information Centre
#15-5440 Argyle Street; at Harbour Quay
250-720-2108
Open daily, July-August; fewer days and shorter hours the rest of the year. Call for information.
Admission free

Displays here tell of the Alberni Valley's surrounding forests and its lumbering heritage. Forestry and mill tours can also be booked here.

Weyerhauser / Alberni Pacific Division
2500 1st Avenue
250-724-7428
Take this two-hour tour to delve into the inner workings of a busy sawmill, from grapplers loading raw logs to the many processes sawing, edging, trimming, sorting, and stacking that create finished lumber products ready for shipment.

Robertson Creek Fish Hatchery
Great Central Lake Road; turn off Highway 4, five kilometres west of Port Alberni
250-724-6521
Open seasonally
Admission free
See autumn salmon runs as well as springtime salmon fry release.

Storm Watching: Vancouver Island's Foul Weather Industry

Waves pound Vancouver Island's west coast during winter storms.

It is early January and in the vastness of the Gulf of Alaska, icy swirls of Arctic air are milling over waves warmed by the Japan Current, arcing north from the tropical Pacific Ocean. In the next few hours the heavy, barometer-plunging atmosphere will sink into downright ugly. Tapping into the jet stream, wind speeds will soon exceed 40 knots, whipping up 10 metre seas that heave and wallow, churning the water into frothy white fury. Old seadogs call the gales "Pacific Howlers," screaming banshees from Mother Nature's bag of ill-tempered tempests that pounce onto the Pacific Northwest coast. Vancouver Island, its crenellated western face nicked and gouged like a prizefighter's scarred jaw juts firmly into the storms' angry swings.

Ideal vacation weather? Actually, yes. For some winter-season visitors to Vancouver Island, a poor weather prognosis couldn't be more promising. Especially along the west coast, where storm after storm spins through, one right after another—some reaching landfall mere hours apart—fickle weather is the premier winter attraction. Sip that first cup of morning latte watching sleet lash against the window-pane, at lunchtime sup al fresco beneath blue skies, but come dinnertime don't forget the umbrella when nipping out into those velvety purple evenings.

A few days on wintry Vancouver Island provide a total change of atmosphere, with the bonus of ample elbowroom. The off-season is ... well, the off-season, and winter accounts for up to 75 percent of the region's average annual 300 centimetres of rainfall. Yet a few showers don't dampen the allure of Vancouver Island's many attractions, and each one is far more accessible without the Easter-to-Thanksgiving throng of visitors. During the high season, when more than three million visitors can't resist the Island's charms, securing a dinner reservation can be enough challenge in and of itself. Venture here after the autumn leaves have skittled about, however, and you don't even need a reservation. This is in addition to delightfully deserted beaches, blissfully empty byways, and hotels ever so happy to see you.

And, of course, there is nothing quite like a thrashing "Old Testament" storm to energize the senses. All along Vancouver Island's Pacific Rim from Port Renfrew to Tofino and beyond resorts and inns facing raucous winds and troubled waters entice visitors with off-season rates and raging weather on the doorstep. Wind-whipped sea spray and the sight of an awesome frothy surf, coupled with a cosy retreat's comforts, are nature and nurturing at its best.

Bamfield

Bamfield Chamber of Commerce

General Delivery, Box 5
Bamfield BC V0R 1B0
250-728-3006
www.alberni.net/bamcham/
Population: 740

Remote and marvellous describes little Bamfield. It's accessible from Port Alberni via 30 nautical miles sailed by MV *Lady Rose*, or, for the land loving, via 85 kilometres of largely unpaved gravel road from Port Alberni. There is also a four-hour route from Victoria via Cowichan Lake, either out of Youbou or Honeymoon Bay, on logging roads mostly. And then of course there is the wilderness trek along the West Coast Trail from Port Renfrew.

Strung along Bamfield Inlet, the village is both charming and workaday. On the inlet's eastern side sits the one-time Trans Pacific Cable Station, now the Western Canadian Universities Marine Biological Station. A seaside boardwalk, decorated with potted flowers, twists and turns along the waterfront, scattered with houses and shops. Indeed, some folks like to say that Bamfield, with its laid-back ambience, is what Tofino was like 20 years ago. Some even call it the "Venice of Vancouver Island;" the inlet is the main street, and residents need boats to get about.

Settled first by the Huu-ay-aht First Nation, the town was named for William Eddy Banfield. He was Barkley Sound's first white settler, government agent, explorer, trader, and all-around enthusiastic supporter of the area's

Bamfield signpost

Pacific Rim Tee Time

Alberni Golf Club
6449 Cherry Creek Road
Port Alberni, BC
250-723-5422
Eighteen holes

The Hollies Executive Golf Course
3133 Nanaimo Highway
Port Alberni, BC
250-724-5333
Nine holes

Long Beach Golf Course
Near airport at Long Beach
Box 998
Ucluelet, BC
250-725-3332
Eighteen holes

The Wickaninnish Inn

Rising from a rocky promontory on the edge of the Pacific Ocean, the weathered cedar Wickaninnish Inn takes advantage of its dramatic location to offer astonishing and outstanding hospitality amid the mystical atmosphere of the coastal rain forest.

Call it rustic elegance. Each of the 46 rooms features a fireplace, floor-to-ceiling windows, deep soaker tub, and a private balcony from which to take in the striking surroundings. Furnishings have been fashioned from recycled old-growth Douglas fir, western red cedar, and driftwood. Natural textures such as sisal carpeting and stone flooring add to the accommodation's casual, yet upscale, ambience.

Add to this the Pointe Restaurant and On-the-Rocks Lounge, which serve award-winning Pacific Northwest cuisine set against a 240-degree panoramic view of the open Pacific, nearby islands, and idyllic Chesterman Beach.

Hand-adzed cedar post-and-beam construction creates soaring 12 metre ceilings, and the proximity to the pounding Pacific surf surging beyond the double-paned windows is breathtaking. Not to be overlooked is the Ancient Cedars Spa, an oasis of restorative experiences with signature treatments that include the Sacred Sea Thalassotherapy and Hot Stone Massage.

It is little wonder that the Wickaninnish Inn has become one of the Pacific Rim's most beloved retreats especially during the raging storms of winter. Guests relish the chance to experience Mother Nature's fury while ensconced in total comfort.

The Wickaninnish Inn & Pointe Restaurant
Osprey Lane at Chesterman Beach
PO Box 250
Tofino BC V0R 2Z0
250-725-3100
800-333-4604
www.wickinn.com

Hot Springs Cove

Situated in 2299 hectare Maquinna Provincial Park, 37 kilometres northwest of Tofino, Hot Springs Cove is the premier Pacific west coast day trip. Floatplanes, water taxis, and whale watching charters pull up to the floating dock, disembarking visitors who walk along two kilometres of boardwalk through rain forest to arrive at the site of Vancouver Island's only known thermal hot springs. Visitors relish the 50°C steaming water that splashes over falls before cooling in a series of shallow pools that trickle into the sea.

commercial possibilities. Apparently, a cartographer's error scribbled the town's spelling of Bamfield not Banfield into history.

Bamfield, despite its isolation, is no stranger to popularity; summertime recreationalists make Bamfield base camp for exploring Barkley Sound and Alberni Inlet. During the salmon fishing season more than a thousand sportfishers reel in comfortable lodging, good meals, and supplies in between casting for salmon. Add to this a near constant stream of scuba divers, hikers, canoeists, and kayakers. Bamfield is the northern start of the West

Coast Trail, 77 kilometres of unparalleled wilderness trekking, and the Broken Group Islands, another section of Pacific Rim National Park Reserve, are only 12 kilometres west of Bamfield.

Bamfield Marine Station
Bamfield Inlet
Bamfield BC V0R 1B0
250-728-3301
Open year-round; guided tours on Saturday and Sunday, May-August, 1 pm-3 pm
Admission charged
In 1902, Bamfield became the site of the eastern terminus of the telegraph cable that snaked across the Pacific Ocean to Australia. Known as the Red Section of an around-the-world British cable system, it linked to other sections spanning the globe to allow worldwide telegraphic communications, the precursor to long-distance telephones.

The station's chateauesque main building (now gone) was designed by the famous Victoria architect Francis Rattenbury and housed the remote site's bachelor staff and their Chinese servants. The concrete cable station is the only structure still standing, and now, as the Bamfield Marine Station, it is used as a study and research centre jointly operated by the universities of Victoria, British Columbia, Calgary, Alberta, and Simon Fraser.

Clayoquot Sound Biosphere

UNESCO, the United Nations Educational, Scientific, Cultural Organization, conferred the designation of a World Biosphere Reserve on Clayoquot Sound in January 2000. The 350,000 hectare area, extending from Esowista Peninsula in the south to north of Estevan Point, encompasses both land and sea. Some 110,000 hectares of the total are also designated ecological reserves or parks. The biosphere includes Flores, Vargas, and Meares islands, as well as some thousand other islands and islets. Essentially, it shelters North America's largest intact low-elevation old-growth temperate rain forest.

Clayoquot Sound is the traditional homeland for a number of groups of the Nuu-chah-nulth; the Tla-o-qui-aht primarily reside on Meares Island at Opitsaht and at Esowista in Pacific Rim National Park. The Toquaht and Ucluelet live south of the

park, and the Ahousaht and Hesquiaht are northwest of the park.

Biosphere reserves are internationally recognized for promoting biodiversity conservation while also demonstrating a balance between nature and people through sustainable development. The administrative arm of the Clayoquot Sound Biosphere Reserve is the Clayoquot Biosphere Trust (CBT), which is governed by the Nuu-chah-nulth First Nation as a non-profit, charitable organization. The CBT strives to maintain a healthy ecosystem within a diversified economy, all amid a varied and vibrant cultural environment. Nuu-chah-nulth living philosophies encompass *lisaak*, "living respectfully"; *Qwa' aak qin teechmis*, "life in balance"; and *Hishuk ish ts'awalk*, "everything is one and interconnected."

Ditidaht First Nations
250-745-3848
Population: 184
This small community of Ditidaht families, located on the northeastern shore of Nitinat Lake, traces its heritage in the area back many, many generations.

Ucluelet

Ucluelet Chamber of Commerce
PO Box 428
Ucluelet BC V0R 3A0
250-726-4641
www.uclueletinfo.com
Info Centre: 100 Main Street, foot of Main Street at Government Wharf
Population: 1753

Yuclutl-aht is a Nuu-chah-nulth word meaning "wind blowing into the bay," a breezy phenomenon still experienced by the small community of First Nations people living on the eastern shore of the Ucluelet Inlet. The area's first European settler was Captain Francis Stuart, but it was Captain William Spring who established a trading post at Spring Cove, acquiring the land by swapping for a barrel of molasses. Early endeavours for the European settlers ran the gamut from fur sealing to sawmilling.

Now the winds of change are blowing across the water to Ucluelet proper, the robust little village hugging the protected shorelines of Ucluth Peninsula, which juts into Barkley Sound. Heritage, nature, and tourism are ushering in a new era, supplementing forestry, seafood processing, commercial fishing, and aquaculture.

Visit the Crow's Nest on Main Street in the building that housed the town's 1908 general store. Up on Peninsula Road stands the old church. With its proximity to Pacific Rim National Park Reserve, it is not surprising that Ucluelet is base camp for a wide range of outdoor activities not only incredible fishing and whale watching, but also kayaking in

Amphitrite Point Lighthouse

the Broken Group Islands, and scuba diving to explore the coast's abundant marine life and, yes, some of its many shipwrecks. Terra firma sports its own activities, notably hiking the Wild Pacific Trail, a five kilometre loop skirting the rugged cliffs of Amphitrite Point.

Canadian Princess

1943 Peninsula Road
Ucluelet BC V0R 3A0
250-726-7771
800-663-7090
www.canadianprincess.com

At one time this was the *William J. Stewart*, a 70-metre-long ship that served for 43 years (1932-75) as a hydrographic survey ship. Constructed of steel, the twin-screw vessel outfitted with steam reciprocating triple expansion engines, was built at Collingwood, Ontario, costing approximately $1 million. It came to Vancouver Island via the Panama Canal. In 1944, the *William J. Stewart* struck Ripple Rock on the Island's east coast, but it later was refloated and returned to duties. The Oak Bay Marine Group of Victoria purchased the ship in 1979, renamed it the *Canadian Princess*, and

Canadian Princess Resort

towed it to Ucluelet, where the ship is now a floating hotel and fishing resort.

Amphitrite Point Lighthouse

Ucluth Peninsula southern tip
Viewing only

Commanding a rocky outcropping at the end of Ucluth Peninsula, Amphitrite Point Lighthouse dates back to 1905. It was erected after the *Pass of Melfort* sank offshore, but at least another 17 vessels have gone down since. Nowadays, this is the Tofino Coast Guard Radio Station.

The roaring Pacific rollers make a dramatic foreground to the mesmerizing sunsets here, and also add a soundtrack for the jaunt along the five kilometre Wild Pacific Trail, which starts here and snakes through the coastal forest, connecting to the He-Tin-Kis boardwalk. In March and April, look for pods of the nearly 20,000 migrating gray whales which skirt the coast on their way to Alaskan feeding grounds. During the winter season, Amphitrite Point is an excellent place at which to experience (at a safe distance) the violent seas churning during storms.

Tofino

Tofino-Long Beach Chamber of Commerce
PO Box 249
Tofino BC V0R 2Z0
250-725-3414
www.tofinobc.org
Visitor Centre: 331 Campbell Street
Population: 1540
Located literally at the end of the road (Highway 4), Tofino is anything but a last-chance sort of locale. Think exhilarating instead. Situated at the tip of Esowista Peninsula, which juts 16 kilometres into Clayoquot Sound, this delightful fishing village and tourism centre derives its name from Vicente Tofino San Miguel, a Spanish rear admiral, astronomer, and

Meares Island rises across the channel from Tofino

hydrographer. John Grice was the first European settler in the area, arriving in 1888.

Today's pretty town encircled by forests (some old growth) is both a centre for the surrounding population of nearly 3000 Nuu-chah-nulth, made up of five communities, along Clayoquot Sound, but also serves as the thriving retreat for Pacific Rim National

Pacific Rim Festivals & Events

March To April
Pacific Rim Whale Festival
Ucluelet, Tofino, and Pacific Rim National Park Reserve
Annual celebration of the gray whale migration up the West Coast.

April
Alberni Valley Giant Spring Craft Fair
Alberni Athletic Hall
Local artists and craftspeople show their creations.
Rhododendron Festival
Ucluelet
The festival features the Rhodo Run, plus walks and drives and a tea party in celebration of the blooming rhododendrons.

June
Port Alberni Harbour Days
Port Alberni Harbour
This annual festival with a boat parade and ship tours, plus water bomber drop

demonstration, is held in conjunction with National Safe Boating Week.
Oceans Day
Pacific Rim National Park Reserve
Beach clean-up events and ocean-themed activities.

July
Canada Parks Day
Pacific Rim National Park Reserve
Celebration of the park with activities and guided hikes.

September
Port Alberni Salmon Festival
Port Alberni
This Labour Day long weekend event features a salmon derby, kids' bullhead derby, and entertainment.
Alberni District Fall Fair
Port Alberni
Community fair with arts and crafts, midway, and agricultural displays and trade show.

Bamfield Kayak Festival
Bamfield
Kayak races, entertainment, and a dance.
Port Alberni "Plummet"
Port Alberni
Amateur and professional downhill cyclists compete for prizes.

October
Robertson Creek Hatchery Open House
Robertson Creek Hatchery
The return of spawning chinook salmon is celebrated with entertainment and exhibits.

December
Harbour Quay Christmas Sailpast
Port Alberni
Nighttime festival with brightly illuminated and decorated boats sailing Port Alberni Harbour for prizes.

Floatplanes arrive and depart from Tofino's bustling marina.

The end of the road at Tofino

Park visitors. Shops, galleries, markets, restaurants, pubs, and nature excursion charters do brisk business during the summer.

Chief among the outdoor activities is whale watching, especially during the March and early April Pacific Rim Whale Festival, coinciding with the height of the gray whale migration. Don't forego Tofino's other nature-loving pursuits such as hiking the 11 kilometre Ahousat Wildside Heritage Trail on nearby Flores Island.

West Coast Maritime Museum / Whale Centre
444 Campbell Street, Tofino
250-725-2132
Open daily, March-October
Admission charged
Presenting a nice mix of Nuu-chah-nulth cultural items, plus exhibits on whales and marine history, this small centre provides an excellent overview of the cetacean life.

Eagle Aerie Gallery
350 Campbell Street
Open daily, March-October
Admission free
Roy Henry Vickers, an artist of the Tsimshian Eagle Clan, designed this longhouse-style gallery. Step inside to see examples of his acclaimed contemporary work that fuses traditional styles with contemporary themes.

Rainforest Interpretive Centre
316 Main Street
250-725-2560
Open daily, March-October
Admission free
Explore the inner workings of a temperate coastal rain forest.

House of Himwitsa
300 Main Street
250-725-2017
Open daily, March-October
Admission free
Stop by the House of Himwitsa to see fine examples of First Nations prints, carvings, and jewellery. Lodging is also available, and whale watching excursions can be booked.

Tofino Botanical Gardens
Mackenzie Beach Road; 1.5 kilometres from Tofino town centre
250-725-1237
Open daily, March-October
Admission charged
Bird blinds and a viewing tower help visitors explore the natural wonders of Vancouver Island's west coast as presented by this five hectare garden and forest site abutting a 2000 hectare wildlife sanctuary and shoreline habitat.

Meares Island
Across from Tofino; accessible via boat or water taxi
In 1985, Nuu-chah-nulth elders declared 8600 hectare Meares Island a tribal park, establishing it as a cultural and nature preserve. The tiny Tla-o-qui-aht village of Opitsaht occupies the island's shore across from Tofino, and the island itself retains ancient forests of hemlock and cedar. The Hanging Garden Cedar, some 2000 years old and six metres in diameter, can be seen on the three kilometre Meares Island Big Trees Trail. Tours of Meares Island by kayak or water taxi run out of Tofino. Lemmens Inlet nearly cuts the island in two, and large mudflats have developed on the island, which are excellent for bird-watchers.

Vargas Island
Five kilometres from Tofino; accessible by boat

Opposite: Kennedy Lake at 69 square kilometres is Vancouver Island's largest lake.

Sandy beaches and access to 5970 hectare Vargas Island Provincial Park are the draws here. The Vargas Island Inn has accommodations, camping sites, plus activities such as kayaking and day trips to nearby natural attractions. Spanish explorer Francisco Eliza originally called the place Isla de Feran, but in 1792 explorers Galiano and Valdes renamed it after Governor Vargas, who had recently recaptured New Mexico for Spain.

Flores Island
20 kilometres northwest of Tofino; accessible by float-plane or water taxi
Head to the Nuu-chah-nulth town of Ahousaht, at Marktosis, to begin the 16 kilometre Ahousaht Wildside Heritage Trail, which heads south and west along beaches and into rain forest to reach 886-metre-high Mt. Flores. South of Marktosis sits Gibson Provincial Marine Park at 142 hectares, and beyond that, to the west is the 7113 hectares of the undeveloped Flores Island Provincial Park.

Hesquiat Peninsula
40 kilometres north of Tofino;

Pacific Rim Parks & Recreation

MacMillan Provincial Park (Cathedral Grove)
Highway 4; 31 kilometres west of Parksville
157 hectares / day use
Only steps from the highway's edge rise some of Vancouver Island's largest old-growth Douglas fir, several more than 800 years old. The park is named for Harvey Reginald MacMillan, BC's first provincial chief forester. He later founded H.R. MacMillan Export Company, which became MacMillan Bloedel. Short hiking trails lead through the forest.

Carmanah Walbran Provincial Park
45 kilometres beyond Nitinat Lake
250-391-2300
16,450 hectares / wilderness camping
Steep and hilly with challenging hikes, this wilderness park holds some of the oldest and tallest known Sitka spruce. The "Carmanah Giant" reaches a height of 95.8 metres and is believed to be BC's tallest tree. Near Cheewhat Lake is a 59-metre-tall western red cedar, thought to be BC's tallest cedar.

Stamp Falls Provincial Park
Off Highway 4; 12 kilometres to entrance
250-337-2400 or 800-689-9025

Martin Mars Water Bombers are anchored at Sproat Lake.

(reservations)
www.discovercamping.ca
234 hectares; 22 campsites
Its pretty falls and cool, clear waters ideal for swimming and snorkelling make this a popular outdoor destination.

Sproat Lake Provincial Park
Off Highway 4; 10 kilometres beyond Stamp Falls Provincial Park turnoff
250-337-2400 or 800-689-9025 (reservations)
www.discovercamping.ca
39 hectares; 59 campsites
Only minutes from Port Alberni, this park features swimming, fishing, and water-skiing. Sproat Lake is also home to the Martin Mars Water Bombers, which use the lake as a runway.

Della Falls (Strathcona Provincial Park)
Southeast corner of Strathcona Provincial Park; 9 kilometres northwest of Highway 4 to the end of Great Central Lake Road, 34 kilometres by boat across Great Central Lake, then 16 kilometres of arduous hiking along Drinkwater Creek
250-954-4600
It's challenging to reach Della Falls, but the reward for experienced hikers is Canada's second highest waterfalls at 440 metres. They are eight times higher than Niagara Falls, and the 11th highest in the world. The hiking season is from May to October, and there are wilderness campsites at 7 kilometres, 12.5 kilometres, and 15.2 kilometres along the trail.

accessible by floatplane or boat Hesquiat Peninsula, at the northwestern edge of Clayoquot Sound, is the traditional homeland for the Hesquiaht people, and the main village is located at Refuge Cove in Sydney Inlet. Lodging and charters to Clayoquot Sound natural attractions, Hesquiat Peninsula Provincial Park, and Hesquiat Lake Provincial Park can be arranged.

Cougar Annie's Garden
Boat Basin, Hesquiat Harbour
Boat Basin Foundation
888-638-2804
www.cougarannie.com
Open daily
Admission free
Ada Annie Rae-Arthur, the legendary recluse who lived here at the head of Hesquiat Harbour, is best known for her deadly aim; she dispatched some 70 cougars in her day. Rae-Arthur's life inspired Margaret Horsfield's acclaimed book *Cougar Annie's Garden.* The heritage garden dating back to 1915 has been preserved and can be visited by charter boat or floatplane tour.

Pacific Rim Parks & Recreation

Taylor Arm Provincial Park
Highway 4; five kilometres beyond the Sproat Lake Park turnoff
250-337-2400
79 hectares / undeveloped campsites
This forested park is best for hiking and fishing.

Kennedy Lake Provincial Park
Off Highway 4; 83 kilometres west of Port Alberni
285 hectares / wilderness camping
Because this park abuts Vancouver Island's largest lake (69 square kilometres), there is a nice two kilometre beach. The lake's waters are hemmed in by steep mountains and are frequented by sudden squalls, making boating dangerous. Clayoquot Arm Provincial Park can be accessed from Kennedy Lake by watercraft.

Clayoquot Arm Provincial Park
Accessible from Kennedy Lake Provincial Park
1490 hectares / wilderness camping
Remote and pristine, this area is accessible from Kennedy Lake by boat or kayak.

Pacific Rim National Park Reserve
Encompasses Long Beach, the Broken Group Islands, and the West Coast Trail
Box 280, 2185 Ocean Terrace Road
Ucluelet BC V0R 3A0
250-726-7721
Long Beach Information Centre (seasonal)
250-726-4212
Pachena Information Centre (seasonal)
250-728-3234
Port Renfrew Information Centre (seasonal)
250-647-5434
http://parkscan.harbour.com/pacrim/
Info Centre: three kilometres northwest of the Ucluelet-Tofino junction on Highway 4
49,962 hectares / campsites and wilderness camping
This world-renowned reserve is divided into three sections: Long Beach, Broken Group Islands, and the West Coast Trail. See the Pacific Rim National Park Reserve box.

Maquinna Provincial Park
37 kilometres north of Tofino via boat or floatplane
2299 hectares / campsites and lodge at Hot Springs Cove
Situated on the shores of this large park is Hot Springs Cove, the site of Vancouver Island's most popular hot springs. The springs' 50°C steaming water cascades into waterfalls and pools before reaching the sea. See the Hot Springs Cove box.

Sydney Inlet Provincial Park
15 kilometres north from Hot Springs Cove
2774 hectares / no facilities
Located on either side of a steep-sided fiord, this is a destination for boaters and kayakers.

Hesquiat Peninsula Provincial Park
40 kilometres north of Tofino via boat or floatplane
7889 hectares / no facilities
Good for coastal hiking and kayaking.

Hesquiat Lake Provincial Park
40 kilometres north of Tofino via boat or floatplane
62 hectares / no facilities
Good for coastal hiking and kayaking.

Sulphur Passage Provincial Park
Upper Shelter Inlet, north of Flores Island
2299 hectares / no facilities
Popular with kayakers, the park is located at Obstruction Island, at the intersection of three channels: Sulphur Passage, Hayden Passage, and Shelter Inlet.

North Central Vancouver Island

Denman and Hornby islands are beloved retreats of North Central Vancouver Island.

F irst Nations people of the west coast of North Central Vancouver Island were the earliest recorded indigenous islanders to encounter Europeans. The Nuu-chah-nulth were visited by numerous British, Spanish, and American fur trading expeditions during the late 1700s, notably by

Captain James Cook in 1778. The dark, thickly furred sea otter pelts secured by these early merchants fetched high prices in Asia and subsequently ushered in a trading surge to Vancouver Island's bountiful shores.

Tahsis and, in particular, Gold River are the west coast gateways to Nootka Sound today. The area is a water recreationalist's wilderness fantasy-come-true with inlets, channels, and coves all backed by thick forest. A journey aboard the MV *Uchuck III*, a working cargo and passenger freighter, is a breathtaking sojourn in this scenically superb, but travel-challenging

geography.

On North Central Vancouver Island's east coast is the Comox Valley and the towns of Comox, Courtenay and Cumberland. Urban centres to the surrounding pastoral farmland of this temperate terrain, they welcome visitors to experience their alpine-to-ocean ambience. In the course of a day it is easy to take in both alpine hiking (or skiing) atop Mount Washington and kayaking in Comox Harbour. Plan the day thoughtfully and a round of golf could be added at one of several excellent nearby links. Just offshore are Denman and Hornby islands,

both relaxing destinations for art lovers and outdoor enthusiasts.

Northward is Campbell River, one of Vancouver Island's undisputed fishing capitals. For more than a century its favourable location — at the mouth of the Campbell River where it flows into Discovery Passage — has lured sportfishers seeking mighty salmon. More adventurous outings await farther out in Discovery Passage; the myriad Discovery Islands, principally Quadra and Cortes islands, present great outdoor recreation amid spectacular natural beauty.

Between the east and

Homemade signs on Hornby Island

west coasts of North Central Vancouver Island sprawls Strathcona Provincial Park. At 254,800 hectares it is Vancouver Island's largest park and also the oldest in BC, put aside for the enjoyment of the people in 1911. Here stands Vancouver Island's highest peak, Mt Golden Hinde, at 2200 metres above sea level. And here too drops Vancouver Island's highest falls, the stunning 440-metre-high cascades of Della Falls, eight times higher than Niagara.

North Central Recommendations

- Explore Comox's many attractions, especially the Comox Air Force Museum and Heritage Airpark and the Filberg Heritage Lodge and Park.
- Don't miss the Comox Valley Farmers' Market if you're in town on a day it convenes.
- See the ancient dinosaur fossils at the Courtenay and District Museum and Paleontology Centre.
- Winter or summer, head to Mount Washinton Alpine Resort for outdoor recreation.
- Take the ferry to Denman and Hornby islands, both great for easy outdoor recreation plus arts and crafts shopping.
- Definitely take time to explore the Museum at Campbell River; its First Nations and pioneer history exhibits are award-winning.
- Book passage aboard the MV *Uchuck III*, a converted 1943 US minesweeper, for a scenic journey into Nootka Sound.
- Take flashlights and don rubber-soled boots for self-guided spelunking through the rooms and passages of the Upana Caves.

The Comox Valley

Comox Valley Visitor Info Centre
2040 Cliffe Avenue
Courtenay BC V9N 2L3
250-334-3234 or 888-357-4471
www.comox-valley-tourism.ca
Population: 65,000

Tucked between the Beaufort Mountains and the Strait of Georgia, the pleasantly pastoral Comox Valley not only holds some of Vancouver Island's most fertile farmland, but also features snow-capped mountains, alpine meadows, rushing rivers, and sandy shorelines. Consequently, the valley's easy access to beaches, mountains, and pretty rural communities makes it an appealing place to live and visit.

Fuelled by the confluence of the Puntledge and Tsolum rivers, the Courtenay River flows into Comox Harbour, one of Vancouver Island's most pronounced tidal estuaries. For over 4000, years people have found the place to their liking, and the indigenous Salish called the place Komoux, or "plenty," noting its bountiful food sources. Europeans arrived in 1792, when Captain George Vancouver anchored HMS *Discovery* in Comox Harbour. However, recent research suggests that Sir Frances Drake might have come across the anchorage as far back as 1579 while seeking the elusive Northwest Passage.

Artists, musicians, and performers have found the Comox Valley special as well, and the region features a number of annual festivals, in addition to its numerous galleries, museums, and theatres.

Denman and Hornby Islands

Denman / Hornby Visitor Services

Denman Island BC V0R 1T0
250-335-2293

Denman Island

www.denmanis.bc.ca
Population: 1250
Only 10 minutes by ferry from Buckley Bay (on Highway 19A), Denman Island is a much beloved escape for its tiny population, many of them potters, artists of all sorts, farmers, and invariably strong naturalists. Natural beauty is a hallmark of the 20-kilometre-long by three- to five-kilometre-wide isle.

It is quite a charmer, with forests, meadows, and shoreline surrounding the occasional idyllic farmstead. Indeed, more than half the island is undeveloped, and its provincial parks — Fillongley, Boyle Point, and Sandy Island — reveal lovely and well-preserved ecosystems.

Denman Village, only a short walk from the ferry dock, is the island's friendly hub; here is found the community school, library, church, hardware store, bookshop, and bakery. The turn-of-the-century general store doubles as the impromptu community gathering-place and is a good stop to pick up snacks and refreshments.

Denman Seniors and Museum Society Activity Centre

1111 Northwest Road; Seniors Community Hall
250-335-0880
Open daily, July-August
Donations accepted
Take a few moments to explore this small repository of First Nations artifacts, fossils, shells, and, in particular, work from the Denman Lace Club.

Elderfield Old-Time Farm

4590 Northwind Trail; off Strachan Road
250-335-2570
www.hornbyisland.com/elderfield
Open daily during the summer, 11 am-3 pm
Admission charged
This eight hectare working farm becomes an olden days homestead when the Bevan / LeBaron family dons old-fashioned clothing and demonstrates traditional farming skills and chores such as egg-collecting, goat milking, and cattle feeding. Farm walks take visitors on an exploration of the orchards and gardens.

Hornby Island

www.hornbyisland.net
Population: 1048
Wee-sized but wonderful, 30-square-kilometre Hornby Island is a haven for its residents and a delight for visitors who come by the thousands during the summer. Lots and lots of crafts — pottery, weaving, candles, water-

The Legend of Queneesh

Queneesh Glacier glistens above the Comox Valley.

Eons ago, an old man dreamed of an approaching flood that would sweep through the Comox Valley, endangering the Comox and Pentlatch peoples. Upon awakening, the old man convinced the villagers to build canoes and weave long cedar ropes.

The flood did indeed come, but the people were ready, and with the rising waters they boarded the canoes and rode the flood higher and higher up into the mountains. Reaching the mighty glacier, Queneesh, the "white whale," the people used their long cedar ropes to lash their canoes to him. As the flood continued, Queneesh floated upon the torrents until the waters receded. He came to rest again upon the mountains and continues to watch over the people of the Comox Valley.

The Comox Museum

colours, you name it — are the reason. The Co-op Store, along with the Ringside Market and a few other small shops, form the island's commercial centre.

Union Bay
Population: 1500
A principal shipping and transport centre during the area's coal mining days, Union Bay offers travellers a hotel, pub, and market. Recreationalists use the boat launch here to access Sandy Island Provincial Marine Park, four kilometres away at the northern end of Denman Island.

Royston
Population: 2125
Some 15 ships have been scuttled off Royston to create a breakwater, calming the churning water to protect nearby booming grounds. Signs along the highway explain a bit about the "Royston Wrecks."

Starting in the late 1930s, the Comox Logging and Railway Co. acquired the scrapped vessels, towed them to their locations, filled them with rock ballast, and sank them. The site holds the

derelict remains of several commercial sailing ships, including a five-masted barquentine and a Cape Horn windjammer, four Royal Canadian Navy war ships, two CPR steam tugs, and two West Coast whalers.

Cumberland
Cumberland Chamber of Commerce and Tourism Information Centre
PO Box 250
Cumberland BC V0R 1S0
250-336-8313
1-866-301-4636
www.island.net/~cumbcham
Tourist Info Centre: 2755
Dunsmuir Avenue, V0R 1S0
Population: 2900
Named for the rich English coal-mining region of Cumbria, this town was founded by coal king Robert Dunsmuir in 1888 as the core of Vancouver Island's east coast coalfields. During its heyday, thousands of Italian, British, Slavic, Chinese, and Japanese immigrant labourers pulled millions of tonnes of black gold from Cumberland mines at the foot of the Beaufort Mountains.

In 1901, Cumberland was

Captain Cook's Discovery

Archeological evidence found on Vancouver Island's west coast suggests that the Nuu-chah-nulth were encountering Asians from across the Pacific Ocean as early as the fifth century. But it wasn't until 1774 that the first European contact was recorded, when Ensign Juan Pérez aboard the Spanish frigate *Santiago* anchored off the west coast of the Island. It was the Nuu-chah-nulth who came out to him.

Captain James Cook of the Royal British Navy, however, established the first lasting European contact. Leading his ships, the *Resolution* and the *Discovery*, in search of the Northwest Passage, Cook explored much of BC's coast-

line from May to October 1778. When he entered into Nootka Sound in the spring of that year, Cook went ashore at Yuquot, an ancient summering village of the Mowachaht, who became the first indigenous people to welcome Europeans to the shores of Vancouver Island. The British named the village Friendly Cove and began trading knives, nails, chisels, and buttons with the Mowachaht, securing animals skins, in particular sea otter pelts, that would later command princely prices in the Far East.

Captain Cook did not see the results of his encounter; he was killed in the Hawaiian Islands in February 1779.

the scene of one of mining's worst disasters: the loss of 64 lives in Number 6 Mine due to an explosion. Cumberland became the flashpoint for labour unrest in 1912 as miners struck against wage cuts and unsafe working conditions. Already, nearly 300 miners had died in Cumberland mines. BC's attorney general, W.J. Bowser, sent in 1000 soldiers to reopen the mines. Cumberland's coal production fell during the 1920s, and operations ultimately ceased in 1966.

The Cumberland of today,

Painter's Lodge

World-famous Painter's Lodge in Campbell River

Painter's Lodge is a sport fishing icon. Originally opened in the 1920s by Ned and June Painter on Campbell River Spit, the venerable fishers' friend started out as a collection of rustic cabins. In 1938 the couple moved the lodge to its present location and successfully operated it as Vancouver Island's premier fishing escape for 10 years before selling the property.

On Christmas Eve 1985, the historic lodge was gutted by fire, and much of the fascinating memorabilia chronicling its history and the story of salmon fishing and the Tyee Club went up in smoke. The lodge was soon rebuilt by the Oak Bay Marine Group, and today it features 94 rooms plus all the amenities, not to mention a creel full of fishing opportunities.

Topping the list are the guided fishing and Zodiac adventures into Discovery Passage. At the lodge's Marine Adventure Centre, seasoned and novice anglers alike can get fishing licences as well as insider tips on fishing the channels and pools of the passage. Transportation to the fishing spots is aboard sturdy Boston whalers, and Helly-Hansen two-piece wet weather gear and rubber boots are provided for guests. However, fishing skill — or luck, as the case may be — is the responsibility of individual patrons.

Painter's Lodge Holiday and Fishing Resort
1625 MacDonald Road
Campbell River BC V9W 4S5
250-286-1102
800-663-7090
www.painterslodge.com

though marred by piles of rusted iron and slag here and there, exudes historic charm. Many vintage buildings and houses still exist, and several have been restored. Of special interest is Doctors Row, with lovely homes; Bridal Row, with its small cottages; and the Pest House, once the quarters for patients at the Isolation Hospital. The town also has a number of heritage trees, including a giant sequoia, a monkey puzzle tree, plus black cottonwood, Japanese larch, grand fir, English yew, and others. Historic walking trails lead past sites of the old mines and old neighbourhoods.

Cumberland Museum and Archives
2680 Dunsmuir Avenue
250-336-2445
www.cumberlandmuseum.ca
Open daily, April-September; closed Sunday, October-March
Admisssion charged

Filled from floor to ceiling with a wealth of artifacts and memorabilia, the Cumberland Museum and Archives presents a fascinating insight into one of Vancouver Island's most colourful boomtowns. Collections range from a priceless assemblage of glassplate negative images of the Japanese community to what may be one of the world's most displays of historic telephones — from turn-of-the-century, nickel-plated candlestick models to the ever-popular 1960s "Princess" line.

Japanese Cemetery, Chinese Cemetery, Municipal Cemetery (Ginger Goodwin's Burial Site)
Cumberland Road, east of Cumberland

The various cemeteries provide an interesting testimony to the diversity of Cumberland's coal mining days, and an amble here reveals poignant reminders of lives lived in toil and turmoil. Of particular note is the gravesite of Ginger Goodwin. This outspoken labour leader was slain in suspicious circumstances in the woods near Comox Lake in 1918.

Comox

Population: 12,252

The town of Comox has preserved the historic flavour of a small seaside, resort-like community. The wharf at Comox Harbour has grown into an extensive marina with a boardwalk promenade, making it a pleasant place to view the many fishing and pleasure boats that use its facilities. Comox is home to many wonderful shops and restaurants, two golf courses, the Filberg Heritage Lodge and Park and the Canadian Forces base, 19 Wing Comox.

Comox Air Force Museum and Heritage Airpark

CFB Comox entrance; Building 11 on Military Row

250-339-8162

Open daily, 10-4

Admission charged

As Comox is a longstanding home of RCAF/CAF squadrons, this facility showcases the history of Canada's West Coast aviation with engaging exhibits. Numerous vintage aircraft are on display at the Heritage Aircraft Park, including a Canadair CF-104 "Starfighter," an Avro CF-100 "Canuck," and a McDonnell CF-101B "Voodoo."

Eclectic architectural styling on Hornby Island

Strathcona Provincial Park

Strathcona Provincial Park

Established in 1911, Strathcona Provincial Park is the oldest in British Columbia and the largest on Vancouver Island. Roughly triangular in shape, the massive tract stretches from the southwest at the head of Herbert Inlet on the west coast to only 13 kilometres shy of Comox Harbour on the east coast and about 65 kilometres south of the 50th parallel of latitude to the north. Within its boundaries rises Mt. Golden Hinde, Vancouver Island's highest peak at 2200 metres, as well as the 440-metre cascades of Della Falls, the highest waterfalls on the Island.

Strathcona is first and foremost a hiker's heaven. Challenging peaks, peaceful meadows, and forested treks are all there in abundance. Campbell River serves as the key gateway to the park, and between there and Gold River, many access points lead to campgrounds and well-marked and maintained trails. The Buttle Lake district offers two popular outings, the Elk River Trail and the Flower Ridge Trail, which are both suitable for hikers of all abilities. To the south, the Comox Valley gives access to the Forbidden Plateau. As its name implies, the region features some challenging high-altitude hikes, in addition to alpine lakes for fishing. Farther south in the park, the Della Falls Trail is a tough two- to three-day trek, but worth the chance to see these magnificent falls, the 11th highest in the world.

Strathcona Provincial Park

Principle access: off Highway 28; accessible via Paradise Meadows/Mount Washington (Hwy 19, exit 130) or Forbidden Plateau Recreation area (hwy 19, exit 127)

254,800 hectares / 161 campsites in two campgrounds plus wilderness camping

The Filberg Heritage Lodge and Park offers lovely gardens and a delightful teahouse.

Filberg Heritage Lodge and Park

61 Filberg Road
250-339-2715
Open daily, grounds from 8 am to dusk
Donations accepted
Set on 3.5 hectares of garden and waterfront, this former estate of R.J. Filberg and his wife Florence McCormack is a lovely place for a morning or afternoon visit. The 1929 stone-and-timber lodge is magnificent, the gardens offer pleasant strolls with more than 100 varieties of trees, the petting farm will delight youngsters, and the teahouse is ideal for anyone seeking a relaxing moment. Each year, the Filberg Festival draws together some 140 artisans for an August long weekend of arts, crafts and musical merriment.

Comox Archives and Museum

1729 Comox Avenue; underneath the Comox Library
250-339-2885
Open Friday and Saturday, 1 pm-4 pm
Donations accepted
Drop into the Comox Archives

Tyee Club

The word Tyee comes from the Chinook language and means "chief" or "great leader." It was used to describe chinook or spring salmon weighing 14 kilograms or more. As the story goes, the Tyee Club was formed by a group of men in 1924. The fishers had concluded that the Tyee salmon was remarkable and therefore it deserved to be celebrated. A club to honour the noble fish was officially created in 1925 with the formulation of a set of rules. It has evolved to include fostering interest in Canadian salmon in general and perpetuating the ideals of good sportsmanship.

You too can join the legendary ranks of anglers who have become members of the Tyee Club. All that's required is to snag a tyee, a 14 kilogram or better chinook salmon. There is a catch, however. Club rules stipulate that, among other conditions, the fish must be caught from a rowboat in Discovery Passage's Tyee Pool, and the extraordinary feat must be done with a hand-operated reel with no more than a 20-pound test line. For more information contact the Tyee Club at 250-287-2724.

and Museum to delve into Comox and Comox Valley history through archival records and photographs. Special exhibitions highlight unique treasures on loan from local residents.

Comox Valley Farmers' Market
Two locations:
Exhibition Grounds (Head-quarters Road); April-October, Saturday, 9 am-12 pm
Downtown Courtenay at Duncan and 4th; June-September, Wednesday, 9 am-12 pm and Thursday, 3 pm-6 pm
250-334-3234
Load up on fresh vegetables and fruits, baked goods, blooming flowers, and local handicrafts at this friendly outdoor market.

The Beaches
Saratoga Beach; 20 kilometres north of Courtenay
Residents and visitors alike enjoy these long, sandy strands, perfect for a picnic and some swimming.

Kitty Coleman Woodland Gardens
6183 Whitaker Road
Open daily
250-338-6901
Admission charged
Cedar bark paths lead through this 10 hectare woodland with thriving heritage rhododendrons — some 3000 — and other plantings. After a stroll, have refreshments at the tearoom.

Courtenay
Population: 19,803
Since the late 1800s, Courtenay has served as the market centre for the Comox Valley. Today it is one of Vancouver Island's fastest growing communities; its population has exploded by nearly 50 percent in the last decade.

Climate and lifestyle are its allure. Here, wrapped around the tidal estuary of the Courtenay River and protected by the Beaufort Mountains to the west, temperatures remain mild. Farms and orchards flourish in the surrounding landscape, and Courtenay itself is a busy commercial centre, its down-town filled with stores, bistros,

The Big Rock – Campbell River's Community Canvas

"Big Rock" outside Campbell River displays local artists' musings.

Known by locals simply as the "Big Rock," the cottage-sized boulder conspicuously lounging upon the beach off Highway 19 outside Campbell River greets passersby — a much-cherished landmark of dubious distinction. The 12-metre-high protrusion is marred and marked with graffiti, the territorial canvas, if you will,

for folks who have something to say or something to draw.

For years Campbell River municipal officers and legislators grappled with the problem of keeping the boastful boulder presentable, but they finally wisely decided to leave well enough alone. As the artwork and scribbles are largely inoffensive — mostly

whimsical drawings and adolescent love notes — the "Big Rock" continues to serve as the mural of choice for would-be artists.

Geologically speaking, the massive chunk of stone is a glacial erratic, once locked in the embrace of an Ice Age glacier, but deposited here as the ice melted away. A prevalent local tale contends that the boulder is actually the remains of an overconfident grizzly bear.

As the story goes, this grizzly bear wished to relocate from the mainland to Vancouver Island and gloated that he could leap his way over the Strait of Georgia. The Great Spirit warned the bruin not to touch the water as he jumped, but unfortunately the braggart bear fell short of his goal, and when his paws touched the surf he was turned forever to stone.

Gold River is the home port for the MV Uchuck III.

coffee shops, boutiques, and markets. For a more sylvan experience of the town, take the Courtenay Riverwalk, beginning behind the Info Centre.

Courtenay is named for Captain George Courtenay, skipper of the British Royal Navy's 50-gun frigate *Constance*. It seems the captain, when off duty, loved to fish the main river leading into Augusta Bay (now Comox Harbour), and in time the place became known as Courtenay's river. With the coming of the nearby settlement, the name was adopted for the emerging town.

Courtenay and District Museum and Paleontology Centre

207 4th Street
250-334-0686
Open daily, May-September; Tuesday to Sunday, October-April
Admission charged
Greeting visitors to the Courtenay and District Museum and Palenontology Centre, housed in the former

post office, is a spectacular fossil of an ornithominid, its back-curved neck and arching tail presenting a dramatic arabesque. Also housed in this vintage 1925 building is an elasmosaur measuring some 10 metres long, which roamed the banks of the Puntledge River 80 million years ago. Indeed, the museum holds some 5000 fossils and is the first stop on the Great Canadian Fossil Trail. First Nations exhibits, and displays showcasing settlement artifacts, round out the museum's excellent collections.

Comox Valley Public Art Gallery

367 4th Street
250-338-6211
Open Tuesday to Saturday, 10 am-5 pm
Donations accepted
Come here to see the work of more than 100 local and Island artists, including jewellery, pottery, woodcrafts, and paintings.

North Central Island Tee Time

Comox Golf Club
1718 Balmoral Avenue
Comox, BC
250-339-4444
Nine holes

Crown Isle Resort and Golf Community
399 Clubhouse Drive
Courtenay, BC
250-337-8212 or 888-338-8439
www.crownisle.com
Eighteen holes

Glacier Green Golf Course
CFB Comox
Comox, BC
250-339-0300
Eighteen holes

Longlands Par 3 Golf Course
1239 Anderton Road
Comox, BC
250-339-6363
Eighteen holes

Mulligans Golf Centre
4985 Cottonwood Road
Courtenay, BC
250-338-2440
Nine holes

Saratoga Golf Course
2084 Saratoga Road
Black Creek, BC
250-337-8212
Nine holes

Sequoia Springs Golf
700 Petersen Road
Campbell River, BC
250-287-4970
www.sequoiasprings.com
Eighteen holes

Storey Creek Golf Club
300 McGimpsey Road
Campbell River, BC
250-923-3673
www.storeycreek.bc.ca
Eighteen holes

Sunnydale Golf and Country Club
5291 North Island Highway
Courtenay, BC
250-334-3060
Eighteen holes

Queneesh Native Gallery and Gift Shop

3310 Comox Road
250-339-7702
Open daily
Admission free

Stop here for a look at excellent Comox First Nation arts, in addition to works from other Pacific Northwest First Nations artisans. The gallery's brochure relates the legend of Queneesh, which was the great white whale to which the Comox and Pentlatch peoples lashed their canoes during the Great Flood (see The Legend of Queneesh box).

Mount Washington Alpine Resort

Strathcona Parkway; exit 130,
Inland Island Highway
250-338-1386
888-231-1499 (reservations)
www.mountwashington.ca

Summer fun and winter frolic find no better home than here in the shadow of 1588 metre Mount Washington. Hiking and mountain biking call visitors to the wild from June to October. Summer activities also feature horseback riding in alpine meadows, ATV tours, Disc golf, fly fishing tours, and special events every weekend. Come the first snowfall, schussers anticipate the opening of alpine and nordic ski-

Sailing Into History Aboard the MV *Uchuck III*

The bridge of the MV Uchuck III

There is perhaps no better way to experience the northern reaches of Vancouver Island's west coast than on the *MV Uchuck III*. Indeed, other than by floatplane or private boat, there is scant means to explore remote Nootka Sound, where Europeans first made contact with the First Nations of British Columbia.

The *MV Uchuck III* is in fact a key link to the remote villages and settlements that comprise the human occupation of this crenellated coastline, a maze of inlets and channels. The 41-metre passenger and freight vessel, formerly a US Navy minesweeper, plies routes from Gold River to Tahsis, Yuquot, Zeballos, and Kyuquot. As it is a working coastal supply ship, passengers can watch the loading and unloading of equipment and supplies at logging camps and other outposts. There are also frequent chances to see wildlife, from black bears wandering the shoreline to eagles soaring overhead to migrating whales.

Nootka Sound Day Trips to Friendly Cove

Departs Wednesday and Saturday, mid-June to mid-September

These summertime sailings take in Yuquot, also known as Friendly Cove, the ancestral home of the Mowachaht people. Passengers may disembark at this national historic site. To and from Yuquot, the *MV Uchuck III* makes supply stops at logging camps, as well as letting off or picking up kayakers.

Kyuquot Adventure

Departs Thursday, year-round

This two-day, overnight excursion explores Nootka Sound and eventually heads up the west coast to the small settlement of Kyuquot. Upon arrival at Kyuquot, passengers have time to explore the harbour-hugging town before dinner. Overnight accommodations are at a local bed & breakfast, followed by an early departure the next morning for the run back to Gold River.

Zeballos Adventure

Departs Monday, year-round

Sailing Nootka Sound and the Esperanza Inlet, the *MV Uchuck III* calls at the coastal community of Zeballos, once known for its gold mines. Passengers disembark, with plenty of time to explore the town before bedding down at a local accommodation. The next day the ship points the compass back toward Gold River, with a few supply stops on the way.

Nootka Sound Service Ltd.

MV Uchuck III
PO Box 57
Gold River BC V0P 1G0
250-283-2325
www.mvuchuck.com

The Discovery Islands

Cape Mudge Lighthouse marks the southern tip of Quadra Island for Discovery Passage mariners.

Look east from Campbell River to spy Discovery Passage. Beyond, in a myriad of channels and waterways, repose the Discovery Islands. Quadra and Cortes are the most visited and offer travellers marvellous scenery and recreation opportunities. The Outer Islands (Read, Maurelle, Sonora, Stuart, East and West Redonda, the Rendezvous Islands, East and West Thurlow, and Raza) are more remote, sporting pristine nature excursions for boaters, kayakers, and sportfishers.

Campbell River Info Centre
PO Box 400, 1235 Shoppers Row
Campbell River BC V9W 5B6
250-287-4636
1-866-830-1113
www.northcentralisland.com
Quadra Island
Population: 3200
A large island (276 square kilometres), Quadra presents many, many recreational opportunities. Fishing is good, and the sheltered harbours,

coves, and scads of tiny inlets are popular with scuba divers, kayakers, and fishers. Heriot Bay is the main town, and there are also the communities of Quathiaski Cove and Cape Mudge. Commercial campsites, lodges, cottages, and fishing resorts are numerous.

Quadra Island is named for Don Juan Francisco de la Bodega y Quadra, an 18th-century Spanish naval officer and, incidentally, a good friend of Captain George Vancouver, who set foot on the island in 1792. The island was originally a homeland for the Coast Salish First Nations, but in the 1800s the Kwagiulth people began living in the area as well, and the We-Wai-Kai band of the Kwagiulth First Nation still lives at Cape Mudge.

Quadra Island is reached by a 12-minute ferry ride from Campbell River.

Cape Mudge Lighthouse
Lighthouse Road; take Herriot Bay Road to Cape Mudge Road and then Lighthouse Road
Rising above a stone-strewn beach, Cape Mudge Lighthouse marks the southern tip of Quadra Island for Discovery Passage mariners.
Cortes Island
www.cortesisland.com
Population: 800
Riddled with tiny harbours and coves, in addition to a constellation of islets, Cortes Island, at 25 kilometres long by 13 kilometres wide, commands the entrance to Desolation Sound, one of British Columbia's most popular boating areas. Squirrel Cove, known for its tidal waterfall, and Gorge Harbour, a narrow channel wedged between precipitous cliffs, are two of the most frequented cruising compass points.

Cortes Island is reached by a 45-minute ferry ride from Quadra Island.

A finely carved thunderbird totem pole greets visitors to Courtenay.

ing, plus snowboarding and snow tubing.

Alpine facilities include more than 50 runs, serviced by a variety of lifts including a new Hawk High-Speed 6-pack, moving 2400 riders per hour. Vertical drop exceeds 500 metres for some runs, ensuring exhilarating skiing. Snowboarders point tips towards a half-pipe and two snowboard parks. The resort's full-service day lodge operates a ski school and equipment rental; the restaurant is open for evening meals and entertainment. Overnight accommodations can be secured at a number of private chalets and condominiums that comprise the Mount Washington village, as well as at the Deer Lodge. Mount Washington also has an RV park.

Puntledge River Hatchery
Powerhouse Road; west on Lake Trail Road, then north on Powerhouse Road
Open daily, year-round
250-338-7444
Admission free
From this viewing site it's possible (depending upon the season) to see chum, pink, coho, and chinook salmon, as well as steelhead trout.

Merville
Population: 865
Acclaimed British Columbia author Jack Hodgins grew up here and drew from his recollections to craft classics such as *Spit Delaney's Island*, Broken Ground, and *The Barclay Family Theatre*. A general store and a gas station provide the basics for the surrounding farms and homes.

Black Creek
Population: 1950
Black Creek is the town centre for a small Mennonite community and also provides services for campers at Miracle Beach Provincial Park.

Campbell River
Campbell River Visitor Info Centre
PO Box 400
Campbell River BC V9W 5B6
250-287-4636
800-463-4FUN
www.vquest.com/crchamber
Visitor Centre: 1235 Shoppers Row, Tyee Plaza
Population: 31,253
Campbell River has long vied for the title of "Salmon Capital of the World," an appellation it certainly can lay claim to. For more than a century, its favourable location — at the mouth of the Campbell River where it flows

into Discovery Passage — has lured sportfishers seeking the big ones. It all started as the result of an 1896 article by Sir Richard Musgrave in the British publication *The Field*, which told of snagging a whopping 31 kilogram salmon at the mouth of the Campbell River. The account forever put the area on fishers' maps. And the monster-sized salmon were there — Tyees, chinook salmon weighing in excess of 14 kilograms, spun the fishing reels of the rich and famous including the King of Siam, John Wayne, and, more recently, Bill Gates and Sean Connery. In 1968 a record was set when the Discovery Passage yielded a mighty 32 kilogram chinook. Today, the Campbell River is one of BC's 19 Heritage Rivers, designated for ongoing restoration efforts to protect the river and its estuaries for spawning salmon.

Still widely regarded for its sportfishing (and increasingly for scuba diving and kayaking), Campbell River is also home to industry, with a state-of-the-art paper and pulp processing plant plus two working mines nearby. Consequently, Campbell River is also the region's busy commercial hub, offering urban amenities with a small-town character.

Discovery Pier
Downtown at Government Wharf / Concession
250-286-6199
Open daily, May-October,
7 am-10 pm
This active pier stretching 185 metres into Discovery Passage offers pleasant strolls night or day. Fishers will be especially delighted, as the pier was built with recreational fishing in mind; the wharf is equipped with rod holders, fish-cleaning tables, and bait stands. The concession sells licences and rents tackle, in addition to serving snacks and ice cream.

Museum at Campbell River
470 Island Highway
250-287-3103
www.crmuseum.com
Open daily, May to September; Tuesday to Sunday, October to May
Admission charged
Set on a bluff overlooking Discovery Passage and Quadra Island, the Museum at Campbell River is a prize. Its First Nations exhibit, "The Treasures of Siwidi" — an installation of fascinating masks set in a darkened theatre with accompanying narration — provides an enthralling insight into First Nations mythology. Other exhibits explore the region's early settlement, logging, and salmon fishing through engaging displays and installations. Step aboard a typical up-Island "floathouse," climb onto a vintage 1919 logging truck, and don't miss the historic film footage of the Ripple Rock explosion that vanquished the troublesome outcropping in Seymour Narrows. Next to the museum is Sequoia Park, where an enormous sequoia reaches heavenward.

Campbell River Public Art Gallery
1235 Shoppers Row
250-287-2261
Open Tuesday to Saturday, July-August; Wednesday to Saturday, September-June
Admission free
Adjacent to the visitor's information centre, this facility presents both touring and local shows by national and international artists and sculptors.

Tidemark Theatre
250-287-7899
Admission charged
Downtown Campbell River's landmark, known for its peppermint pink facade, is the region's performing arts venue with a seasonal roster of engagements.

Transformations on the Shore
Rotary Beach Seawalk
Admission free
The 4.2 kilometres of the Rotary Beach Seawalk are lined with whimsical outdoor sculptures, all created in the annual driftwood carving contest (held July 1 weekend).

Wei Wai Kum House of Treasures
1370 Island Highway
250-286-1440
www.houseoftreasures.com
Open daily
Admission free
This retail outlet for First Nations' artists is as much a contemporary museum as it is a store. Come here to see excellent masks, jewellery, totem poles, and other arts and crafts. At their newly installed Gildas Theatre, local First Nations share dances, songs, and stories of the Laichwiltach people.

Campbell River Optical Marine Museum
102-250 Dogwood Street
250-287-2052
Open daily
Admission charged
Come here to see a variety of marine artifacts.

North Central Island Festivals & Events

FEBRUARY
Heritage Tea
Enjoy old time luxury at the Filberg Lodge, Comox

APRIL
Snow to Surf Relay Race
Mount Washington
Teams compete in a race from Mount. Washington down to the Comox Marina.

MAY
Cumberland Empire Days
Cumberland
Festivities and food make this a great family event.
North Island Hot Jazz Festival
May 30- June 1, ontinuous jazz and dancing in downtown Courtenay.
Painters at Painters
(late May)
An annual gathering of western Canada's top artists at Painters Lodge in Campbell River. Meet the artists, attend workshops, demonstrations, and round table discussions.
Juggler's Festival
Quadra Island (early May)
Various locations on the island, amazing jugglers from all around converge on Quadra.

MID-MAY – OCTOBER
Arts & Edibles Market, *Campbell River* Taste local wares and view the work of regional artists. Held ever Sunday at the Tyee Plaza.

JUNE
Union Bay Days
Union Bay
Annual fair with games, displays, food, etc.
Denman Island Home and Garden Tour
Denman Island
Participants get the chance to explore several remarkable

gardens and homes not generally open to the public.
Annual Great Walk
Tahsis (June 7)
Put you're your feet to the test on challenging and beautiful routes.
Transformations on the Shore
(June 26 to June 30)
This annual wood carving contest takes place at the Frank James Park in Willow Point and features carvers from all over the world.

JULY–AUGUST
Heritage Puppet Theatre
Enjoy the antics of our Heritage Puppet Theatre at the Campbell River Museum daily throughout the summer.

JULY
Quadra Island Canada Day
Celebrate Canada Day island style with fun events all day for the whole family.
Vancouver Island Music Fest
Courtenay
Three-day event with musicians and performers from across Canada and the world.
Comox Nautical Days
Marina Park, Comox
Family event with canoe jousting, a bathtub race, clam chowder cookoff, and the Ceremony of the Flags.
Comox International Air *Show and Armed Forces Day*
CFB Comox, Comox
Ground displays of aircraft plus an air show by Canadian and American aerobatic flyers.

AUGUST
Filberg Festival
Filberg Heritage Lodge and Park, Comox
Annual 4-day event with 140 artisans and entertainment.

Hornby Festival of the Arts
Hornby Island
This 10-day event brings together Canadian artists for shows and seminars.
Courtenay Rodeo
Norwood Equestrian Centre, Courtenay
Rodeo events from bronco busting to steer wrangling.
Annual Wine Festival
Wine and food tastings. Call 888-231-1499 for details.
Campbell River Salmon Festival and Loggers Sports
This annual event takes place at Nunn's Creek Park and includes loggers sports, Stage of Stars (concert), petting zoo and many activities for the whole family.

SEPTEMBER-OCTOBER-NOVEMBER
Return of the Salmon
Visit rivers or hatcheries in the region to watch the return of the salmon to spawn. This is a wonder of nature that is unique to our region.

SEPTEMBER
Comox Valley Art Studio Tour
Courtenay (gallery on 4th St.)
Visit 15-20 art studios on this do-it-yourself tour

NOVEMBER
Moonlight Magic
Courtenay downtown
Annual event with street entertainment and refreshments.
Comox Valley Christmas Arts & Crafts Fair
Comox Recreation Centre
100 artisans display their creations.

DECEMBER
Santa Claus Parade
Courtenay downtown
Parade with floats, carollers, and bands.

Haig-Brown House Education Centre

2250 Campbell River Road
250-286-6646
www.heritage.gov.bc/haig/haig.htm
or oberon.ark.com/~kdbhbh/
Open daily
Admission charged

This BC Heritage Site is the one-time home of Roderick Haig-Brown, noted conservationist and author. Besides tours of the 1923 farmhouse, the centre offers a variety of workshops and retreats, including writers' seminars and grandparent / grandchild fly-fishing outings. The Haig-Brown Kingfisher Creek Society fostered, and continues, work to restore the west and east branches of Kingfisher Brook (now creek), which flows into the Campbell River.

NorskeCanada / Elk Falls Division

Elk Falls Mill Road; four kilometres north of Campbell River on Highway 19
250-287-5594, call for reservations
Tours run May to August; Monday to Friday at 10 am; second tour Tuesday and Thursday at 1 pm
Admission free

Experience the inner workings of the Norske pulp and paper mill during the two-hour tours.

Seymour Narrows and Ripple Rock

11 kilometres north of Campbell River

Up until 1958, the perilous peaks of Ripple Rock — the "Devil Beneath the Sea — lurked only metres below the surface of the passage, where the feisty current can flow at more than 10 knots. The mariners' nightmare, which over the years claimed more

Floatplanes offer practical transportation to and from remote Gold River.

than 100 lives and scuttled some two dozen ships, was dispatched, blown to bits, by one of the most thunderous non-atomic blasts in history. It took miners nearly two years to tunnel from Maud Island and then pack enough explosives to pulverize the submerged rock. At its ignition, the detonation rocketed more than 600,000 tonnes of rock and water 300 metres into the air. Four kilometres north of Campbell River on Highway 19, a stop at the Seymour Narrows Lookout grants a view of the treacherous passage. Two kilometres farther north on the highway is the starting point for the Ripple Rock Trail, a four kilometre hike through forest to an excellent overlook of the waterway.

Nootka Sound

Honoured as the birthplace of British Columbia, Nootka Sound was where First Nations people welcomed Captain James Cook in 1778. The Gold River area is also the traditional home of the Mowachaht and Muchalaht of the Nuu-chah-nulth peoples.

Gold River

Gold River Visitor Info Centre

PO Box 610
Gold River BC V0P 1G0
250-283-2418 or 250-283-2202
www.village.goldriver.bc.ca
Visitor Centre: Highway 28 and Scout Lake Road
Open mid-May to Sept.
Population: 1786

An "instant town," Gold River sprang up in 1965 to support a pulp mill located 12 kilometres downriver at Muchalat Inlet. Sadly, the mill closed in 1998 and the town largely relies on tourism now.

And there is much to offer visitors; Gold River is known for its steelhead fishing, and the town offers all the conveniences and supplies to support kayakers and boaters wishing to explore the wonders of remote and wild Nootka Sound. Recently, scuba diving has flourished here as enthusiasts marvel at the pristine underwater world of Nootka Sound.

Nootka Sound Service

Muchalat Inlet; 12 kilometres south of Gold River town centre
250-283-2515 or 250-283-2325
Admission charged

Passengers are welcome to board the MV *Uchuck III*, a converted 1943 US

Gold River is known for its steelhead fishing.

minesweeper, now a working freighter, for a scenic journey as the ship plies Nootka Sound, supplying remote communities. See the Sailing into History Aboard the MV *Uchuck III* box.

Yuquot (National Historic Site)
Mowachaht / Muchalaht First Nations Band Office
Ahaminaquus Tourist Info Centre
Box 459, Gold River BC V0P 1G0
www.yuquot.ca
800-238-2933 or
250-283-7464 (band office)
Population: 3

Situated at the southeastern end of Nootka Sound, Yuquot is the ancient summering grounds of the Mowachaht, who became the first indigenous people to welcome European visitors to the shores of Vancouver Island. In 1778, sailors under the command of Captain James Cook entered the sound and were escorted by the Mowachaht through the treacherous waters to the call of "*nootka*" or "circle around," a warning to their pale-looking guests to avoid the perils of submerged rocks here and there. The British named the village Friendly Cove and began trading with the Mowachaht, whom they called Nootka, securing sea otter pelts in particular, which fetched high prices in the Far East and subsequently ushered a surge of traders to Vancouver Island's bountiful shores.

During the 1770s, Yuquot was visited by numerous British, Spanish, and American fur-trading expeditions. In time, conflicts arose between the English and Spanish governments over the sovereignty of the increasingly profitable area. In 1789, the Spanish laid their claim to Yuquot by building a fort and settlement, Santa Cruz de Nutka. Representatives from both European kingdoms attempted, unsuccessfully, to resolve the conflict, but it was the decline in the fur industry of the early 1800s that finally brought an answer to the disagreement — the Spanish abandoned Yuquot, no longer finding it of commercial interest.

Yuquot was declared a national historic site in 1923, and today only one Mowachaht family still resides there, but the church and other buildings remain. Mowachaht-guided tours are available during the summer, coinciding with the arrival of the MV *Uchuck III*, which calls here on Wednesday and Saturday.

Upana Caves
Head Bay Forest Road; 17 kilometres west of Gold River
Admission free

Take flashlights and don rubber-soled boots for self-guided spelunking through the rooms and passages of the Upana Caves. There are 15 known entrances to the extensive cave system. In all, passages run for some 450 metres and take approximately one hour to cover.

Conuma Salmon Hatchery
Head Bay Forest Road; 40 kilometres west of Gold River
250-283-7148
Open daily, 8 am-4 pm
Admission free

Stop at the Conuma Salmon Hatchery to see coho, chum, chinook, and steelhead.

Tahsis
Tahsis Chamber of Commerce
PO Box 278
Tahsis BC V0P 1X0
250-934-6344 or 250-934-5555
www.villageoftahsis.com
Population: 896

A hardworking community of primarily Western Forest

Products Ltd. sawmill employees at the head of Tahsis Inlet, Tahsis is also a favourite base for recreationalists — from kayakers to fishers, spelunkers to whale watchers. Don't forget walkers, too; the annual "Great Walk" from Tahsis to Gold River in early June brings together more than 1000 hoofers who tackle this tough, 70-kilometre heel-to-toe jaunt.

Reachable by a well-maintained gravel road, Tahsis is more easily accessible via the

North Central Island Parks & Recreation

Fillongley Provincial Park
Denman Island; Lambert Channel facing Hornby Island
250-954-4600 or 800-689-9025 (reservations)
www.discovercamping.ca
23 hectares / 10 campsites
A long sand and shell beach, backed by Douglas fir and red cedar, offers great views of Texada Island.

Sandy Island Provincial Marine Park
Denman Island; north end
250-334-4600
18 hectares / limited camping
Only accessible by water, this is a favourite with kayakers.

Boyle Point Provincial Park
Denman Island; south end
250-954-4600
125 hectares / day use
Trails through old-growth Douglas fir lead to great lookouts over Eagle Rock and the Chrome Island lighthouse.

Tribune Bay Provincial Park
Hornby Island; southeast end
250-334-4600
95 hectares / day use
Some of BC's finest white beaches and warmest waters are found here. Tidal pools and shallow coves are excellent for beachcombing.

Helliwell Provincial Park
Hornby Island; southeast end
250-334-4600
69 hectares / day use
Take the five kilometre walk that encircles the park; it offers great views from the cliff tops to Flora Island, where sea lions congregate during the spring.

Mt. Geoffrey Regional Park
Hornby Island; Shingle Spit Road, right on Central Road, right to Strachan Road
250-334-6000
300 hectares / day use
Good trails lead to lookouts with great views.

Public Shellfish Reserve
Adjacent to Baynes Sound Rest Area; 89 kilometres north of Nanaimo
This one-kilometre beach is open for daily harvesting of no more than 15 oysters in the shell (half a litre shucked), 25 butter clams, 12 razor clams, and 75 little neck clams. See the Red Tide box.

Forbidden Plateau Recreation Area (Strathcona Provincial Park)
Mt. Becher's lower slopes; exit 127, Inland Island Highway
This former ski area has many good hiking trails to lakes and meadows.

Nymph Falls Regional Nature Park
Forbidden Plateau Road
250-334-6000
55 hectares / day use
Situated on the Puntledge River, trails lead to the falls and good swimming holes.

Seal Bay Regional Nature Park
Bates Road; north of Comox
250-334-6000
150 hectares / day use
With some 20 kilometres of hiking trails, this park is excellent for hikers; there is good wildfowl watching as well.

Goose Spit Regional Park
Hawkins Road (aka Balmoral); south of Comox
250-334-6000
Six hectares / day use
This sandbar jutting into Comox Harbour offers swimming and lots of bird-watching. Windsurfers like the small park as well.

Miracle Beach Provincial Park
Off Highway 19; 24 kilometres north of Courtenay
250-337-8181
137 hectares / 201 campsites
Only 20 minutes north of Courtenay, this long sandy beach park is perfect for picnics and sandcastle building. Check at the Miracle Beach Nature House for a list of activity programs.

Mitlenatch Island Provincial Marine Park
North end of the Strait of Georgia; 13 kilometres northeast of Miracle Beach
250-337-2400
155 hectares / day use
Though this island park is only accessible by boat, bird-watchers flock here to see nesting glaucous-winged gulls, pelagic cormorants, and other avian species.

Oyster River Regional Park
29 kilometres north of Courtenay
250-334-6000
Five hectares / day use
The Woodhus Slough is located here, and along with the adjoining marsh and beach plain supports some 200 species of birds and 200 species of plants.

regular sailings of the MV *Uchuck III*, as well as by Air Nootka. A marina, fuel dock, boat launch, plus accommodations are available.

Tahsis Museum
Rugged Mountain Road,
Info Centre
250-934-6667
Open daily, June-August

Admission charged
In a restored bunkhouse, the Tahsis Museum displays an interesting collection of local artifacts.

North Central Island Parks & Recreation

Rebecca Spit Provincial Marine Park
Quadra Island; east side of Drew Harbour
250-337-2400
177 hectares / day use
A short BC Ferries trip delivers visitors to this beautiful park with a 1.5 kilometre sand spit, popular with beachcombers and kayakers.

Octopus Islands Provincial Marine Park
Quadra Island; northeast side
250-337-2400
109 hectares / wilderness camping
Only accessible by watercraft, the park is a cluster of small islands, favoured by kayakers.

Smelt Bay Provincial Park
Cortes Island; southwest end
250-337-2400 or 800-689-9025
www.discovercamping.ca
16 hectares / 22 campsites
Known for the thousands of smelt which spawn here, the beach is good for swimming and watersports.

Mansons Landing Provincial Marine Park
Cortes Island; west side, north of Smelt Bay
250-337-2400
100 hectares / day use
Nice beaches and calm waters for paddlers make this sheltered cove popular.

Hague Lake Regional Park
Cortes Island; on Hague Lake, opposite Cortes Motel
250-334-6000
13 hectares / day use
On the eastern shores of Hague Lake, this forest was logged in the 1920s — until

the steam donkey exploded. Its remains are still visible.

Von Donop-Hathayim Provincial Marine Park
Cortes Island; Von Donop Inlet
250-954-4600
1277 hectares / wilderness camping
The Klahoose First Nation and BC Parks manage this park together to protect its saltwater lagoons and tidal marshes.

Elk Falls Provincial Park
Highway 28; one kilometre west of Highway 19
250-337-2400 or 800-689-9025 (reservations)
www.discovercamping.ca
1086 hectares / 122 campsites at Quinsam Campground
Many good hiking trails, plus fishing and swimming holes are located here at the confluence of the Campbell and Quinsam rivers.

Loveland Bay Provincial Park
Camp 5 Road (aka Brewster Road); five kilometres west of Highway 19, past John Hart Dam
250-337-2400 or 800-689-9025 (reservations)
www.discovercamping.ca
30 hectares / 47 campsites, two group campsites
This popular park features good swimming and canoeing, plus lots of hiking trails.

Strathcona Provincial Park
Principle access: off Highway 28; accessible via Paradise Meadows/Mt. Washington (Hwy 19, exit 130) or Forbidden Plateau Recreation area (hwy 19, exit 127) 254,800 hectares / 161 campsites in

two areas,
and wilderness camping
Hikers of all abilities relish this park, which is filled with alpine meadows, mountain and ocean views, and lush forests. Great wildlife viewing possibilities. See the Strathcona Provincial Park box.

Bligh Island Provincial Marine Park
Muchalat Inlet; near Gold River
250-954-4600
4455 hectares / wilderness camping
Kayakers and sportfishers love this remote recreation area, which embraces forested islands known as the Spanish Pilot group. The island is named for Vice-Admiral William Bligh, famed captain of the *Bounty*, who was set adrift by mutineers and survived a 3618-mile voyage in an open boat. Bligh was master aboard Captain Cook's *Resolution* when it called at Vancouver Island in 1778.

Morton Lake Provincial Park
MacMillan Bloedel, Menzies Bay Division; 20 kilometres north of Campbell River
250-954-4600
67 hectares / 24 campsites
Small park with good family camping, fishing, hiking, and swimming.

Rock Bay Provincial Marine Park
Highway 19; 37 kilometres north of Gold River to Rock Bay Road, then 10 kilometres east
250-954-4600
525 hectares / limited camping
This rocky headland features some sheltered bays, plus walking trails and fishing.

North Vancouver Island

The seaside village of Kyuquot is situated on Walters Island in Kyoquot Sound.

I t is the pristine wilderness and impressive outdoor recreation opportunities that attract most travellers to the farthest reaches of Vancouver Island. Encompassing the entire northern tip — hemmed in on the east by the Queen Charlotte Strait and open to the wild Pacific Ocean on the west —

North Vancouver Island is blissfully devoid of urbanization. Here the towns are small, the people friendly and hard working, and the great outdoors is always at the front door. Temperate rain forest covers most of the terrain, interspersed with mountains, lakes, and clear running rivers. There is still a feeling of the frontier here.

Highway 19, the main route up the Island, narrows to two lanes and tunnels through thick interior forest, with tall trees walling in the road on either side for kilometre after kilometre. Only some 3 percent of the Island's population lives here, and what traffic is encountered is usually a logging

truck, or RVs and SUVs towing campers or boats, with kayaks and bikes strapped on. The region has long been devoted to logging, mining, and

commercial fishing, but increasingly tourism is adding to the local economy.

Port McNeill and Port Hardy, both east coast harbour

North Island Recommendations

- Check out the Salmon River Wildlife Reserve at Kelsey Bay to marvel at osprey, trumpeter swans, hawks, and ducks.
- Strap on some skis for alpine and cross-country skiing at Mt. Cain Alpine Park.
- Pay a visit to the Port McNeill Heritage Museum to examine the area's pioneer and logging history; don't miss the "World's Largest Burl" near Port McNeill.

- Take the ferry to Cormorant Island and explore Alert Bay and its many First Nations sites, especially the U'mista Cultural Centre.
- Take the ferry to Malcolm Island, visiting the pretty town of Sointula and its heritage museum.
- Venture along logging roads to historic Ronning's Gardens outside Holberg; the horticultural legacy seen here is worth the trip.

Opposite: Alert Bay on Cormorant Island is rich with First Nations artifacts.

towns, are the largest communities, offering a complete range of visitor services. Port McNeill makes a good base from which to plan excursions into the Nimpkish Valley and to the west coast, for a visit to the small historic town of Zeballos. Closer at hand is the delightful village of Telegraph Cove, a pretty settlement built on stilts over the surf and famous for its whale watching excursions and kayaking. Offshore from Port McNeill are Cormorant and Malcolm islands. The town of Alert Bay on Cormorant is one of Vancouver Island's most intriguing First Nations historical destinations, while Sointula, on Malcolm, was

Robson Bight

Also called the Michael Bigg Ecological Reserve, in honour of the late Dr. Michael Bigg, whose research added immensely to the understanding of killer whales, Robson Bight protects 1248 hectares of irreplaceable killer whale habitat. This is the site of one of the killer whales' favourite rubbing beaches. Northern resident whales are often seen wriggling across the smooth pebbles in the shallows for hours at a time, perhaps for the sheer enjoyment, but also no doubt scraping off a few pesky parasites in the process.

Interestingly, the behavior is only evident in the northern resident killer whale population, and not in southern or transient whale groups, suggesting to researchers that this cetacean tradition has developed over several generations.

once the site of a Finnish utopian community.

Farther north, Port Hardy welcomes travellers with a wealth of year-round outdoor activities. From sportfishers to divers to kayakers to inveterate hikers, recreational enthusiasts find ample options for pursuing their passion, and Cape Scott Provincial Park at the far northern tip of the Island won't disappoint even the most experienced outdoors person. Port Hardy is also the BC Ferries terminal for excursions to mid-coast mainland British Columbia, the Inside Passage, and Prince Rupert.

Strathcona Park Lodge and Outdoor Education Centre

Upper Campbell Lake;
Highway 28, 38 kilometres
west of Highway 19
250-286-3122
www.strathcona.bc.ca
Sign up for family excursions, wilderness skill programs, or outdoor summer camps at the Strathcona Park Lodge and Outdoor Education Centre. Two programs of special note are the Canadian Outdoor Leadership Training (COLT) for adults 19 or older. This intensive 105-day program hones land- and water-based outdoor skills, promotes environmental awareness, and provides valuable insight into experiential education platforms. For young adults 12 to 18 years old, Wilderness Youth Leadership Development summer camps are available.

Boliden / Westmin Resources Mine

South end Buttle Lake; 12
kilometres from Ralph River
campground
250-287-9271
Taking an escorted tour of the

Kayakers

Boliden / Westmin Resources mine at Myra Falls offers a rare opportunity to see the inner workings of a copper and zinc mining operation.

Sayward-Kelsey Bay

Sayward Chamber of
Commerce
PO Box 70
Sayward BC V0P 1R0
250-282-5512
www.sayward.com
Population: 432; area
population: 1400
Farming, fishing, and logging, particularly the logging operations of MacMillan Bloedel, are the lifeblood of the Salmon River Valley, and Sayward-Kelsey Bay is the principal commercial centre. Kelsey Bay's wharf was once the terminus for the BC Ferries' Inside Passage route from Prince Rupert, and now the harbour is the only public small-craft anchorage on the Johnstone Strait between Campbell River and Port McNeill. The Salmon River, which drains into Johnstone Strait at Kelsey Bay, is known for its large steelhead, and at the river's mouth is the Salmon River Wildlife Reserve, an

avian haven for osprey, trumpeter swans, hawks, and ducks.

Plan a stop at the Cablehouse Cafe, about one kilometre beyond Sayward Junction. The cafe was constructed with 2700 metres of wire rope, 26 tonnes in all. Most of the cable is two-inch skyline logging cable, used primarily during the 1950s.

Mt. Cain Alpine Park
Highway 19; follow the signs
Mt. Cain Alpine Park Society
Box 1225
Port McNeill BC V0N 2R0
888-668-6622
www.island.net~cain

It can be rough going to reach Mt. Cain Alpine Park, but rewards await. In summer, hiking is superb through wildflower-filled meadows up to shimmering, clear lakes. Come winter, 1646-metre Mt. Cain delivers a 450-metre vertical drop and 18 downhill runs serviced by T-bars and handle-tows. Moreover, Mt. Cain offers 20 kilometres of unmarked cross-country trails. Hostel-style accommodation is available, and there is a day lodge with equipment rental and lessons.

Woss and the Nimpkish Valley
Population: 600

The Nimpkish Valley is known for its trout fishing, hunting, logging, and, lately, its windsurfers, who love the breezes puffing across Nimpkish Lake. Woss, a Canadian Forest Products community, honours its logging legacy with an antique steam locomotive prominently displayed. Services found here include a motel, coffee shop, and gas station.

Zeballos
Zeballos Village Office
PO Box 127
Zeballos BC V0P 2A0
250-761-4070
www.zeballos.com
Population: 265

A thriving gold mining town from 1938 to 1943, Zeballos is a sleepier place these days. Some mining exploration still goes on, though the main commercial enterprises now are focused on fishing, logging, and tourism. Zeballos makes an excellent base for boat trips into the waterways and inlets of Nootka Sound. In particular, kayakers come to Zeballos to access Catala Island and Nuchatlitz provincial parks, and the islands of Kyoquot Sound.

Zeballos Museum
Maquinna Avenue
250-761-4070 or 250-761-4229 (winter)
Open Tuesday to Saturday, July-August
Admission charged

Pull in at the Zeballos Museum to delve into artifacts and

Killer Whales

Killer whales travel in matriarchal family groups, or pods, usually consisting of mothers and their young. Pod sizes vary. They generally contain five to 20 individuals, but some have as many as 50 members. Males stay with their mothers as long as she is alive, but females split off to join other pods. Pods emit unique sets of calls and clicks when foraging, travelling, and socializing. When resting, members of a pod line up abreast of each other, synchronizing their breathing.

Individual killer whales are recognized by their dorsal fins, their saddle patches, plus their scars and nicks. Dr. Michael Bigg pioneered the identification method, and thanks to his efforts there have been some 480 killer whales documented in British Columbia waters. Of this total, about 300 are specialized fish eaters and stay year-round; they are grouped as "resident" whales. About 200 of the resident killer whales have been spotted in the Johnstone Strait, making this area the most consistently reliable spotting location around Vancouver Island. The remaining whales are called "transients"; they are travelling whales that visit the area but don't stay.

Killer whales swim at speeds of two to eight kilometres per hour, often in tight groups, but they can sometimes be dispersed over several square kilometres. Individual dive sequences generally are composed of one long dive lasting about three to four minutes, with subsequent shorter duration dives of 20 to 30 seconds.

At birth, killer whales are slightly more than two metres long, while fully grown females may reach eight metres, and mature bulls ten metres. Male dorsal fins may be two metres tall, while female dorsal fins usually measure one metre high. Cows may live as long as 75 years and bulls about 50 years. During a typical life, a cow may raise five offspring, though she may give birth to more. Many calves die before the age of five.

memorabilia from the area's gold mining history. Here too you will learn the tale of Spanish explorer Lt. Ciriaco Cevallos, who visited the region in 1791 and lent Zeballos his name.

Kyuquot

Kyuquot Band Office
General Delivery
Kyuquot BC V0P 1J0
250-332-5259
Population: 275
Situated on Walters Island in

Charming Telegraph Cove is strung along boardwalks lining the shoreline.

The Forestry Industry

Logging companies are major employers for Vancouver Island residents.

As one of Vancouver Island's top employers, the forestry industry in its many forms — from logging operations to sawmills and pulp processing plants — is a constant presence on the Island. Many of the roads into the Island's backcountry are logging roads, reaching deep into the forests. Logging trucks zoom up and down the highways delivering raw timber to mills. And towns from Port Renfrew to Port Hardy have stakes in the forestry business.

It is Captain Edward Stamp who is credited with opening Vancouver Island's first sawmill at Port Alberni in 1860. Early logging methods were decidedly laborious, not to mention dangerous. Essentially, two men would fell trees using huge crosscut saws, and after the massive timbers were stripped, the logs would be dragged off by teams of horses or oxen to a nearby pond or lake. Booms of logs were graded and sorted before being sent off to the mill for processing into lumber and shipment to markets around the world.

Nowadays, the process is similar, but is carried out with high-technology efficiency and considerably more concern for the environment. Large corporations such as Weyerhaeuser, Timber West, Western Forest Products, and Norske Skog have made massive investments to sustain and perpetuate the commercial viability of forests and their harvest for production of lumber, pulp, and paper.

These companies are eager to give visitors a glimpse of their fascinating operations on guided tours, which come in three basic formats:

Forest Tours – These excursions venture into forests to see active logging sites, where massive machinery harvests logs and loads logging trucks. Knowledgeable driver / guides explain the intricacies of logging methods, as well as local natural history. Excursions usually take four to five hours.

Sawmill Tours – These are tours of working sawmills, where guides detail the processes that take raw timber and turn it into usable lumber products. Tours generally last about two hours.

Pulp and Paper Mill Tours – These tours examine working pulp mills, and guides explain

Kyoquot Sound, the village of Kyuquot is only accessible via floatplane or the MV *Uchuck III*, which calls here once a week to ferry passengers and deliver supplies. Kyuquot houses a store, post office, restaurant and a few homes. Across the bay at Houpsitas is the Kyuquot First Nation village, home for both the Kyuquot and Checleset peoples. Visitors are asked to register at the band office before entering.

Kayakers favour Kyuquot as a base from which to launch wilderness excursions to several remote provincial parks: Rugged Point, Tahsish-Kwois, Big Bunsby, and Brooks Peninsula. Contact BC Parks Strathcona District at 250-954-4600 for information on accessing these wilderness areas.

Telegraph Cove
Port McNeill and District
Chamber of Commerce
PO Box 129
Port McNeill BC V0N 2R0
250-949-9094 / 800-903-6660
www.vinva.bc.ca
Population: 6
Cute and charming describes pretty Telegraph Cove, a diminutive village perched upon pilings and strung together by raised boardwalks running about the cove's shoreline. Back before World

The Forestry Industry

the processes in which pulp is transformed into sheets, then dried and wrapped for shipment, or processed into various types of paper. These tours usually last about an hour.

Forestry And Mill Tours
Weyerhaeuser /
Chemainus Mill
2860 Victoria Street
Chemainus, BC
250-246-9793
Open Tuesday and Thursday, May-September, 12:30 pm-2 pm
Admission free
Explore a working sawmill equipped with state-of-the-art technology.
Weyerhaeuser / Island Phoenix Mill
900 Phoenix Way
Nanaimo, BC
250-722-4138
Open by appointment only
Admission free
One of the largest automated sawmills on the coast, this tour showcases the entire sawmilling process.
Alberni Forest Information Centre
#15-5440 Argyle Street; at Harbour Quay
Port Alberni, BC

250-720-2108
Open daily, July-August; fewer days and shorter hours the rest of the year. Call for information.
Admission free
Visit the interesting forestry displays here, and sign up for a forest tour to see actual logging operations.
Weyerhauser / Alberni Pacific Division
2500 1st Avenue
Port Alberni, BC
250-724-7428
Tours run Tuesday and Wednesday, July-August, 10 am
Take this two-hour tour, which delves into the inner workings of a busy sawmill, from grapplers loading raw logs to the many processes — sawing, edging, trimming, sorting, and stacking — that create finished lumber products ready for shipment.
North Island Forestry Tours
1245 Shoppers Row
Visitor Information Centre,
Tyee Plaza
Campbell River, BC
250-286-4636
Tours run Tuesday and Wednesday, July-August, 9 am
Admission charged
Join a knowledgeable guide

for an excursion into the nearby forest to see logging operations.
NorskeCanada / Elk Falls Division
Elk Falls Mill Road; four kilometres north of Campbell River on Highway 19
250-287-5594, call for reservations
Tours run May to August, Monday to Friday at 10 am; second tour Tuesday and Thursday at 1 pm
Admission free
See the Norske pulp and paper mill at work during the two-hour tours.
North Island Discovery Centre
Highway 19; near junction with Beaver Cove Road, four kilometres south of Port McNeill
250-956-1446
Open daily, May-September, 10 am-4:30 pm
Forestry tours on Monday, Wednesday, Friday at 10 am
Admission free
Besides free forestry tours, the centre offers a wealth of information on the forest industry.

Logging trucks haul timber from sorting sites to mills.

The world's largest burl

A logger deftly sorts and positions floating logs.

War I, Telegraph Cove was the northern terminus for a telegraph line running from tree limb to tree limb up Vancouver Island's eastern coast. The 1920s brought a sawmill to Telegraph Cove, and it operated until the 1980s. Nature tourism took over when Stubbs Island Charters introduced BC's first killer whale-spotting excursion company. Other charter outfitters followed, and now Telegraph Cove is renowned as one of the world's best locales for seeing killer whales.

Robson Bight is the reason. About 20 kilometres down Johnstone Strait, the Tsitika River enters the channel,

forming submerged gravelly beaches, the perfect place for killer whales to skim across the rocks for a good belly rub. Robson Bight (Michael Bigg) Ecological Reserve encompasses 1248 hectares of the whales' habitat, and some 300 killer whales frequent the area. About 200 are "northern residents" and another 85 are "southern residents" that often migrate into the straits of Georgia, Haro, and Juan de Fuca. If you're within 15 kilometres of Robson Bight, tune in to ORCA-FM, station CJKW at 88.5, to hear broadcasts of killer whale vocalizations.

North Island Discovery Centre
Highway 19; near junction with Beaver Cove Road, four kilometres south of Port McNeill
250-956-1446
Open daily, May-September, 10 am-4:30 pm
Forestry tours on Monday, Wednesday, Friday at 10 am
Admission free
This information centre is jointly operated by several forest companies; forestry and logging tours can be booked here. Take along a lunch and wear sturdy footwear and long pants for the outings.

Beaver Cove Dryland Sort
Beaver Cove Road; 13 kilometres from Highway 19
Lookout and information signs located at the eastern end of the sorting grounds
Take a few moments here to see Canada's largest dryland log-sorting facility, an operation of Canadian Forest Products. The Nimpkish Valley annually accounts for more than a million cubic metres of logs, hauled by truck to the Englewood Railway, which then freights them to Beaver Cove where they are sorted and scaled. From here, mighty tugs with 2000-horse-

Totem pole near Port McNeill

power engines embark on seven-day tows to Vancouver, each transporting 11 booms of logs in their wake. At Vancouver, the logs are processed into lumber, hardboard, pulp, and paper.

Port McNeill

Port McNeill and District Chamber of Commerce
PO Box 129
Port McNeill BC V0N 2R0
250-956-3131
www.portmcneill.net
Population: 3114

A modern townsite set upon a sloping hillside dropping down to a sheltered harbour and downtown waterfront, Port McNeill is named after William Henry McNeill, an American sea captain who first visited here in the 1830s as an employee of the Hudson's Bay Company. McNeill later returned to the area and helped establish the Fort Rupert coal mines.

Port McNeill today is a vibrant anchorage, its population engaged primarily in forestry, fishing, and tourism. It makes an ideal staging

Cape Scott Provincial Park

Named Cape Scott by Captain James Stranger in 1786 to honour his fur trading partner and Bombay merchant benefactor David Scott, the northernmost tip of Vancouver Island is still, after more than two centuries, a land of rugged shoreline, graceful sandy beaches, coves, inlets, lakes, rivers — and little human impact. The moist forested uplands of red and yellow cedar, pine, hemlock, and fir receive some 375 to 500 centimetres of rain annually. High winds and rain can be expected any time of year.

Cape Scott is, after all, smack-dab in the path of the tumultuous Pacific Ocean tempests, careening in one after another like drunken sailors after a night's binge. Shipwrecks by the dozens — the *Maggie Mac* in 1892, the *Galiano* in 1918, the *Black Barnacle* in 1938, the *Northolm* in 1943, and on and on — are grim reminders of the northern tip's temperamental nature. On a gentler note, Cape Scott is home to elk, deer, bear, cougar, wolves, and waterfowl species by the score as the park lies within the route of the Pacific Flyway. Its highest point is Mt. St. Patrick, rising 415 metres above sea level, and Eric Lake, at 44 hectares, is the largest body of water.

Embracing some 15,070 hectares of terrain and 23 kilometres of coastline from Nissen Bight in the north to San Josef Bay in the south, it is not a place for the inexperienced nature lover. The only access is via a 67-kilometre-long logging road from Port Hardy through Holberg, which ends at the San Josef Bay trailhead.

Although traditionally the homeland of three First Nations peoples — the Tlatlasikwala, the Nakumgilisala, and the Yutlinuk — the area was largely abandoned in the 1850s. A group of Danish pioneers from the United States started a settlement in 1897 and attempted to overcome the formidable obstacles of remoteness, severe weather, and poor soil conditions, but ultimately abandoned their dreams. Scant evidence remains of these pioneers: a few dilapidated buildings slowly succumbing to nature and the names they gave local landmarks like Nels Bight, Hansen Lagoon, Frederiksen Point.

After the turn of the century, more immigrants arrived, settlers from Washington State and Canada's prairie provinces establishing themselves at the former Danish settlements. By 1913 the area's population numbered more than 1000, but the same hardships encountered by earlier settlers soon overcame these intrepid souls as well. By the beginning of World War I, the community was all but done for. In 1942 a small radar station was established at Cape Scott, operating for only three years during World War II.

Cape Scott Provincial Park
BC Parks District Manager
Box 1479
Parksville BC V9P 2H4
250-954-4600
15,070 hectares / campground at San Josef River trailhead and wilderness camping

point for whale watching, diving, and sportfishing excursions into Broughton Strait and the channels cutting between the many offshore islands and islets. Port McNeill is also the embarkation point for the Alert Bay-Sointula Ferry (250-339-0444), which heads to Cormorant and Malcolm islands.

Port McNeill Heritage Museum
351 Shelly Crescent; off Broughton Boulevard
250-956-9898
www.portmcneill.net/museum.htm
Open daily, May-September; weekends only, October-April
Admission charged
Step into this log building to examine artifacts and mementos largely associated with the area's pioneer and forestry history.

World's Largest Burl
1.5 kilometres north of Port McNeill
Just off the road hunkers the world's largest burl, cut from a 351-year-old spruce. It weighs in at 20 tonnes and measures 13.5 metres around. It was discovered by surveyors 40 kilometres south at the head of the Benson River.

Cormorant Island
Alert Bay Info Centre
Bag Service 2800
Alert Bay BC V0N 1A0
250-974-5024
Population: 1800
Both tiny (3.2 square kilometres) Cormorant Island and its town, Alert Bay, were named for British warships, HMS *Cormorant* and HMS *Alert*, which surveyed the coastal waters here from 1845 to 1861. Today the island is the home of the 'Namgis people of the Kwakwaka'wakw First Nation,

though the Nimpkish River, on the other side of Broughton Strait, was their ancestral homeland and the place they lived until the 1870s. The establishment of a salmon saltery and church mission on Cormorant Island brought the 'Namgis here to work and live and eventually stay.

Alert Bay
Tourism Alert Bay Association
250-974-5213
800-690-TABA
www.alertbay.com
or
www.village.alert.bc.ca
Visitor Centre: 116 Fir Street
Attractive Alert Bay, hugging the waterfront around the harbour, is a compact seaside village, the oldest in the North Island region. As it is rich in the cultural history of the Kwakwaka'wakw, particularly the 'Namgis, visitors are invariably impressed with its historical significance, as well as the town's many totem poles and other First Nations artifacts.

The main part of town running along Front Streets offers a nice walking tour, for there are many historic buildings: the 1923 Court House, once the office, living quarters, and lockup for provincial police; the 1900 Alert Bay Indian Day School, now the Council Hall; the 1892 Christ Church; plus the 1925 St. George's Hospital, among many others.

With its close proximity to

Alert Bay is home to a wealth of totems.

the Robson Bight Ecological Reserve, Alert Bay is an excellent departure point for whale watching excursions.

U'mista Cultural Centre
Front Street; left from ferry dock
250-974-5403
www.umista.org
Open daily, May-September; Monday to Friday, October-April
Admission charged
Housed in this modern interpretation of a

North Island Tee Time

Seven Hills Golf and Country Club
Port Alice Highway; one kilometre off Highway 19
250-949-9818
Nine holes

Port Alice Golf and Country Club
Port Alice Highway; beyond Port Alice townsite
250-284-3213
Nine holes

Alert Bay is the oldest community in North Vancouver Island.

Kwakwaka'wakw Big House is an amazing wealth of ceremonial masks and regalia, basketry, and woodcarvings. Repatriated in 1979, these artifacts of the Kwakwaka'wakw were confiscated by the Canadian government in the 1920s when it enforced laws banning potlatch ceremonies. Of particular interest are the ornamental copper pieces that recorded significant life events and business transactions of their owners. The centre takes its name from a traditional Kwakwaka'wakw term signifying the return, through ransom or retaliatory raid, of slaves or goods.

To take in a performance of 'Na'nakwala dance at the traditional Big House, call 250-974-5501 or 250-974-2626.

Alert Bay Library and Museum
118 Fir Street
250-974-5721
Open daily, July-August; Wednesday, Friday, and Saturday, September-June
Admission free
Next door to the visitor centre, a browse through the Alert Bay Library and Museum reveals Kwakwaka'wakw and pioneer artifacts, plus archival photos.

World's Tallest Totem Pole
Outside 'Namgis Big House; near the U'mista Cultural Centre
The *Guinness Book of Records*

validated this pole, topped by a Sun Mask 52.7 metres above the ground, as the world's tallest from 1973 to 1994. Natives in Victoria raised a taller one — 2.1 metres higher — but citizens' concern for safety brought it down by 1997, re-establishing Alert Bay as the home of the planet's most towering totem pole. The figures on the pole represent tribes of the Kwakwaka'wakw.

Nearby is the Alert Bay Big House, modelled on the traditional communal residences of the Kwakwaka'wakw.

'Namgis Burial Grounds
Front Street; right from ferry dock
Stately totem poles adorn this

North Island Festivals & Events

JUNE
The Great Walk
Gold River
North America's toughest walkathon goes for 64km from Gold River to Tahsis.

Port Alice Rumble Mountain Rage
Port Alice
Vancouver Island's most northern cross-country mountain bike race across rugged trails and scenic paths.

JULY
Port Hardy FILOMI Days
Port Hardy / Carrot Park
This summer festival celebrates the area's three biggest industries — fishing, logging, and mining — honouring the "FI," "LO," and "MI" mainstays of the local economy.

AUGUST
Alert Bay SeaFest
Cormorant Island, Alert Bay
Fun-filled festival with lots of games and activities such as Family Feud, Ladies'/Mens'

Skiff Races, Adult/Youth/Child Lip Sync's, Seafest Cabaret, Mr. & Mrs. Strong Person, Skiff Races, Soapbox Derby, 'Na'Nakwala Dancers, Crowning of Mr. & Mrs. Seafest, and more.

Port McNeill Orca Festival
Port McNeill
Good times for residents and visitors alike with a parade, soap box derby, mini-train rides, watermelon eating contest, three-legged races, arm wrestling competition, salmon barbeque, plus many other diversions.

SEPTEMBER
Zeballos Fall Fair Logger Sports
Zeballos
Agricultural exhibits, arts and crafts displays, salmon barbeque, beer garden, and logger events top the list of activities at this annual get-together for family, friends, and visitors.

Residents of Sointula on Malcolm Island are primarily commercial fishers.

Monkey puzzle trees at Ronning's Garden.

sacred century-old cemetery of the 'Namgis, and visitors are asked to respect the site by viewing the totems only from the street.

Alert Bay Ecological Park
Entrances off East Hemlock Street or Alder Road
A BC Wildlife viewing area, Alert Bay Ecological Park offers glimpses of ravens, eagles, and other birds, plus possibly an elusive tortoise who was released here years ago and every once in a while pops up to amuse visitors. Boardwalks and trails wind through this unusual landscape of hemlock and pine draped with moss, as well as stands of gnarly old cedar snags.

Malcolm Island
Port McNeill and District
Chamber of Commerce
PO Box 129
Port McNeill BC V0N 2R0
250-956-3131
www.portmcneill.net or
www.island.net/~sointula
Population: 800
Unsuccessfully settled first by a British temperance society, and then by utopian Finnish immigrants at the turn of the century, Malcolm Island is far

more diversely populated these days, though its hardworking residents are still primarily commercial fishers and some farmers. Visitors will find a pleasant, genuinely friendly atmosphere that is certainly not over-touristy. Sointula is the main village, tidy and compact, with small shops and businesses running along First Street. From here a network of gravel roads leads off into the island's interior, with the combination of Mitchell Bay, Big Lake, and Pulteney Point roads running the entire 28 kilometre length of the island from Donegal Head to Pulteney Point.

Sointula
Sointula, "A Place of Harmony," was conceived in 1901 as a Finnish cooperative community by the charismatic philosopher / playwright Matti Kurikka. Although his utopian experiment failed in less than five years, some 100 Finns stayed on, establishing themselves as fishers and farmers. Even up to the 1970s the lingua franca of the island was principally Finnish.

Today less than 50 percent

of the population is of Finnish descent, and due to the reduction of fishing licences, commercial fishing as a livelihood has nearly disappeared. Sointula is therefore a quieter place these days, though its co-op general store welcomes an increasing number of recreation-minded visitors who come to Malcolm Island to bike its backroads, kayak its lovely coves and bays, troll its waters on fishing charters, or bird-watch the mudflats of Rough Bay.

Sointula Finnish Museum
First Street; left from ferry dock
250-973-6353 or 250-973-6764
Open daily, May-September
Admission charged
Take a stroll through the tiny Sointula Finnish Museum to ponder the many, many artifacts, mementos, and keepsakes

Port Alice
Village of Port Alice
PO Box 130
Port Alice BC V0N 2N0
250-284-3391
www.village.port-alice.bc.ca
Population: 1371
Dramatically situated at the head of Neroutsos Inlet on

Quatsino Sound, Port Alice is a modern logging and pulp mill town. Indeed, it was British Columbia's first "instant municipality," erected to the original town four kilometres up the inlet. Alice Whalen, who gave her name to the town, was a member of the Whalen family, which operated three pulp mills in the area. Freshwater and saltwater activities are easy to come by,

and there are many hiking opportunities in the surrounding mountains. The Port Alice Golf Country Club is one of Vancouver Island's most challenging nine-hole courses, as well as being the western-most golf course in Canada.

Kwakiutl / Beaver Harbour / Fort Rupert
Port Hardy and District Chamber of Commerce
PO Box 249
Port Hardy BC V0N 2P0
250-949-7622
www.ph-chamber.bc.ca
Beaver Harbour is also called Kwakiutl, which is the name of its Kwakwaka'wakw First Nation community. And it is also called Fort Rupert, for

North Island Parks & Recreation

Schoen Lake Provincial Park
Highway 19; follow the signs
250-954-4600
8430 hectares / 10 campsites
Schoen Lake is one of the Island's most beautiful, especially when the reflection of 1802-metre-high Mt. Schoen ripples in its waters. Mountain and meadow hikes lead off from the lake. Nisnak Meadows is a profusion of wildflowers in late spring and summer.

Woss Lake Provincial Park
Woss Lake; south end
250-954-4600
6634 hectares / wilderness camping
This park, which can be reached by a five-kilometre-long logging road or by boat, is heavily forested and good for experienced trekkers.

Little Hustan Caves Regional Park
Zeballos Road
Good for inexperienced spelunkers, the cave system features a cathedral entrance and a river that appears and reappears with the rock formations.

Brooks Peninsula Provincial Park
North of Kyuquot; accessible by boat from Fair Harbour and Kyuquot
250-954-4600

51,631 hectares / wilderness camping
With no development or trails, and with definitely rugged terrain, this is only for experienced outdoors folks. The peninsula's shores are home to Canada's re-establishing population of sea otters, descendants of Alaska otters transplanted here in the 1960s.

Nimpkish Lake Provincial Park
Southwest shores of Nimpkish Lake; 11 kilometres beyond Zeballos Road
3950 hectares / no facilities
Access points to trails and viewpoints are marked along Highway 19 as it follows the 22-kilometre-long lake.

Marble River Provincial Park
Marble River Recreation Area; 13 kilometres from Highway 19
250-954-4600
1512 hectares / campsites at Marble River Recreation Area
Following either side of the shallow river from its mouth up along Quatsino Narrows, and from Varney Bay to Rupert Inlet, the park has limited hiking trails; most spots can be reached by boat.

God's Pocket Provincial Marine Park
Island group north of Port Hardy
2025 hectares / no facilites

(God's Pocket Resort is nearby)
This cluster of islands at the entrance to the Queen Charlotte Strait off Port Hardy is favoured by divers and sportfishers.

Raft Cove Provincial Park
West of Holberg, 14 kilometres
250-954-4600
405 hectares / wilderness camping
It takes about 40 minutes to hike to the cove, which is a good place for surfing and kayaking.

Cape Scott Provincial Park
End of Road; 68 kilometres west of Port Hardy
250-954-4600
22,131 hectares / campground at San Josef River trailhead and wilderness camping
Rugged and untamed, this park features wilderness experiences, especially the 30 kilometre hike to Cape Scott Lighthouse.

Scott Islands Provincial Park
10 kilometres off the northern tip of Vancouver Island
250-954-4600
6125 hectares / no facilities
This park encompasses Lanz and Cox islands, along with three ecological reserves: Anne Valle (Triangle Island), Beresford Island, and Sartine Island. Accessible only by private boat or charter.

this is the site of the Hudson's Bay Company outpost established in 1849 to exploit the nearby coal fields. Fort Rupert closed in 1882, and only a crumbling chimney remains.

Coal Harbour
Port Hardy and District
Chamber of Commerce
PO Box 249
Port Hardy BC V0N 2P0
250-949-7622
www.ph-chamber.bc.ca
Population: 200

The massive jawbone of a blue whale — some six metres long — greets visitors to the tiny hamlet of Coal Harbour. Although it was briefly the site of a coal mining operation in the 1800s, Coal Harbour spent more time as a lively whaling station after World War II. Some 70 workers once crewed the whaling ships sailing from the harbour, and another 85 residents toiled in the processing plant where catches were sliced and diced into steaks and fillets (for humans), packaged into pet food and stock feed, and even rendered into machine oil.

Quatsino
Port Hardy and District
Chamber of Commerce
PO Box 249
Port Hardy BC V0N 2P0
250-949-7622
www.ph-chamber.bc.ca
Population: 100

Accessible from Coal Harbour via water taxi, this small community was settled in the late 1800s. St. Olaf's Anglican Church dates from 1896 and still holds services today. Most visitors come to fish for salmon, cod, or red snapper; do some berry picking; or simply stroll along the beaches.

Port Hardy is North Vancouver Island's principal commercial centre.

Port Hardy
Port Hardy and District
Chamber of Commerce
PO Box 249
Port Hardy BC V0N 2P0
250-949-7622
www.ph-chamber.bc.ca
Info Centre: Market Street
near docks
Population: 5283

This is North Vancouver Island's principal commercial centre, offering numerous services and stores, plus many accommodation facilities and restaurants. Archaeological evidence suggests that the Port Hardy area was occupied as far back as 8000 years ago, but white settlers arrived here only in 1904. Pioneers from England and the United States came to take advantage of attractive land deals. Prosperity eluded the fledgling village, however, and by 1914 only 12 families remained.

Port Hardy endured, however, and its proximity to phenomenal wilderness recreation is supplementing its traditional mining, fishing, and logging economy. Hailed once as "King Coho Country," government closure of the coho fishery in 1998 to protect diminishing stocks has left most sportfishers angling for halibut, in addition to pink, sockeye, and chinook salmon. Port Hardy is also the embarkation point for kayakers and hikers heading to remote Cape Scott and Brooks Peninsula provincial parks, or to the island clusters of God's Pocket Provincial Marine Park at the entrance to Queen Charlotte Strait. BC Ferries sail up the Inside Passage to Prince Rupert and to the BC mainland's central coast from Bear Cove, just outside Port Hardy.

Port Hardy Museum and Archives
7110 Market Street
250-949-8143
Open Tuesday, Thursday, and Saturday afternoons
Admission charged

Explore the area's Kwakwaka'wakw legacy as well as Port Hardy's and northern Vancouver Island's settlement and development.

Quatse River Salmon Hatchery
Hardy Bay Road; off Highway 19
250-949-9022
Open daily

A totem near Winter Harbour

Winter Harbour was so named in the 1800s for its protected cove.

Admission free
A BC Wildlife Watch viewing site where visitors can see coho, chinook, and chum salmon and take nature walks along the river.

Shoe Tree
Highway 19; 13 kilometres west of Port Hardy
Look to the roadside to spot a 22-metre-high cedar snag draped with hundreds of shoes, donated by visitors from around the world. The quirky tradition arose when a local Holberg resident nailed six pairs of his son's shoes to the old tree's base.

Holberg
Port Hardy and District Chamber of Commerce
PO Box 249
Port Hardy BC V0N 2P0
250-949-7622
www.ph-chamber.bc.ca
Population: 200
Holberg was founded in 1895 by Danish immigrants, who named their new home after the Danish dramatist Baron Ludvig Holberg. Logging was (and is) Holberg's business, and at one time it claimed to

have the "world's largest floating logging camp." Facilities have since moved to land. For more than 30 years, up until 1991, the town hosted the Canadian Forces Station Holberg, a 300-personnel radar base engaged in North America's defense system.

Ronning's Garden
14.5 kilometres west of Holberg; a 10 minute walk from parking area along the old San Josef wagon road
No phone
Open daily
Admission free
Sheltered in the midst of thick forest sprouts the horticultural legacy of Bernt Ronning, a Norwegian-born bachelor who set up home here in 1915, working primarily as a trapper and camp cook, and stayed until his death in the mid-1960s. As Ronning cleared his land, he sowed seeds and planted cuttings from trees and plants from across the globe. Today the garden is best known for its male and female specimens of Chilean monkey puzzle trees, two of the largest and oldest in BC, and a pair of only a handful

of this type of tree in North America that produces viable seeds. These beauties, in addition to rare Himalayan rhododendrons, plus scads of daffodils, bluebells, and sweet woodruff, still flourish thanks to the care and upkeep of retired lighthouse keepers Ron and Julia Moe.

Winter Harbour
Port Hardy and District Chamber of Commerce
PO Box 249
Port Hardy BC V0N 2P0
250-949-7622
www.ph-chamber.bc.ca
Population: 55
Ships that tucked into the protected cove during winter in the 1800s gave Winter Harbour its name. But it was also known as Queenstown, then Leeson Harbour, before taking on the moniker of Winter Harbour again in the 1940s. A tiny settlement of, primarily, commercial fishers, main street is a three-plank-wide boardwalk waterfront connecting to the dock and marina. Sportfishers will find several charter companies.

Index

Photographic Credits

All photos by the author except for
page 13 by Rob Melnychuk, courtesy of the Wickaninnish Inn
pages 18-21 courtesy of BC Archives
pages 27-32 Dennis and Esther Schmidt
pages 48-49,128-129 John Walls
page 159 courtesy Tourism North Central Island

About the Author

Award-winning writer and photographer Dan Klinglesmith has travelled the world extensively, but Canada holds a special place in his heart. He has visited and written about nearly every province, especially British Columbia and in particular Vancouver Island. Dan calls Vancouver Island a treasure of the world and easily one of its most rewarding destinations.

Dan Klinglesmith is the author of several other books for Altitude Publishing including *Colorado, An Altitude SuperGuide* and *Colorado, A History in Photographs*. Currently, Dan is based in Denver, Colorado.